The Army of the Kingdom of Italy 1805–1814

Uniforms, Organisation, Campaigns

Stephen Ede-Borrett

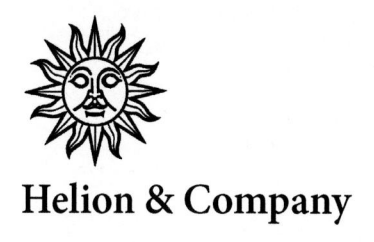

Helion & Company

This book is respectfully dedicated to

Bridget Bentley, Kesh Kotecha, Sarah Thompson, Juliet Bugby
My friends. They were good times, thank you.

And to my partner Mary
Without whose encouragement it would probably never have been finished.

Helion & Company Limited
Unit 8 Amherst Business Centre
Budbrooke Road
Warwick
CV34 5WE
England
Tel. 01926 499 619
Email: info@helion.co.uk
Website: www.helion.co.uk
Twitter: @helionbooks
Visit our blog http://blog.helion.co.uk/

Published by Helion & Company 2022
Designed and typeset by Serena Jones
Cover designed by Paul Hewitt, Battlefield Design (www.battlefield-design.co.uk)

Text © Stephen Ede-Borrett 2022
Images © as individually credited

Front cover: Prince Eugène de Beauharnais, by Johann Heinrich Richter. Hermitage Museum, St Petersburg.

Every reasonable effort has been made to trace copyright holders and to obtain their permission for the use of copyright material. The author and publisher apologise for any errors or omissions in this work, and would be grateful if notified of any corrections that should be incorporated in future reprints or editions of this book.

ISBN 978-1-911628-49-1

British Library Cataloguing-in-Publication Data.

A catalogue record for this book is available from the British Library.

All rights reserved. No part of this publication may be reproduced, stored in a retrieval system, or transmitted, in any form, or by any means, electronic, mechanical, photocopying, recording or otherwise, without the express written consent of Helion & Company Limited.

For details of other military history titles published by Helion & Company
Limited, contact the above address, or visit our website: http://www.helion.co.uk

We always welcome receiving book proposals from prospective authors.

Contents

Preface	iv
Introduction: The Napoleonic Kingdom of Italy, 1805–1814	vi
Italy in the Napoleonic Period, 1796–1814 (*Encyclopaedia Britannica* 1911)	x
Note on Terminology and Unit Titles	xxii
1. General Officers and Staff	25
2. Guardia Reale (Royal Guard)	44
3. Cavalleria di Linea (Cavalry of the Line)	92
4. Fanteria di Linea (Infantry of the Line)	118
5. Artigleria di Linea, etc. (Line Artillery and Support Units)	162
6. Naval Units	188
Appendix I: The Order of the Iron Crown	194
Appendix II: Illustrative Strength Returns	198
Appendix III: The Armée d'Italie at the Battle of the Mincio, 8 Febr. 1814	204
Appendix IV: Glossary of Uniform Patterns and Types	207
Colour Plate Commentaries	220
Bibliography	226

Preface

This work is not intended to be a detailed study of the service and history of the Army of the Kingdom of Italy, although they are both covered superficially. Neither is it intended as an history of Italy or even the Kingdom during this period.[1] It is primarily a work of uniformology – a study of the changes in the uniforms and equipment of the units of the Army of the Kingdom of Italy (*not*, in Napoleonic terms, the Army of Italy, on which see below), and for completeness those parts of the navy who served alongside that army in land campaigns.

The format for each unit that I have chosen to use is that formulated by the late W.J. Rawkins in his books published by Anschluss Publishing. Over the years I have seen many ways of presenting this information but his is, in my opinion, undoubtedly the best and, in the vein of Isaac Newton, I readily acknowledge the debt that I owe him in copying his format.

I have tried not to be pedantic over many details of a uniform and state that this source is right and this one wrong – uniformology is not such an exact science. In many cases it is highly probable that both original sources may be correct and that variations in many aspects of a uniform changed from issue to issue, or even tailor to tailor, and may thus have often been seen alongside each other. This may have been the period of elegant uniform but Colonels still followed their personal whims on many things, strict precise uniformity simply did not exist in most units and many old or outdated items of uniform or equipment continued to be issued until stocks were exhausted. What are given here are, therefore, both the regulations – when they existed, the Kingdom's army seemed remarkably lax on such things, which were usually, although not always, quite clear – and many of the numerous recorded variations to them.

Whilst there are *brief* overviews of each unit's organisational changes during the period these were frequent and, particularly in the Royal Guard, were at best barely completed before the next was ordered. It is also worth noting that the theoretical establishments were rarely achieved, as some of the actual strengths quoted will amply show.

Many obsolete patterns of uniforms from the Army of the abolished republics continued to be worn, again particularly in the Royal Guard,

---

1 For this the author would highly recommend Juan Carlos Carmignani and Gilles Boué (Marie-France Renwick trans.), *Napoleon and Italy: A Military History of Napoleonic Italy, 1805–1815* (Paris: Histoire & Collections, 2016).

PREFACE

until 1806/1807 whatever the new regulations might say (a similar situation existed in almost all armies of almost every era). I have not tried to cover these 'older' uniforms since to do so would increase the size of this work exponentially to no real effect and they are thus mentioned only in passing. It is, however, hoped that these earlier uniforms may be covered in a later volume on the Armies of the Italian Republics.

Whilst much of this material has been collected over many years my thanks must go particularly to those authors whose works are cited in the bibliography, especially Piero Crociano, whose series in the long-gone and much lamented English-language *Tradition Magazine* first sparked my interest in the Kingdom of Italy and whose work provided the skeleton for me to build on. Also to Art Etchells and to Laurent Claudet for sharing the fruits of their researches and their libraries, to Peter Heath of Anschluss Publishing, the publisher of W. J. Rawkins' books, and to Fabrice and Sophie Dalamare of Uniformologie who found so many of the illustrations and sources that I have used. My thanks also to my partner Mary who has patiently read the manuscript and corrected many of my errors.

Lastly my apologies to native speakers of Italian, my own Italian is very basic and I apologise if I have mangled your language at any point.

Stephen Ede-Borrett
April 2022

Introduction: The Napoleonic Kingdom of Italy, 1805–1814

The Kingdom of Italy came into being on 17 March 1805, when the Italian Republic was dissolved, and Napoleon, who had been President of the Republic, was elevated to the throne as the new Kingdom's monarch. The 24-year-old Eugène de Beauharnais, Napoleon's stepson, was nominated as viceroy. Napoleon was crowned with the Iron Crown of Lombardy in Milan Cathedral on 26 May 1805 and took the full title of 'Emperor of the French and King of Italy'.

The Republic ceased to exist upon the creation of the Kingdom but its constitution was never formally abolished although a series of constitutional statutes completely altered it:

The first, proclaimed on 19 March just two days after the creation of the Kingdom, when Napoleon was declared King, established that the monarchy was to be hereditary and the King's sons would succeed to the throne, even if the French and the Italian crowns were separated after Napoleon's death.

The second, dated 29 March, regulated the Regency, the major officials of the Kingdom, and the oaths to be taken by the army, the civil service, and the populace.

In practice, however, the third statute of 5 June 1805 was the new Constitution of the Kingdom: the King was to be head of state, and had the full powers of government; in his absence, his powers were in the hands of the viceroy; respectively these were Napoleon and Eugène de Beauharnais. The Consulta, Legislative Council, and speakers, were all merged into a new council of state, whose recommendations and motions were advisory only, and not binding on either the head of state or the viceroy. The legislative body, the old parliament, theoretically remained in being or at least was not formally abolished, but after 1805 it was not called again.

By a statute of 16 February 1806 the proclamation of 19 March of the previous year was amended and Eugène and his heirs were nominated as the heirs to the Kingdom upon Napoleon's death.

The last of the important statutes was that of 21 September 1808, which created a new nobility of dukes, counts and barons; and two further statutes, of 15 March 1810, established an annuity for the members of the Royal Family.

The Kingdom of Italy initially comprised the territories of the old Italian Republic: the former Duchies of Milan, Mantua, and Modena, with the western part of the Republic of Venice, part of the Papal States in The Romagna, and

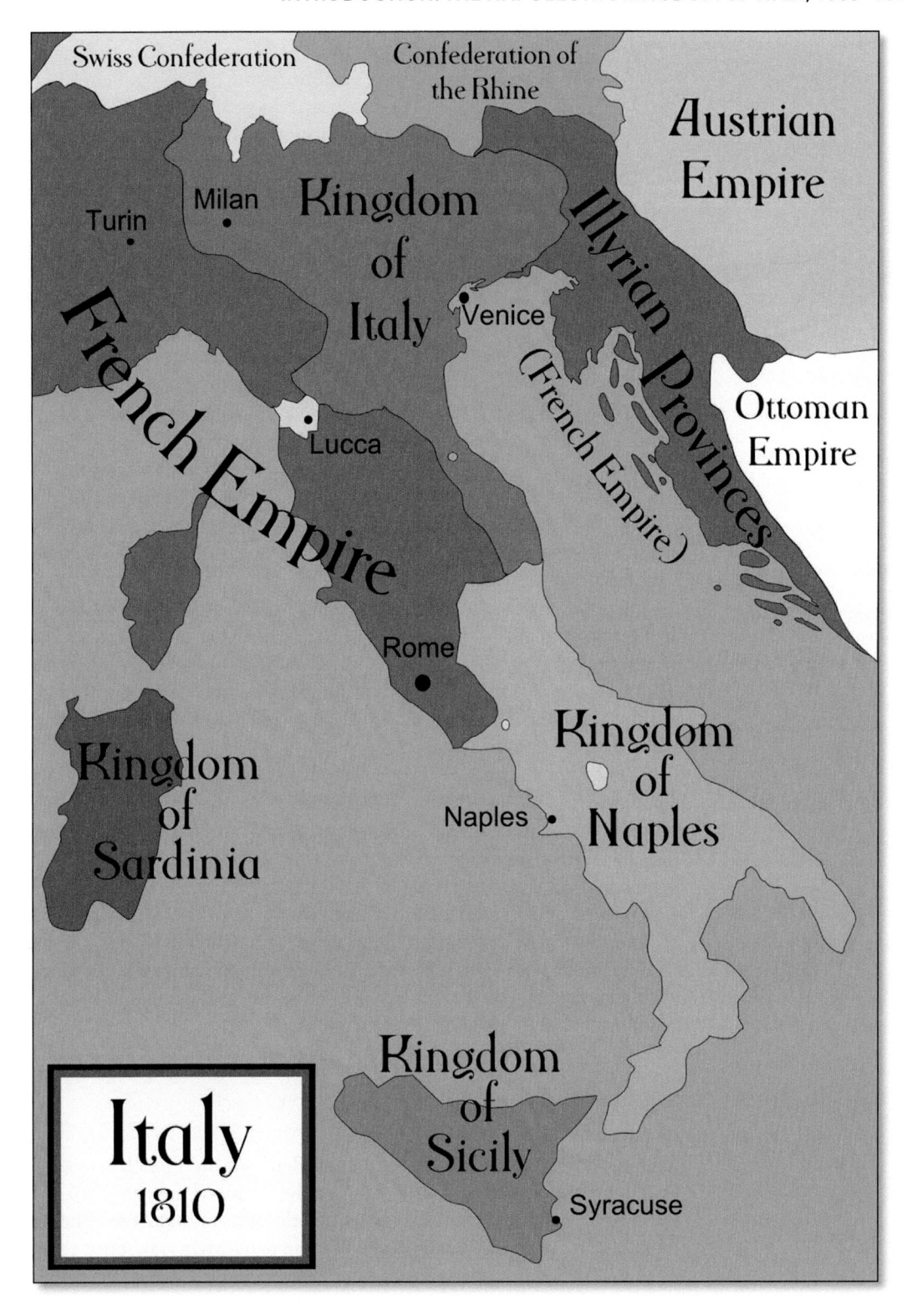

INTRODUCTION: THE NAPOLEONIC KINGDOM OF ITALY, 1805–1814

Italy in 1810 showing the Kingdoms' boundaries. The Principality of Lucca (see main text) stands out as an obvious anachronism. (Created by Aibdescalzo, Mapmaster via Wikimedia Commons)

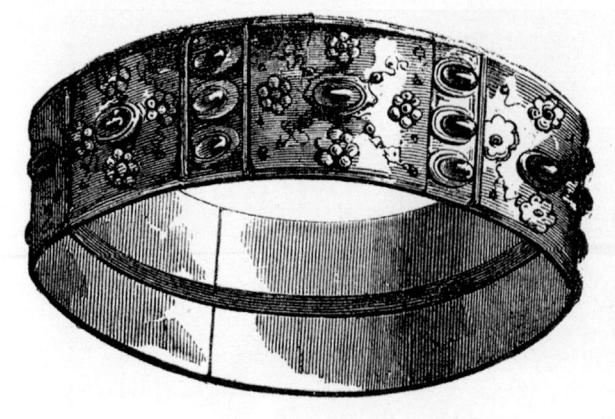

The Iron Crown of Lombardy (image: public domain). Note that this is what the crown actually *looks like although when used as a badge by the Kingdom's army it was shown with a 'spiked' upper edge. The Iron Crown was similarly illustrated on the Kingdom's coat of arms. Although interestingly it is shown in this form on the commemorative medal struck to celebrate Napoleon's coronation as King of Italy.*

the province of Novara. After the defeat of the Third Coalition and the subsequent Treaty of Pressburg of 1 May 1806, Austria surrendered the remaining part of the Venetian territories, including Istria and Dalmatia down to Cattaro (today Kotor). All of these were incorporated in the Kingdom of Italy although, at the same time Massa and Carrara were transferred to the Principality of Lucca and Piombino, ruled by Elisa Bonaparte.[1] Then, on 24 May 1806, The Duchy of Guastalla was annexed and added to the Kingdom.

By the Convention of Fontainebleau with Austria of 10 October 1807, Italy ceded Monfalcone to Austria and gained Gradisca, putting the new border on the River Isonzo.

In Spring 1808 Marshal Marmont annexed the Republic of Ragusa, which was then added to the Kingdom, and on 2 April 1808, following the dissolution of the Papal States, the Kingdom annexed the present-day Marches.

This was the Kingdom at its maximum extent, with 6,700,000 inhabitants and 2,155 cities, towns and villages.

The final changes to the Kingdom's borders came following the defeat of Austria in 1809. Napoleon and Maximilian, King of Bavaria, signed the Treaty of Paris on 28 February 1810, deciding an exchange of territories which also involved the Kingdom of Italy: Bavaria ceded the Southern Tyrol to the Kingdom of Italy, which in its turn ceded Istria and Dalmatia (with Ragusa) to France.

Napoleon abdicated the throne of the Kingdom of Italy on 11 April 1814 at the same time as he abdicated the throne of France. Eugène was on the Mincio with the Army and attempted to have himself crowned as his stepfather's successor but there was little enthusiasm from the Senate and on 20 April a Provisional Regency Government was appointed. Three days later Eugène surrendered and was exiled to Bavaria. On 28 April the Austrians occupied Milan and over the next month the previous monarchies in Modena, Romagna and Piedmont were re-established. The remaining territories of the Kingdom were annexed by Austria on 12 June 1814, no vestiges of the Napoleonic Kingdom of Italy were allowed to survive.

The Armée d'Italie

It should be noted that in the Orders of Battle of the French armies of the First Empire the Armée d'Italie was *not* the Army of the Kingdom of Italy, although it invariably included the main field units of that Army. The Armée d'Italie was a mainly French force stationed in what was, post 1805, the

---

1   Maria Anna Elisa Bonaparte Baciocchi Levoy (3 January 1777–7 August 1820), younger sister of Napoleon, Emperor of the French and King of Italy. She was the only one of Napoleon's sisters to hold independent political power.

Kingdom of Italy, primarily to keep a 'watch' on the Austrian Empire who, Great Britain excepted, between 1791 and 1815 spent a greater period at war with France than any other country.

The status reports of the Armée d'Italie amply demonstrates this:[2]

Date	Total Strength	French	Italian	
1805, Vendémiare 8	65,257	60,191	5,066	
1806, 1 April	56,653	50,143	6,510	
1807, 15 September	94,291	76,609	18,484	
1808, 1 July	75,799	57,257	18,542	
1809, 1 April	108,542	77,543	28,285	+ 2,714 Neapolitans
1814, 15 January	45,025*			

* The last, and incomplete, status report of the Armée d'Italie.

The Iron Crown of Lombardy

Throughout the Kingdom of Italy's existence the 'Iron Crown' of Lombardy featured strongly in its iconography. Tradition states that the crown was made for Theodelinda, Queen of the Lombards (*c.* 570–628),[3] and was supposed to incorporate the iron from one of the nails of the True Cross. Theodelinda's crown was made of six separate plates of gold, set with precious gems, over an iron circlet structure, hence the term 'Iron Crown'.

Upon Theodelinda's death in 628, the crown was deposited in Monza Cathedral (along with a[nother] piece of the True Cross), where it is still preserved. When Charlemagne took the throne of Lombardy in 774 the Iron Crown was used for his coronation, and this tradition was continued at the subsequent coronations of Holy Roman Emperors when they were crowned King of Lombardy, it was thus natural that Napoleon should also do so.

---

2   From *Napoleon and Italy: A Military History of Napoleonic Italy, 1805–1815*, Juan Carlos Carmigniani and Gilles Boué, trans. Marie-France Renwick (Paris: Histoire & Collections, 2016), p.221. Also see Appendix III.

3   Theodelinda, Queen of the Lombards, was the daughter of Duke Garibald I of Bavaria. In 588 she married Authari, King of the Lombards, and after his death in 590 his successor, Agilulfas, the following year. She exerted a great amount of influence in restoring Nicene Christianity to a position of primacy in Italy against its rival, Arian Christianity. She built a number of churches throughout Lombardy and Tuscany, including the Cathedral of Monza, dedicated to Saint John the Baptist.

Italy in the Napoleonic Period, 1796–1814 (*Encyclopaedia Britannica*, 1911)

The campaign of 1796 which led to the awakening of the Italian people to a new consciousness of unity and strength is detailed in the article 'Napoleonic Campaigns'. Here we can attempt only a general survey of the events, political, civic and social, which heralded the Risorgimento in its first phase. It is desirable in the first place to realise the condition of Italy at the time when the irruption of the French and the expulsion of the Austrians opened up a new political vista for that oppressed and divided people.

For many generations Italy had been bandied to and fro between the Habsburgs and the Bourbons. The decline of French influence at the close of the reign of Louis XIV left the Habsburgs and the Spanish Bourbons without serious rivals. The former possessed the rich duchies of Milan (including Mantua) and Tuscany; while through a marriage alliance with the house of Este of Modena (the Archduke Ferdinand had married the heiress of Modena) its influence over that duchy was supreme. It also had a few fiefs in Piedmont and in Genoese territory. By marrying her daughter, Maria Amelia, to the young duke of Parma, and another daughter, Maria Carolina, to Ferdinand of Naples, Maria Theresa consolidated Habsburg influence in the north and south of the peninsula. The Spanish Bourbons held Naples and Sicily, as well as the Duchy of Parma. Of the nominally independent states the chief were the kingdom of Sardinia, ruled over by the house of Savoy, and comprising Piedmont, the isle of Sardinia and nominally Savoy and Nice, though the two provinces last named had virtually been lost to the monarchy since the campaign of 1793. Equally extensive, but less important in the political sphere, were the Papal States and Venetia, the former torpid under the obscurantist rule of pope and cardinals, the latter enervated by luxury and the policy of unmanly complaisance long pursued by doge and council. The ancient rival of Venice, Genoa, was likewise far gone in decline.

The small states, Lucca and San Marino, completed the map of Italy. The worst governed part of the peninsula was the south, where feudalism lay heavily on the cultivators and corruption pervaded all ranks. Milan and Piedmont were comparatively well governed; but repugnance to Austrian rule in the former case, and the contagion of French Jacobinical opinions in the latter, brought those populations into increasing hostility to the rulers.

ITALY IN THE NAPOLEONIC PERIOD, 1796–1814

The democratic propaganda, which was permeating all the large towns of the peninsula, then led to the formation of numerous and powerful clubs and secret societies; and the throne of Victor Amadeus III, of the house of Savoy, soon began to totter under the blows delivered by the French troops at the mountain barriers of his kingdom and under the insidious assaults of the friends of liberty at Turin. Plotting was rife at Milan, as also at Bologna, where the memory of old liberties predisposed men to cast off clerical rule and led to the first rising on behalf of Italian liberty in the year 1794. At Palermo the Sicilians struggled hard to establish a republic in place of the odious government of an alien dynasty. The anathemas of the pope, the bravery of Piedmontese and Austrians, and the subsidies of Great Britain failed to keep the league of Italian princes against France intact. The grand-duke of Tuscany was the first of the European sovereigns who made peace with, and recognized the French republic, early in 1795. The first fortnight of Napoleon's campaign of 1796 detached Sardinia from alliance with Austria and England. The enthusiasm of the Italians for the young Corsican 'liberator' greatly helped his progress. Two months later Ferdinand of Naples sought for an armistice, the central duchies were easily overrun, and, early in 1797, Pope Pius VI was fain to sign terms of peace with Bonaparte at Tolentino, practically ceding the northern part of his states, known as the Legations. The surrender of the last Habsburg stronghold, Mantua, on the 2nd of February 1797 left the field clear for the erection of new political institutions.

Already the men of Reggio, Modena and Bologna had declared for a democratic policy, in which feudalism and clerical rule should have no place, and in which manhood suffrage, together with other rights promised by Bonaparte to the men of Milan in May 1796, should form the basis of a new order of things. In taking this step the Modenese and Romagnols had the encouragement of Bonaparte, despite the orders which the French directory sent to him in a contrary sense. The result was the formation of an assembly at Modena which abolished feudal dues and customs, declared for manhood suffrage and established the Cispadane Republic (October 1796).

The close of Bonaparte's victorious campaign against the Archduke Charles in 1797 enabled him to mature those designs respecting Venice. On a far higher level was his conduct towards the Milanese. While the French directory saw in that province little more than a district which might be plundered and bargained for, Bonaparte, though by no means remiss in the exaction of gold and of artistic treasures, was laying the foundation of a friendly republic. During his sojourn at the castle of Montebello or Mombello, near Milan, he commissioned several of the leading men of northern Italy to draw up a project of constitution and list of reforms for that province. Meanwhile he took care to curb the excesses of the Italian Jacobins and to encourage the Moderates, who were favourable to the French connexion as promising a guarantee against Austrian domination and internal anarchy. He summed up his conduct in the letter of the 8th May 1797 to the French directory, 'I cool the hot heads here and warm the cool ones'. The Transpadane Republic, or, as it was soon called, the Cisalpine Republic, began its organized life on the 9th July 1797, with a brilliant festival at Milan. The constitution was modelled on that of the French directory, and, lest there should be a majority of clerical or Jacobinical deputies, the French Republic through its general, Bonaparte, nominated and appointed the first deputies and administrators of the new government. In the same month it was joined by the Cispadane Republic; and the terms of the treaty of Campo Formio (October 17, 1797), while fatal to the political life of Venice, awarded to this now considerable state the Venetian territories west of the river Adige. A month later, under the pretence of stilling the civil strifes in the Valtelline, Bonaparte absorbed that Swiss district in the Cisalpine Republic, which thus included all the lands between Como and Verona on the north, and Rimini on the south.

Early in the year 1798 the Austrians, in pursuance of the scheme of partition agreed on at Campo Formio, entered Venice and brought to an end its era of independence which had lasted some 1100 years. Venice with its mainland territories east of the Adige, inclusive of Austria and Dalmatian, went to the Habsburgs, while the Venetian isles of the Adriatic (the Ionian Isles) and the Venetian fleet went to strengthen France for that eastern expedition on which Bonaparte had already set his heart. Venice not only paid the costs of the war to the two chief belligerents, but her naval resources also helped to launch the young general on his career of eastern adventure. Her former rival, Genoa, had also been compelled, in June 1797, to bow before the young conqueror, and had undergone at his hands a remodelling on the lines already followed at Milan. The new Genoese republic, French in all but name, was renamed the Ligurian Republic.

Before he set sail for Egypt, the French had taken possession of Rome. Already masters of the papal fortress of Ancon, they began openly to challenge the pope's authority at the Eternal City itself. Joseph Bonaparte, then French envoy to the Vatican, encouraged democratic manifestations; and one of them, at the close of 1797, led to a scuffle in which a French general, Duphot, was killed. The French directory at once ordered its general, Berthier, to march to Rome: the Roman democrats proclaimed a republic on the 15th February 1798, and on their invitation Berthier and his troops marched in. The pope, Pius VI, was forthwith hauled away to Siena and a year later to Valence in the south of France, where he died. Thus fell the temporal power. The 'liberators' of Rome thereupon proceeded to plunder the city in a way which brought shame on their cause and disgrace (perhaps not wholly deserved) on the general left in command, Masséna.

These events brought revolution to the gates of the Kingdom of Naples, the worst-governed part of Italy, where the boorish king, Ferdinand IV (*il rè lazzarone*, he was termed), and his whimsical consort, Maria Carolina, scarcely held in check the discontent of their own subjects. A British fleet under Nelson, sent into the Mediterranean in May 1798 primarily for their defence, checkmated the designs of Bonaparte in Egypt, and then, returning to Naples, encouraged that court to adopt a spirited policy. It is now known that the influence of Nelson and of the British ambassador, Sir William Hamilton, and Lady Hamilton precipitated the rupture between Naples and France. The results were disastrous. The Neapolitan troops at first occupied Rome, but, being badly handled by their leader, the Austrian general, Mack, they were soon scattered in flight; and the Republican troops under General

Championnet, after crushing the stubborn resistance of the lazzaroni, made their way into Naples and proclaimed the Parthenopaean Republic (January 23, 1799). The Neapolitan Democrats chose five of their leading men to be directors, and tithes and feudal dues and customs were abolished. Much good work was done by the Republicans with his army beyond the river Mincio, ten days earlier during their brief tenure of power, but it soon came to an end owing to the course of events which favoured a reaction against France. The directors of Paris, not content with overrunning and plundering Switzerland, had outraged German sentiment in many ways. Further, at the close of 1798 they virtually compelled the young king of Sardinia, Charles Emmanuel IV, to abdicate at Turin. He retired to the island of Sardinia, while the French despoiled Piedmont, thereby adding fuel to the resentment rapidly growing against them in every part of Europe.

The outcome of it all was the War of the Second Coalition, in which Russia, Austria, Great Britain, Naples and some secondary states of Germany took part. The incursion of an Austro-Russian army, led by that strange but magnetic being, Suvarov, decided the campaign in northern Italy. The French, poorly handled by Schérer and Sérurier, were everywhere beaten, especially at Magnano (April 5) and Cassano (April 27). Milan and Turin fell before the allies, and Moreau, who took over the command, had much difficulty in making his way to the Genoese coast-line. There he awaited the arrival of Macdonald with the army of Naples. That general, Championnet's successor, had been compelled by these reverses and by the threatening pressure of Nelson's fleet to evacuate Naples and central Italy. In many parts the peasants and townsfolk, enraged by the licence of the French, hung on his flank and rear. The republics set up by the French at Naples, Rome and Milan collapsed as soon as the French troops retired; and a reaction in favour of clerical and Austrian influence set in with great violence. For the events which then occurred at Naples, so compromising to the reputation of Nelson, Sir William Hamilton was subsequently recalled in a manner closely resembling a disgrace, and his place was taken by Paget, who behaved with more dignity and tact.

Meanwhile Macdonald, after struggling through central Italy, had defeated an Austrian force at Modena (June 12, 1799), but Suvarov was able by swift movements utterly to overthrow him at the Trebbia (June 17–19). The wreck of his force drifted away helplessly towards Genoa. A month later the ambitious young general, Joubert, who took over Moreau's command and rallied part of Macdonald's following, was utterly routed by the Austro-Russian army at Novi (August 15) with the loss of 12,000 men. Joubert perished in the battle. The growing friction between Austria and Russia led to the transference of Suvarov and his Russians to Switzerland, with results which were to be fatal to the allies in that quarter. But in Italy the Austrian successes continued. Melas defeated Championnet near Coni on the 4th November; and a little later the French garrisons at Ancona and Coni surrendered. The tricolour, which floated triumphantly over all the strongholds of Italy early in the year, at its close waved only over Genoa, where Masséna prepared for a stubborn defence. Nice and Savoy also seemed at the mercy of the invaders. Everywhere the old order of things was restored.

The death of the aged Pope Pius VI at Valence (August 29, 1799) deprived the French of whatever advantage they had hoped to gain by dragging him into exile; on the 24th March 1800 the conclave, assembled for greater security on the island of San Giorgio at Venice, elected a new pontiff, Pius VII.

Such was the position of affairs when Bonaparte returned from Egypt and landed at Fréjus. The contrast presented by his triumphs, whether real or imaginary, to the reverses sustained by the armies of the French directory, was fatal to that body and to popular institutions in France. After the coup d'état of Brumaire (November 1799) he, as First Consul, began to organize an expedition against the Austrians (Russia having now retired from the coalition), in northern Italy. The campaign culminating at Marengo was the result. By that triumph (due to Desaix and Kellermann rather than directly to him), Bonaparte consolidated his own position in France and again laid Italy at his feet. The Austrian general, Melas, signed an armistice whereby he was to retire on the 4th June, Masséna had been compelled by hunger to capitulate at Genoa; but the success at Marengo, followed up by that of Macdonald in north Italy, and Moreau at Hohenlinden (December 2, 1800), brought Emperor Francis to sue for peace which was finally concluded at Lunéville on the 9th February 1801. The Cisalpine and Ligurian Republics (reconstituted soon after Marengo) were recognized by Austria on condition that they were independent of France. The rule of Pius VII over the Papal States was admitted; and Italian affairs were arranged much as they were at Campo Formio: Modena and Tuscany now reverted to French control, their former rulers being promised compensation in Germany. Naples, easily worsted by the French, under Miollis, left the British alliance, and made peace by the treaty of Florence (March 1801), agreeing to withdraw her troops from the Papal States, to cede Piombino and the Presidii (in Tuscany) to France and to close her ports to British ships and commerce. King Ferdinand also had to accept a French garrison at Taranto, and other points in the south.

Other changes took place in that year, all of them in favour of France. By complex and secret bargaining with the court of Madrid, Bonaparte procured the cession to France of Louisiana, in North America, and Parma; while the duke of Parma (husband of an Infanta of Spain) was promoted by him to the duchy of Tuscany, now Italy, renamed the Kingdom of Etruria. Piedmont was declared to be a military division at the disposal of France (April 2 1801); and on the 21st September 1802, Bonaparte, then First Consul for life, issued a decree for its definitive incorporation in the French Republic. About that time, too, Elba fell into the hands of Napoleon. Piedmont was organized in six departments on the model of those of France, and a number of French veterans were settled by Napoleon in and near the fortress of Alessandria. Besides copying the Roman habit of planting military colonies, the First Consul imitated the old conquerors of the world by extending and completing the road-system of his outlying districts, especially at those important passes, the Mont Cenis and Simplon. He greatly improved the rough track over the Simplon Pass, so that, when finished in 1807, it was practicable for artillery. Milan was the terminus of the road, and the construction of the Foro Buonaparte and the completion of the cathedral added dignity to the Lombard capital. The Corniche road was improved; and public Works in various parts of Piedmont, and the Cisalpine and Ligurian Republics attested the foresight and wisdom of the great organizer of industry and quickener of human energies. The universities of Pavia and Bologna were reopened and made great progress in this time of peace and growing prosperity. Somewhat later the Pavia canal was begun in order to connect Lake Como with the Adriatic for barge-traffic.

The personal nature of the tie binding Italy to France was illustrated by a curious incident of the winter of 1802–1803. Bonaparte, now First Consul for life, felt strong enough to impose his will on the Cisalpine Republic and to set at defiance one of the stipulations of the treaty of Lunéville. On the pretext of consolidating that republic, he invited 450 of its leading men to come to Lyons to a consulta. In reality he and his agents had already provided for the passing of proposals which were agreeable to him. The deputies having been dazzled by fétes and reviews, Talleyrand and Marescalchi, ministers of foreign affairs at Paris and Milan, plied them with hints as to the course to be followed by the consulta; and, despite the rage of the more democratic of their number, everything corresponded to the wishes of the First Consul. It remained to find a chief. Very many were in favour of Count Melzi, a Lombard noble, who had been chief of the executive at Milan; but again Talleyrand and French agents set to Work on behalf of their master, with the result that he was elected president for ten years. He accepted that office because, as he frankly informed the deputies, he had found no one who 'for his services rendered to his country, his authority with the people and his separation from party has deserved such an office'. Melzi was elected vice-president with merely honorary functions. The constitution comprised a consulta charged with executive duties, a legislative body of 150 members and a court charged with the maintenance of the fundamental laws. These three bodies were to be chosen by three electoral colleges consisting of (a) landed proprietors, (b) learned men and clerics, (c) merchants and traders, holding their sessions biennially at Milan, Bologna and Brescia respectively. In practice the consulta could override the legislature; and, as the consulta was little more than the organ of the president, the whole constitution may be pronounced as autocratic as that of France after the changes brought about by Bonaparte in August 1802. Finally we must note that the Cisalpine now took the name of the Italian Republic, and that by a concordat with the pope, Bonaparte regulated its relations to the Holy See in a manner analogous to that adopted in the famous French concordat promulgated at Easter 1802. It remains to add that the Ligurian Republic and that of Lucca remodelled their constitutions in a way somewhat similar to that of the Cisalpine.

Bonaparte's ascendancy did not pass unchallenged. Many of the Italians retained their enthusiasm for democracy and national Kingdom independence. In 1803 movements in these directions took place at Rimini, Brescia and Bologna; but they were sharply repressed, and most Italians came to acquiesce in the Napoleonic supremacy as inevitable and indeed beneficial. The complete disregard shown by Napoleon for one of the chief conditions of the treaty of Lunéville (February 1801) – that stipulating for the independence of the Ligurian and Cisalpine Republics - became more and more apparent every year. Alike in political and commercial affairs they were for all practical purposes dependencies of France. Finally, after the proclamation of the French empire (May 18, 1804) Napoleon proposed to place his brother Joseph over the Italian state, which now took the title of kingdom of Italy. On Joseph declining, Napoleon finally decided to accept the crown which Melzi, Marescalchi, Serbelloni and others begged him to assume. Accordingly, on the 26th May 1805, in the cathedral at Milan, he crowned himself with the iron crown of the old Lombard kings, using the traditional formula, 'God gave it me: let him beware who touches it'. On the 7th June he appointed his stepson, Eugène Beauharnais, to be Viceroy. Eugène soon found that his chief duty was to enforce the will of Napoleon. The legislature at Milan having ventured to alter some details of taxation, Eugène received the following rule of conduct from his stepfather: 'Your system of government is simple: the emperor wills it to be thus'. Republicanism was now everywhere discouraged. The little republic of Lucca, along with Piombino, was now awarded as a principality by the emperor to Elisa Bonaparte and her husband, Bacciocchi. In June 1805 there came a last and intolerable affront to the Emperors of Austria and Russia, who at that very time were seeking to put bounds to Napoleon's ambition and to redress the balance of power. The French Emperor, at the supposed request of the doge of Genoa, declared the Ligurian Republic to be an integral part of the French empire. This defiance to the sovereigns of Russia and Austria rekindled the flames of war. The third coalition was formed between Great Britain, Russia and Austria, Naples soon joining its ranks. While Masséna pursued the Austrians into their own lands at the close of 1805, Italian forces under Eugène and Gouvion St Cyr held their ground against allied forces landed at Naples. After Austerlitz (December 2, 1805) Austria made peace by the treaty of Pressburg, ceding to the Kingdom of Italy her part of Venetia along with the provinces of Istria and Dalmatia. Napoleon then turned fiercely against Maria Carolina of Naples upbraiding her with her 'perfidy'. He sent Joseph Bonaparte and Masséna southwards with a strong column, compelled the Anglo-Russian forces to evacuate Naples, and occupied the south of the peninsula with little opposition except at the fortress of Gaeta. The Bourbon court sailed away to Palermo, where it remained for eight years under the protection afforded by the British fleet and a British army of occupation. On the 15th February 1806 Joseph Bonaparte entered Naples in triumph, his troops capturing there two hundred pieces of cannon. Gaeta, however, held out stoutly against the French. Sir Sidney Smith with a British squadron captured Capri (February 1806), and the peasants of the Abruzzi and Calabria soon began to give trouble. Worst of all was the arrival of a small British force in Calabria under Sir John Stuart, which beat off with heavy loss an attack imprudently delivered by General Réynier on level ground near the village of Maida (July 4). The steady volleys of Kempt's light infantry were fatal to the French, who fell back in disorder under a bayonet charge of the victors, with the loss of some 2700 men. Calabria now rose in revolt against King Joseph, and the peasants dealt out savage reprisals to the French troops. On the 18th July, however, Gaeta surrendered to Masséna, and that Marshal, now moving rapidly southwards, extricated Réynier, crushed the Bourbon rising in Calabria with great barbarity, and compelled the British force to re-embark for Sicily. At Palermo Queen Maria Carolina continued to make vehement but futile efforts for the overthrow of King Joseph. It is more important to observe that under Joseph and his ministers or advisers, including the Frenchmen Roederer, Dumas, Miot de Melito and the Corsican Saliceti, great progress was made in abolishing feudal laws and customs, in reforming the judicial procedure and criminal laws on the model of the Code Napoléon, and in attempting the beginnings of elementary education. More questionable was Joseph's policy in closing and confiscating the property of 213 of the richer monasteries of the land. The monks were pensioned off, but though the confiscated property helped to fill the empty coffers of the state, the measure aroused widespread alarm and resentment among that superstitious people.

The peace of Tilsit (July 7 1807) enabled Napoleon to press on his projects for securing the command of the Mediterranean, thenceforth a fundamental axiom of his policy. Consequently, in the autumn of 1807 he urged on Joseph the adoption of vigorous measures for the capture of Sicily. Already, in the negotiations with England during the summer of 1806, the emperor had shown his sense of the extreme importance of gaining possession of that island, which indeed caused the breakdown of the peace proposals then being considered; and now he ordered French squadrons into the Mediterranean in order to secure Corfu and Sicily. His plans respecting Corfu succeeded. That island and some of the adjacent isles fell into the hands of the French (some of them were captured by British troops in 1809–10); but Sicily remained unassailable. Capri, however, fell to the French on the 18th October 1808, shortly after the arrival at Naples of the new King, Murat.

This ambitious Marshal, brother-in-law of Napoleon, foiled in his hope of gaining the crown of Spain, received that of Naples in the summer of 1808, Joseph Bonaparte being moved from Naples to Madrid. This arrangement pleased neither of the relatives of the Emperor; but his will now was law on the continent. Joseph left Naples on the 23rd May 1808; but it was not until the 6th September that Joachim Murat made his entry. A fortnight later his consort Caroline arrived, and soon showed a vigour and restlessness of spirit which frequently clashed with the dictates of her brother, the emperor and the showy, unsteady policy of her consort. The Spanish national rising of 1808 and thereafter the Peninsular War diverted Napoleon's attention from the affairs of south Italy. In June 1809, during his campaign against Austria, Sir John Stuart with an Anglo-Sicilian force sailed northwards, captured Ischia and threw Murat into great alarm; but on the news of the Austrian defeat at Wagram, Stuart sailed back again.

It is now time to turn to the affairs of central Italy. Early in 1808 Napoleon proceeded with plans which he had secretly concerted after the treaty of Tilsit for transferring the Infanta of Spain who, after the death of her consort, reigned at Florence on behalf of her young son, Charles Louis, from her kingdom of Etruria to the little principality of Entre Douroe of Portugal. Etruria reverted to the French empire, but the Spanish princess and her son did not receive the promised indemnity. Elisa Bonaparte and her husband, Bacciocchi, rulers of Lucca and Piombino, became the heads of the administration in Tuscany, Elisa showing decided governing capacity. The last part of the peninsula to undergo the Gallicizing influence was the papal dominion. For some time past the relations between Napoleon and the pope, Pius VII, had been severely strained, chiefly because the emperor insisted papacy, on controlling the church, both in France and in the kingdom of Italy, in a way inconsistent with the traditions of the Vatican, but also because the pontiff refused to grant the divorce between Jerome Bonaparte and the former Miss Patterson on which Napoleon early in the year 1806 laid so much stress. These and other disputes led the emperor, as successor of Charlemagne, to treat the pope in a very highhanded way. 'Your Holiness (he wrote) is sovereign of Rome, but I am its Emperor'; and he threatened to annul the presumed donation of Rome by Charlemagne, unless the pope yielded implicit obedience to him in all temporal affairs. He further exploited the Charlemagne tradition for the benefit of the continental system, that great engine of commercial war by which he hoped to assure the ruin of England. This aim prompted the annexation of Tuscany, and his intervention in the affairs of the Papal States. To this the pope assented under pressure from Napoleon; but the latter soon found other pretexts for intervention, and in February 1808 a French column under Miollis occupied Rome, and deposed the papal authorities. Against this violence Pius VII protested in vain. Napoleon sought to push matters to an extreme, and on the 2nd April he adopted the rigorous measure of annexing to the Kingdom of Italy the papal provinces of Ancona, Papal Urbino, Macerata and Camerina. This measure, which seemed to the pious an act of sacrilege, and to Italian patriots an outrage on the only independent sovereign of the peninsula, sufficed for the present. The outbreak of war in Spain, followed by the rupture with Austria in the Spring of 1809, distracted the attention of the emperor. But after the occupation of Vienna the conqueror dated from that capital on the 17th May 1809 a decree virtually annexing Rome and the Patrimonium Petri to the French empire. Here again he cited the action of Charlemagne, his 'august predecessor', who had merely given 'certain domains to the bishops of Rome as fiefs, though Rome did not thereby cease to be part of his empire'. In reply the Pope prepared a bull of excommunication against those who should infringe the prerogatives of the Holy See in this matter. Thereupon the French general, Miollis, who still occupied Rome, caused the Pope to be arrested and carried him away northwards into Tuscany, thence to Savona; finally he was taken, at Napoleon's orders, to Fontainebleau. Thus, a second time, fell the temporal power of the papacy. By an imperial decree of the 17th February 1810, Rome and the neighbouring districts, including Spoleto, became part of the French empire. Rome thenceforth figured as its second city, and entered upon a new life under the administration of French officials. The Roman territory was divided into two departments – the Tiber and Trasimenus; the Code Napoléon was introduced, public works were set on foot and great advance was made in the material sphere. Nevertheless the harshness with which the emperor treated the Roman clergy and suppressed the monasteries caused deep resentment to the orthodox.

There is no need to detail the fortunes of the Napoleonic states in Italy. One and all they underwent the influences emanating from Paris; and in respect to civil administration, law, judicial procedure education and public works they all experienced great benefits, the results of which never wholly disappeared. On the other hand, they suffered from the rigorous measures of the continental system, which seriously crippled trade at the ports and were not compensated by the increased facilities for trade with France which Napoleon opened up. The drain of men to supply his armies in Germany, Spain and Russia was also a serious loss. A powerful Italian corps marched under Eugène Beauharnais to Moscow, and distinguished itself at Malo-Jaroslavitz, as also during the horrors of the retreat in the closing weeks of 1812. It is said that out of 27,000 Italians who entered Russia with Eugène, only 333 saw their country again. That campaign marked the beginning of the end for the Napoleonic domination in Italy as else-where. Murat, left in command of the Grand Army at Vilna, abandoned his charge and in the next year made overtures to the allies who coalesced against Napoleon. For his vacillations at this time and his final fate, here it must suffice to say that the uncertainty caused by his policy in 1813–1814 had no small share in embarrassing Napoleon and in precipitating the downfall of his power in Italy. Eugène Beauharnais, viceroy of the kingdom of Italy, showed both constancy and courage; but after the battle of Leipzig (October 16–19, 1813) his power crumbled away under the assaults of the now victorious Austrians. By an arrangement with Bavaria, they were able to march through Tirol and down the valley of the Adige in force, and overpowered the troops of Eugène whose position was fatally compromised by the defection of Murat and the dissensions among the Italians. Very many of them, distrusting both of these kings, sought to act independently in favour of an Italian republic. Lord William Bentinck with an Anglo-Sicilian force landed at Leghorn on the 8th March 1814, and issued a proclamation to the Italians bidding them rise against Napoleon in the interests of their own freedom. A little later he gained possession of Genoa. Amidst these schisms the defence of Italy collapsed. On the 16th April 1814 Eugène, on hearing of Napoleon's overthrow at Paris, signed an armistice at Mantua by which he was enabled to send away the French troops beyond the Alps and entrust himself to the consideration of the allies. The Austrians, under General Bellegarde, entered Milan without resistance; and this event precluded the restoration of the old political order.

The arrangements made by the allies in accordance with the treaty of Paris (June 12, 1814) and the Final Act of the congress of Vienna (June 9, 1815), imposed on Italy boundaries which, roughly speaking, corresponded to those of the pre-Napoleonic era. To the Kingdom of Sardinia, now reconstituted under Victor Emmanuel I, France ceded its old provinces, Savoy and Nice; and the allies, especially Great Britain and Austria, insisted on the addition to that monarchy of the territories of the former republic of Genoa, in respect of which the king took the title of Duke of Genoa, in order to strengthen it for the duty of acting as a buffer state between France and the smaller states of central Italy. Austria recovered the Milanese, and all the possessions of the old Venetian Republic on the mainland, including Istria and Dalmatia. The Ionian Islands, formerly belonging to Venice, were, by a treaty signed at Paris on the 5th November 1815, placed under the protection of Great Britain. By an instrument signed on the 24th April 1815, the Austrian territories in north Italy were erected into the kingdom of Lombardo-Venetia, which, though an integral part of the Austrian empire, was to enjoy a separate administration, the symbol of its separate individuality being the coronation of the Emperors with the ancient iron crown of Lombardy ('Proclamation de l'Empereur d'Autriche, &c.', April 7, 1815, State Papers, ii. 906). Francis IV, son of the Archduke Ferdinand of Austria and Maria Beatrice, daughter of Ercole Rinaldo, the last of the Estensi, was reinstated as duke of Modena. Parma and Piacenza were assigned to Marie Louise, daughter of the Austrian emperor and wife of Napoleon, 'on behalf of her son, the little Napoleon', but by subsequent arrangements (1816–1817) the duchy was to revert at her death to the Bourbons of Parma, then reigning at Lucca. Tuscany was restored to the grand-duke Ferdinand III of Habsburg-Lorraine. The Duchy of Lucca was given to Marie Louise of Bourbon-Parma, who, at the death of Marie Louise of Austria, would return to Parma, when Lucca would be handed over to Tuscany. The Pope, Pius VII, who had long been kept under restraint by Napoleon at Fontainebleau, returned to Rome in May 1814, and was recognized by the congress of Vienna (not without some demur on the part of Austria) as the sovereign of all the former possessions of the Holy See. Ferdinand IV of Naples, not long after the death of his consort, Maria Carolina, in Austria, returned from Sicily to take possession of his dominions on the mainland. He received them back in their entirety at the hands of the powers, who recognized his new title of Ferdinand I of the Two Sicilies. The rash attempt of Murat in the autumn of 1815, which led to his death at Pizzo in Calabria, enabled the Bourbon dynasty to crush malcontents with all the greater severity. The reaction, which was dull and heavy in the dominions of the pope and of Victor Emmanuel, systematically harsh in the Austrian states of the north, and comparatively mild in Parma and Tuscany, excited the greatest loathing in southern Italy and Sicily, because there it was directed by a dynasty which had aroused feelings of hatred mingled with contempt.

There were special reasons why Sicily should harbour these feelings against the Bourbons. During eight years (1806–1814) the chief places of the island had been garrisoned by British troops; and the commander of the force which upheld the tottering rule of Ferdinand at Palermo naturally had great authority. The British government, which awarded a large annual subsidy to the king and queen at Palermo, claimed to have some control over the administration. Lord William Bentinck finally took over large administrative powers, seeing that Ferdinand, owing to his dullness, and Maria Carolina, owing to her very suspicious intrigues with Napoleon, could never be trusted. The contest between the royal power and that of the Sicilian estates threatened to bring matters to a deadlock, until in 1812, under the impulse of Lord William Bentinck, a constitution modelled largely on that of England was passed by the estates. After the retirement of the British troops in 1814 the constitution lapsed, and the royal authority became once more absolute. But the memory of the benefits conferred by 'the English Constitution' remained fresh and green amidst the arid waste of repression which followed. It lived on as one of the impalpable but powerful influences which spurred on the Sicilians and the democrats of Naples to the efforts which they put forth in 1821, 1830, 1848 and 1860.

This result, accruing from British intervention, was in some respects similar to that exerted by Napoleon on the Italians of the mainland. The brutalities of Austria's white coats in the north, the unintelligent repression then characteristic of the house of Savoy, the petty spite of the duke of Modena, the medieval obscurantism of pope and cardinals in the middle of the peninsula and the clownish excesses of Ferdinand in the south, could not blot out from the minds of the Italians the recollection of the benefits derived from the just laws, vigorous administration and enlightened aims of the great emperor. The hard but salutary training which they had undergone at his hands had taught them that they were the equals of the northern races both in the council chamber and on the field of battle. It had further revealed to them that truth, which once grasped can never be forgotten, that, despite differences of climate, character and speech, they were in all essentials a nation.

Note on Terminology and Unit Titles

Throughout, this work uses Italian military terminology for ranks and titles and section headings, although occasionally not in the body text but only when exact equivalents exist (i.e. you will sometimes find 'captain' not '*capitano*' and '1st Regiment' and not '1° Reggimento', etc.)

The reason for doing this is to maintain a consistency that is usually lacking in English-language works on the Italian Army whereby '*sottotenente*' would become 'second lieutenant', '*fanteria*' would become 'infantry' (or even 'foot') but 'Cacciatori a cavallo' would at best become simply 'chasseurs a cheval', in itself a French term not an English one … it is thus easier and clearer to use the original Italian.

An anomaly worth mentioning is that the French term 'sabre-briquet' is used for the infantry pattern short sword. There is no really accurate translation of this term and the weapon was a direct and exact copy of that in use by the French Army, so the French term seems appropriate.

The English equivalents of the original Italian are immediately obvious in most cases but included below is a glossary of Italian to English ranks and titles that may occasionally be of help. It is also useful to bear in mind that the command structure and rank titles were often copied from the French Army on which the Army of the Kingdom of Italy was modelled.

Italian	English	Notes
Aiutante	Adjutant	to a battalion
Aiutante-sottufficiale	Adjutant NCO	to a company
Ammiraglio	Admiral	
Artigliere	Gunner	
Primo artigliere	1st class gunner	
Autista	Driver	Drove artillery limbers, supply wagons, etc.
Bracciante	Worker	Literally 'labourer'
Brigadiere	Corporal	Cavalry
Cacciatore	Chasseur	Centre company, light infantry
Capitano	Captain	

NOTE ON TERMINOLOGY AND UNIT TITLES

Italian	English	Notes
Capo di squadrone	Squadron commander	Roughly a major
Capo di battaglione	Battalion commander	Roughly a lieutenant-colonel
Chirurge-maggiore	Surgeon-major	Regimental senior surgeon
Chirurge	Surgeon	
Comandante	Commander	Naval rank
Cornette	Hornist	
Corporale	Corporal	Infantry
Caporale-furiere	Quartermaster corporal	To a company
Caporale-tamburo	Corporal-drummer	Responsible for the drummers of a unit
Colonnello	Colonel	
Colonnello sotto	No equivalent	A rank somewhere between colonel and lieutenant-colonel
Contrammiraglio	Rear Admiral	
Generale di brigata	Brigadier-general	
Generale di divisione	Major-general	
Furiere	Quartermaster	
Maggiore	Major	
Maestro-artigiano	Master artisan	On a regimental staff
Maniscalco	Farrier	
Musicanti	Bandsmen	
Porta aquila	Eagle bearer	A title, not a rank, the holder would have held a military rank
Quartiermastro	Quartermaster	To a battalion or regiment.
Sergente	Sergeant	
Sergente-maggiore	Sergeant-major	
Sotto-chirurgo	Assistant surgeon	
Sottotenente	2nd Lieutenant	Roughly the equivalent of the British rank of ensign, itself a rank still in use during this period
Sottufficiale	NCO	
Tenente	Lieutenant	
Tamburo	Drummer	

THE ARMY OF THE KINGDOM OF ITALY 1805–1814

Italian	English	Notes
Tamburo-maggiori	Drum-major	Responsible for both drummers and musicians within a unit. The next in line above the *caporale-tamburo*
Tromba-maggiori		Trumpet-major
Trombettista	Trumpeter	
Veterinario	Veterinarian	
Vice ammiraglio	Vice admiral	
Zappatore	Sapper	

1

General Officers and Staff

As with many, perhaps most, of the uniforms of the Army of the Kingdom of Italy those of the Italian general officers closely followed the pattern of that worn by their French equivalents. However, the basic colour of the uniform for the Italian general officers and staff was dark green in place of the French blue.

Again, as with the general officers the uniform of the *aiutanti* and staff echoed that of their Fremch counterparts.

Eugène Rose de Beauharnais, Viceroy of Italy

(Paris, 3 September 1781–Munich, 21 February 1824)[1]

1805	7 Jun	Proclaimed Viceroy of Italy
	13 Dec	Promoted to Général de Division in the French Army
1806	3 Jan	Appointed Commander-in-Chief of the Armée d'Italie
1809	16 Apr	Battle of Sacile
	14 Jun	Battle of Raab
	5–6 Jul	Battle of Wagram
1812	18 Apr	Leaves Milan for the Russian campaign as commander of IV Corps of the Grande Armée (see Appendix)
	19 Aug	Battle of Smolensk
	7 Sep	Battle of Borodino
	24 Oct	Battle of Maloyaroslavets
1813	16 Jan	Appointed Commander of the Grande Armée when Murat left the Army to return to Naples
	5 Apr	Battle of Möckern

---

1 Eugène is buried in the Church of St Michael in Munich. He had been created Duke of Leuchtenberg by his father-in-law Maximilian I Joseph, King of Bavaria on 14 November 1817. The title became extinct with the death of the 8th Duke, Sergei Georgievich, in Rome in 1974, although the title is claimed by the line of Nicolas Alexander Fritz de Beauharnais, through a morganatic marriage.

	1–2 May	Battle of Lützen
	22 Nov	Eugène refuses the Allies' offers to abandon Napoleon
1814	8 Feb	Battle of the Mincio
	16 Apr	Signs the Armistice at Milan
	23 Apr	Surrenders the Army at Mantua. (Napoleon abdicates on 22 June)

Uniform

Eugène is shown in a portrait by Richter[2] in a uniform essentially that described below for general officers but with gold lace on the bicorne, a dark blue coat with a dark blue collar, both embroidered with gold oak leaf design, and all buttons gilt. The oak leaf embroidery covers the front of the coat, along both sides of the opening, and also follows around the lower edge and down into the tails. The heavy bullion-fringed epaulettes are gold. He does not wear a sash and the narrow red waist belt is laced gold with a gilt clasp. His sword has a gilt hilt, gilt sword strap and knot, and gilt scabbard. Richter shows Eugène wearing a dark blue cloak over the coat but there is no indication of lining colour for either cloak or coat.

Richard Knötel's plate of Eugène in *Grosse Uniformenkunde*[3] shows a somewhat simpler uniform, taken from an illustration by Albrecht Adam of Eugène in campaign dress during the 1812 campaign, in contrast to Richter's portrait showing gala or full dress. The coat has the oak leaf embroidery only on the collar of the dark blue coat which has black Polish cuffs edged with two lines of gold piping, and black turnbacks with gold eagle badges. The horse furniture is a red shabraque with a wide gold lace just inside the edge and gold fringe along the very edge; the red double pistol holster covers have a similar edging. Another illustration by Albrecht Adam of Eugène in 1812 shows essentially the same uniform but with dark blue breeches in place of white.

In both Richter's portrait and Knötel's plate the Viceroy is shown with all but the lower two buttons of the coat undone to show a white shirt beneath and the red sash of the Légion d'Honneur worn *under* the coat. Albrecht Adam shows a similar conceit in his illustrations of Eugène in 1812 confirming that this is almost certainly how the Viceroy usually appeared, and obviously the Viceroy's personal preference.

A contemporary picture by Lejeune shows Eugène at Borodino again in essentially the same uniform as that shown by Albrecht Adam, including the eccentricity of it being fastened by only the lower two buttons,[4] obviously a personal conceit of Eugène.

---

2   Johann Heinri Richter, 1803–1845. Painting in the Leuchtenberg Collection in Munich.
3   Richard Knötel, *Grosse Uniformenkunde* (Rathenow: Max Babeuzien, 1890–1914). Band III, Nr 58.
4   F. G. Hourtoulle, *Borodino, The Moskova: The Battle for the Redoubts* (Paris: Histoire & Collections, 2000), p. 87.

GENERAL OFFICERS AND STAFF

Eugene de Beauharnais, Duke of Leuchtenberg post 1815. Artist Unknown.

THE ARMY OF THE KINGDOM OF ITALY 1805–1814

Eugène de Beauharnais at the Battle of Borodino (7 September 1812). Engraving by Albrecht Adam, published in Munich c. 1820, after a sketch made at the time. Eugène is clearly shown with his coat buttoned/unbuttoned in his own eccentric style. (Courtesy Anne S. K. Brown Collection)

Aide-de-Camp to the Viceroy

The aides-de-camp to the viceroy wore the uniform of an *aiutante* (see below) with epaulettes of a *capo di battaglione* and a silver aiguillette on the right shoulder. The cuffs of the coat were trimmed with silver lace; the breeches were dark green decorated with silver lace Hungarian knots on the thighs and a wide silver stripe on the outer seam. The waistcoat was light blue with silver lace at the front and lower edges, and silver frogging at each button and buttonhole. The boots were Hungarian pattern with silver lace trim and tassels. Horse furniture followed that for the *aiutanti*, again see below.

An illustration of an aide-de-camp to Eugene, dated to *c.* 1811, shows an alternative, Hussar-style, uniform:

Headwear
Black/brown colpack with a red bag, unusually hanging on the right-hand side, with silver piping and tassel. Tall white plume at the front above a national cockade. Silver metal chin scales.

Coat
Red, hussar-style dolman with mid-blue collar edged with broad white/silver lace, mid-blue pointed cuffs with four broad white/silver lace chevrons above. White silver lace frogging and three rows of silver buttons.

Red pelisse edged in white fur, four white/silver broad lace chevrons on the sleeves. White/silver frogging and silver buttons.

Blue and white barrel sash with white/silver cords.

Breeches etc.
Mid-blue overalls with two broad white/silver stripes down the outside and blue straps under the boot. Note, there is no evidence of leather inserts.

Equipment
Black boots, but because they are worn underneath overalls the pattern is unknown. Dark red cartouche box strap edged in a broad silver lace worn over the left shoulder. On the front is a silver heart-shaped plate with silver chains attaching the plate to another higher up. The cartouche box cannot be seen, but speculation would suggest that this would have been the small cavalry style, perhaps in fashionable red leather rather than black.

Straight cavalry sabre with a brass, single-bar hilt carried in an all-steel scabbard from a white waist belt, mainly hidden by the barrel sash, and white suspension straps. White sword knot and tassel.

Horse Furniture
Because the figure is shown dismounted there is no evidence of horse furniture. This may have been a similar pattern to that used by the *aiutante*, which appears to have been of a general style used throughout the Staff.

A list of Eugène's eight aides at Borodino, together with short biographies of each, is given by Dr F. G. Hourtoulle in *Borodino, The Moskova: The Battle for the Redoubts*.[5]

Generali (General Officers)

Headwear
General officers wore a black bicorne, often velvet faced in full dress, trimmed at the upper edge with elaborate silver lace, which usually incorporated a laurel and oak leaf design, and with silver tassels at the outer tips. Beneath the large national cockade was a silver rosette secured by a wide, deep silver cockade strap which almost reached the lower edge of the hat and was finished with a silver button. The outer edges of the bicorne were trimmed with a feather trim, silver for the viceroy, white for general of division and black for general of brigade. For parade dress the hat was further decorated with a tall white feather plume with short red and green feathers at the base.

Coat
The coat was of a cut similar to that of the regulation coat of French Generals: single-breasted, surtout style with high upright collar, plain squared cuffs

---

5 F. G. Hourtoulle, *Borodino, The Moskova: The Battle for the Redoubts* (Paris: Histoire & Collections, 2000), p. 87.

THE ARMY OF THE KINGDOM OF ITALY 1805–1814

Italien.

Vice-König Eugen.   General.   Adjutant.   Kriegscommissar der Garde.

Das Italienische Heer unter Vice-König Eugen.
1812.

Vice-König Eugen trägt auf der von uns benutzten, der Zeit selbst entstammenden Vorlage eine von der Italienischen Generalsuniform durchaus abweichende Montur — einen zweireihigen blauen Rock mit schwarzen Abzeichen, letztere goldgestickt. Die Schossspiegel zeigen goldene Adler. Die Italienische Generalsuniform zeigt die in der Armee besonders bevorzugte Zusammenstellung von grün, roth und weiss (Silber). Der Adjutant trägt einen grünen Surtout mit hellblauen Abzeichen und weissen Knöpfen. Als besonderes Adjutantenabzeichen um den linken Oberarm eine weisse Armbinde.

Knötel, Uniformenkunde. Band III. No. 58.   Verlag von Max Babenzien in Rathenow.

and long tails without turnbacks but open at the rear with a double vent. This coat was dark green lined red, with red collar and cuffs. It was closed at the front with nine silver buttons embossed with the Imperial eagle. The front of the coat was trimmed with elaborate silver embroidery extending down to the edge and a similar embroidery decorated both sides of the rear vents. The same embroidery embellished the upper and front edge of the collar and upper edge of the cuffs. Nine batons of the embroidery sometimes also appeared on the coat's breast, each baton running out from a button or buttonhole. Epaulettes were silver with thick crescents and heavy bullion fringe; the straps were lace embroidered and decorated with two stars for *generale di brigata* and three for *generale di divisione*.

The silver silk waist sash was knotted at the left hip and ended with heavy silver bullion tassels for both the viceroy and for general officers. The silver sash for *generale di divisione* was worked through with diagonal red stripes, which for *generale di brigata* showed light blue stripes.

Breeches etc.
Breeches were white and worn with high, cuffed heavy cavalry–style boots with brass spurs. General officers' dark green, high-collared greatcoats were of the cavalry pattern with silver lace on the edges of the collar and shoulder straps.

Equipment
Waist belts were the light cavalry pattern in black leather edged with silver braid and with a silvered 'S' buckle and silver fittings. The regulation sword had a gilded hilt (when worn, many officers wore privately purchased swords of their own choice of style, as in the French Army the 'Mameluke style' was popular), the sword knot followed the colouring of the waist sash. Scabbards were silver-plated steel, or black leather with gilt fittings.

Horse Furniture
General officers' shabraques were similar to those of dragoon officers and of dark green cloth with a double wide silver lace trim piped silver at the outer edge, each stripe separated by a welt of dark green, the triple pistol holster covers were decorated in the same way. The viceroy used a shabraque of the same pattern but with the addition of a heavy bullion fringe at the very outer edge. Saddles and harness were black leather, the latter trimmed with silver lace. All buckles and fittings were silver-plated.

General Pino

Pino is shown in an unpublished study by Louis de Beaufort 'after Boisselier', in an otherwise unique uniform, but its very uniqueness makes it worth recording.

Headwear
A brass dragoon pattern helmet with brown fur turban and a black shiny leather peak bound in brass and with brass chinscales. The houpette is white and the helmet has a tall red plume at the left side mounted in a brass socket.

Facing page; Knötel Plate III/58. Eugène, general officers and staff of the Army of Italy. From left: Eugène, general officer, adjutant, military commissary attached to the Royal Guard. Colouring as in the text. (Author's collection)

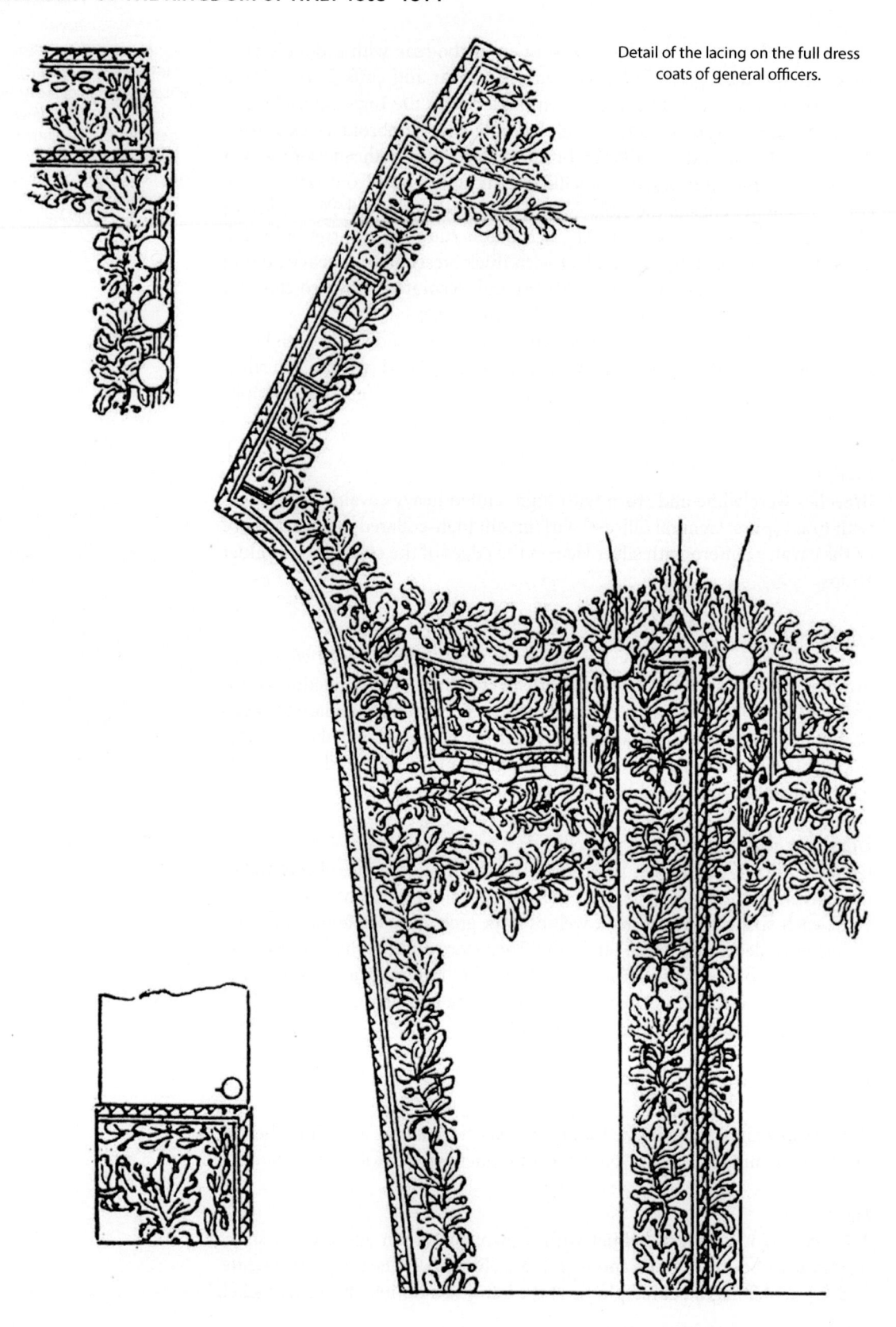

THE ARMY OF THE KINGDOM OF ITALY 1805–1814

Detail of the lacing on the full dress coats of general officers.

GENERAL OFFICERS AND STAFF

Close up detail of the collar and cuff lace. The buttons were probably of the same design as worn by the Guard: an Imperial eagle below the Imperial Crown. On the breast of the eagle was an oval design within which was a star crowned with the Iron Crown (although the author has been unable to confirm this from any contemporary source). H. Malibran, *Guide à l'Usage des Artistes et des Costumiers* (Paris: Combet et Cie, 1907).

Coat
Dark blue habit style with white squared lapels, white collar and white turnbacks, all piped white. The cuffs cannot be seen in the illustration because Pino is wearing white gauntlet-cuffed gloves. All buttons are brass and the epaulettes are full, heavy-fringed pattern in gold. Over his right shoulder he is wearing the red silk sash edged green of the Légion d'Honneur.

Breeches etc.
White waistcoat with brass buttons, white breeches and black heavy cavalry pattern boots

Equipment
White waist belt over the waistcoat with a large square buckle. Heavy-cavalry pattern sword with brass hilt and a gilt sword knot and tassel in an all steel scabbard carried from white slings with brass buckles.

Aiutante-Comandante (Aide-de-Camp Commandant)

Headwear
Black bicorne edged silver with cockade and cockade strap as for general officers.

Coat
In full dress *aiutante-comandante* wore a dark green long-tailed habit with pointed lapels and plain cuffs without cuff flaps. The coat had dark green facings, piped silver and red unpiped turnbacks. The collar was decorated with two horizontal batons of lace, each with a small button at the front; the cuffs had similar batons of vertical lace with a silver button at the top.

On campaign the above coat was usually replaced with the undress coat: the usual pattern surtout with facings as above. This coat was also worn when not on duty and for 'walking-out dress'. A full *colonnello*'s silver epaulettes were worn on both patterns of coat.

Breeches, etc.
Breeches and waistcoats were white for parade and full dress and dark green for campaign dress; buttons were silver. Boots were of the cuffed heavy cavalry pattern with silvered spurs. Greatcoats were of the dark green cavalry pattern with silver batons on the collar, as on the coat.

Equipment
Light cavalry sabre with silvered or gilded hilt, silver sword knot and tassel, black leather scabbard with gilt fittings. The sword was worn from a hussar-style belt of black leather with silver lace trim and silvered fittings.

Horse Furniture
Was the same pattern as that used by general officers with a double, wide silver band at the edge of the shabraque.

GENERAL OFFICERS AND STAFF

Aiutanti (Aides-de-Camp)

Headwear
Black bicorne hat with national cockade and silver cockade strap and tassels. The plume was coloured to indicate the staff level to which the officer was assigned (see below).

Coat
The full dress coat was a dark green short-tailed habit-veste, with pointed lapels, Polish cuffs and 'a la Soubise' pockets. The coat had collar, cuffs and lapels of sky blue and turnbacks of dark green piped sky blue, the pockets were piped sky blue.

In undress and on campaign *aiutanti* wore a dark green surtout coat with collar, cuffs, turnbacks and piping as on the full dress coat.

Epaulettes of rank were worn on both patterns of coat and the arm sash of an *aiutante* was tied above the elbow on the left arm with the tassels hanging on the outside of the arm. This sash, and the bicorne plume, was coloured to denote the staff level to which the aide-de-camp was assigned (note not the officer's actual, personal rank).

	Sash	Plume
Brigade	Sky blue trimmed silver	Sky blue over green
Division	Red trimmed silver	Sky blue over red
Corps/Army	White trimmed silver	Sky blue over red

Breeches etc.
The breeches were green with silver Hungarian knots on the thighs and a silver stripe along the outer seam. The waistcoat was sky blue with silver lace 'frogging' and trim for parade, and plain dark green for undress and campaign. The boots were Hungarian pattern with silver lace and tassel.

Equipment
Waist belts were black leather and sabres were of the pattern used by officers of the light cavalry, with a silver sword knot and tassel.

Horse Furniture
As for the *aiutante-comandante* but with a single wide silver lace band.

Revisori Militari (Military Auditors)

Revisori militari, who were exclusively officers, were a part of the General Staff and were, as the name implies, responsible for checking the accounts of the Army.

Headwear
Black bicorne with national cockade and a silver cockade strap and tassels

Coat
The coat was of the same cut as that of the general officers but was bright red, with dark green collar and plain round cuffs and piping to the horizontal pockets. There was a single line of silver lace at the edge of the collar and the cuffs and on the pockets. Like the generals' coat it had no turnbacks. All buttons were silvered. Inspectors wore a light blue sash, with silver fringe, around the waist over the coat. Sub-inspectors had a green sash with a gold fringe. Revisiori attached to the Guard wore a silver aiguillette on the right shoulder.

Breeches etc.
Breeches and waistcoats were white for parade and full dress and dark green for campaign dress; again buttons were silver. Boots were of the cuffed heavy cavalry pattern with silvered spurs.

Equipment
Officers' pattern sword with silvered or gilded hilt, silver sword knot and tassel, black leather scabbard with gilt fittings. The sword was carried on a black leather waist belt with silver lace trim and silvered fittings, worn under the coat and over the waistcoat.

Horse Furniture
The shabraque and pistol holsters were of the same pattern as that used by general officers but in red with wide silver lace edge.

Revisore Capo (Chief Auditor)

The uniform was generally the same as above but with some minor additional decoration.

Headwear
As above with the addition of silver lace along the edge and white plumes.

Coat
The coat was of the same colouring and cut as the auditors but had double silver lace on the collar and a silver 'oak leaf' design lace down the front of the coat and around the cuffs and the edges of the coat's tails. His sash was red with a silver fringe.

Commissari di Guerra (Military Commissaries)

Commissari di Guerra were responsible for arranging and organising quarters and the supply services for the Army both on campaign and during peacetime. Note, the uniform was generally similar in cut and style to the *revisori militari*.

Headwear
Black bicorne with national cockade and a silver cockade strap and tassels.

Coat
The coat, of the same cut as that of the general officers, was light blue with a bright red collar and plain round cuffs and piping to the horizontal pockets. Like the generals' and the auditors' coats it had no turnbacks. The coat fastened with nine silvered buttons.

Commissari on the General Staff had a double silver lace edge to the collar, cuffs and pockets and the silver oak leaf pattern lace on the front of the coat and around the tails; *commissari* attached to divisions had a single silver lace on the collar, cuffs and pockets, whereas *commissari* 'ordinari' had silver lace only on the collar and cuffs. *Commissari aiutanti* had silver lace only on the collar but with a narrow dark green lace inside it.

As with the *revisori*, *commissari* attached to the Guard had a silver aiguilette at the right shoulder.

Breeches etc.
Breeches and waistcoats were white for parade and full dress and dark green for campaign dress; again buttons were silver. Boots were of the cuffed heavy cavalry pattern with silvered spurs.

Equipment
Officers' pattern sword with silvered or gilded hilt, silver sword knot and tassel, black leather scabbard with gilt fittings. The sword was carried on a black leather waist belt with silver lace trim and silvered fittings, worn under the coat and over the waistcoat.

Horse Furniture
The shabraque and pistol holsters were of the same pattern as that used by general officers and auditors but were light blue with silver lace.

THE ARMY OF THE KINGDOM OF ITALY 1805–1814

The following full-page engravings (the originals are hand coloured) portray the Army of Italy in review in 1805, 1807 and 1812. These engravings are three of the five (the remaining two show the Armies of the various pre-Kingdom Republics) that were published in *Sulla Milizia Cisalpino-Italiana. Cenni Storico Statistici dal 1796 al 1814*: Alesandro Zanoli (Milan: Borroni e Scotti, 1845). They are remarkably

GENERAL OFFICERS AND STAFF

accurate and are perhaps the first post-Napoleonic celebrations of the Kingdom's army. The Milan Fireman of the Pompieri Della Città di Milano (centre of the engraving on the following page, with his back to the viewer) was copied essentially unchanged by Knötel on his III/45 (see notes that follow). Most other units can also be identified on these plates. Colouring as described in the text.

THE ARMY OF THE KINGDOM OF ITALY 1805–1814

GENERAL OFFICERS AND STAFF

THE ARMY OF THE KINGDOM OF ITALY 1805–1814

GENERAL OFFICERS AND STAFF

2

The Guardia Reale (Royal Guard)

The Guardia Reale of the Kingdom of Italy came into existence by a royal decree of 20 June 1805. Outwardly it appears to have been organised on the same lines as the French Garde Impériale with most of the units corresponding with those of that body although this superficial similarity is illusory albeit that the Guardia Reale was, like the Garde Impériale, a self-contained force of all arms.

The decree creating the Guardia Reale gave it an initial structure of three defined parts:

Guardie d'Onore (Guards of Honour)
Guardie Veliti (Velite Guards)
Guardie della Linea (Guards of the Line)

More detail on each individual unit is given below under the appropriate section but it should be noted that the first two were essentially training schools for officers whereas only the latter followed the French Imperial Guard system of recruiting veterans from the line, albeit that its title suggests it is the least prestigious of the three.

To be eligible for admission to the regiments of the Guardie della Linea a recruit was supposed to have had five years' service and a good disciplinary record but as these units absorbed the Presidential Guard units (see below) initially at least they were composed of men who had no service record and had simply joined the latter direct from civilian life.

Throughout its existence the Guardia Reale, and to a lesser extent the line regiments, contained a number of French officers. Initially these French officers were considered senior to any Italian officer of the same rank, regardless of length of service. However by a decree of 21 May 1808 Eugène set out that French and Italian officers were to be considered equal with seniority determined only by length of service of rank.

Facing page: the units of the Royal Guard. Plate 48 of Dr Lienhart & R. Humbert, *Les Uniformes de l'Armée Française. Recueil d'Ordonnances de 1690 à 1894, Volume 5* (Leipzig: Ruhl, 1894). (Author's collection)

THE GUARDIA REALE

Tome V. Pl. 48.

TROUPES ALLIÉES. — ITALIE.
GARDE ROYALE.

Grenadier. — Carabinier. — Vélite Grenadier. — Vélite Carabinier. — Chasseur. — Officier. (Vélites grenadiers.)

Garde d'honneur. Cie de Milan.
Garde d'honneur. Cie de Bologne.
Garde d'honneur. Cie de Brescia.

Garde d'honneur de Bologne. — République cisalpine. Tambour. — Garde royale. Officier d'artillerie à pied. — Grenadier de la Garde.

Garde d'honneur. Officier. Cie des Romagnes.
Garde d'honneur. Cie des Romagnes.
Garde d'honneur. Cie de Venise.

Dragon. — Trompette des Dragons. — Artillerie à pied.¹) — Train d'artillerie. — Gendarmerie d'élite.

¹) Nous n'avons pas reproduit l'uniforme de l'artillerie à cheval de la Garde royale, ce dernier étant pareil à celui du corps correspondant dans Garde impériale française. Nous y renvoyons nos lecteurs.

Dr. Lienhart et R. Humbert.

Cavalry of the Royal Guard

Organisation

The cavalry of the Royal Guard comprised:

Guardia Reale d'Onore of 4, later 5, companies
Dragoni Della Guardia Reale, of 2 squadrons
Gendarmeria Scelta Della Guardia Reale of 1 company strength

The personal escort for the viceroy was customarily provided by the Dragoni Della Guardia Reale and not by the Guardia Reale d'Onore as might have been expected – an unkind observer might perhaps suggest that Eugène felt safer if his escort was provided by the regular army proper …

Guardia Reale d'Onore (Royal Guards of Honour)

History and Organisation
The unit[1] had its origins in the City Guards of Honour that had escorted Napoleon on his entry into Italy even before the Kingdom was proclaimed.[2] These aristocratic bodies were not strictly military units in any sense but were akin to the local landed classes dressing in military uniform to feel important for the day. Napoleon disbanded these local groups with the intention of using their manpower to form the Royal Guards of Honour and tie himself closer to the aristocracy of his new Kingdom.

The four, later five, companies of the Guardia Reale d'Onore of the Royal Guard were each recruited from one of the four principal departments of the Kingdom and bore the subsidiary title of that department. The recruiting departments were:

1st Company 'Milano':	Olona, Agogna, Lario, Adda
2nd Company 'Bologna':	Reno, Crostolo, Panaro, Mincio
3rd Company 'Brescia':	Serio, Alto Po, Mella, Adige
4th Company 'Romagna':	Rubicone, Basso Po

In 1806, when the Venetian territories were absorbed into the Kingdom of Italy, a 5th company, 'Venezia' was raised from the departments created within the new territory.

---

1 It is not technically correct to refer to the companies as a 'unit' before 1806, or even perhaps 1808, since they existed as separate companies, but it is so much more convenient to do so, for which the author asks the reader's indulgence.
2 Similar local Gardes d'Honneur existed throughout France and even in the Netherlands. They frequently seized the honour of escorting the Emperor when he was in their area, though they were militarily insignificant.

The regiment[3] was considered as a training school for officers and the other ranks as 'officer cadets' who could be promoted into the line cavalry regiments with the rank of 2° *Tenente* after two years' service.

All rank and file were required to be literate in both Italian and French and have a private income of at least 1,200 Milan Lira per year, which, as in the Velites, was to be paid to the State. The initial voluntary enlistment from the sons of the wealthy proved to be unpopular and enlistment was therefore subsequently made compulsory for any who fulfilled the criteria. Discipline and duties were light and the companies even had their own grooms, probably for this reason the unit proved less than successful when it participated in the 1809 and 1812 campaigns.

The officers of Guardia Reale d'Onore, as with the officers of the French Imperial Guard, held a double rank of grading over the line officers, thus a *sottotenente* of the Guardia Reale d'Onore ranked as a *capitano* in the line, etc.

The company establishment was laid out in a decree of 6 August 1805 as:

1 *capitano*
1 *sottotenente*
4 *marescialli d'alloggio*
8 *brigadieri*
2 *trombettieri*
86 *guardie*
1 *tenente*
1 *maresciallo d'alloggio capo*
1 *brigadiere furiere*
1 *maniscalo*
1 *tamburino*

Within this establishment three *brigadieri*, 36 *guardie*, and the *tamburo* were to be dismounted.

The *trombettieri*, the *tamburo* and the *maniscalo* were recruited from the line cavalry and were not 'guards' in the same sense as the troopers.

All companies were commanded by their own officers and there was no form of regimental organisation or overall command, a situation that added to the chaotic affairs and lack of discipline of the unit, or more strictly, units. To overcome this the 'Regolamento di Disciplina Interna ed Administrazione Della R. Guardie d'Onore'[4] were issued on 7 August 1806 and Gaetano Battaglia, the *capitano* of the 1st Company 'Milano', was given overall command of the five companies with the acting rank of *maggiore* and with the intention that they should be commanded as a single unit.

On 30 March 1807 a company of grooms was formally added to the regimental establishment. The company was formed as five squads of 25, each under a head groom and each squad assigned to a specific company.

Finally, on 14 March 1808 a small regimental staff of *chirurge*, assistant *chirurge* and a *veterinario* was created, and then later in the same year a second *tenente* was added to the 1st Company allowing Battaglia to command the regiment with less responsibility for his own company. At the same time it was decided that all of the companies were to be mounted which also resulted in the tamburo being removed from the company establishments.

---

3   Whether the companies should ever truly be considered as a 'regiment', even after the creation of the staff in 1808, is arguable but again it is a convenient shorthand to refer to them as such.
4   'Regulations of Internal Discipline and Administration…'

Despite all of these theoretical establishments, in 1809 the unit could only raise enough personnel for a single composite company to accompany the army into the field. In July 1807 the Guards mustered a strength of only 374 all ranks against an establishment of 535 (see Appendix II for the illustrative strength of the Guard). However when the Army of Italy joined the Grand Armée for the Russian campaign of 1812 the five companies were essentially at establishment.

In 1813 the Guards who returned from the campaign in Russia were transferred into the line as officers of the reformed Army, and only a single company was raised for the new army. This single company had a new establishment of:

1 *capitano*	2 *tenente*
2 *sottotenente*	1 *maresciallo d'alloggio capo*
6 *marescialli d'alloggio*	1 *brigadiere furiere*
10 *brigadieri*	2 *maniscalo*
1 *brigadiere trombettiere*	3 *trombettier*
124 *guardie*	

It was uniformed as the 4th Company 'Romagna'.

On 16 May 1814, the Guardie d'Onore were the first unit of the Royal Guard to be formally disbanded, having already transferred the majority of its personnel to other units.

In the 10 years of its existence a total of 895 men had passed through its ranks, of whom 450 were promoted to officers in other units, 106 were discharged for wounds or illness, and 193 were killed or taken prisoner (mainly in Russia).

Service

1805	Nov	Observation Corps against Venice
1809		One composite company drawn from all troops joined the Army after the Battle of Sacile on 16 April.
	8 May	Battle of the Piave
	14 Jun	Battle of Raab
	5 Jul	Battle of Wagram (108 officers and men)
		No officer casualties, killed or wounded, are recorded during the campaign
1812	7 Sep	Battle of Borodino
	24 Oct	Battle of Maloyaroslavetz
	16 Nov	Battle of Krasnoi
	28 Nov	Battle of the Beresina?

1812		During the campaign Martinien records as 'Killed or Disappeared': 5 *capitani* 13 *tenenti* (2 of whom were killed in action) 1 *chirurge* (killed in action)
1813–1814		Various skirmishes during the defence of the Kingdom but no officers are recorded as killed or wounded during these campaigns
1814	8 Feb	Battle of the Mincio (119 officers and men)

Uniform

From late 1805 until 1810,[5] at the very latest, each company of the Guards had a unique uniform. Whilst much of the general equipment was the same as that in use post 1810, and described below, the 1805 coats were:

1st Company 'Milano': Red coat with blue collar, lapels cuffs and turnbacks, silver buttons and eagles on the turnbacks
2nd Company 'Bologna': White coat with blue facings
3rd Company 'Brescia': Blue coat with crimson facings
4th Company 'Romagna': Green coat faced red
5th Company 'Venezia': Green coat faced orange

Initially buttonholes were piped silver although this distinction was officially abolished in August 1806. Horse furniture appears to have been of the company facing colour, piped silver. *Trombettieri* generally wore reversed colours but a contemporary illustration shows a *trombettista* in a yellow coat faced light blue and with a white helmet crest, unfortunately the company is not recorded, although 'Bologna' would seem the most likely and it is possible that the illustration is *c.* 1811 and not from the early period.

The 'traditional' uniform was introduced as a cost reduction exercise as many families were unwilling to pay the high cost of equipping their sons, resulting in the Guards being severely understrength even at the beginning of 1809. The new uniform was laid down by decree and thus is more completely documented. Since the coats were issued annually the 'change' would have been fairly swiftly effected.

Headwear

The helmet was brass (similar in appearance to that worn by the French carabiniers after the 1810 dress regulations) with a black woollen caterpillar crest, the lower portion of the helmet, excluding the peak, was a steel 'band' with a crowned[6] 'N' in brass at the front. The peak, chin scales and plume holder were brass and in full dress a white plume was worn at the left-hand

---

5 Alain Pigeard, 'Les Gardes d'Honneur du Royaume d'Italie', *Tradition No.117, Janvier 1997* (Paris: Tradition, 1996), pp. 12–16. gives a date of 1812 for this change but all other sources consulted put it much earlier.
6 'Crowned' in any reference to the Kingdom of Italy's Army means, of course, with the Iron Crown of Lombardy, not the French Imperial Crown.

THE ARMY OF THE KINGDOM OF ITALY 1805–1814

Right, and facing page: Trooper's helmet, Guardia Reale d'Onore. Brass skull, steel turban edged in brass, brass 'N' and crown, black woollen caterpillar crest, brass crest holder and chin scales, black leather peak bound in brass. (Private collection, photo © and courtesy of Laurent Claudet)

side. The brass crest holder comb was in the form of an eagle with swept back wings; the wings formed the side of the crest, the chest the front of the crest and the eagle's head protruded forward below the caterpillar crest. Whilst some examples of this elaborate helmet actually survive it is arguable how widespread its use really was after 1807, however at some point before 1812 this helmet with its elaborate crest holder had definitively been replaced with the more usual plain brass one. This change may have been at the same time as the change of coat colour but would, no doubt, have taken some time to 'work through' the whole unit since helmets, unlike coats, were not replaced annually.

The 'Pokalem' pattern fatigue caps were dark green with piping of the company colour. After 1808 a unique pattern of fatigue cap seems to have come into use; it was similar in appearance to the German feldmutz with soft crown and wide headband and a small patch at the crown from which a short cord and tassel hung, the colouring being the same as for the Pokalem.

Coat
The full dress coat was the uniform pattern dark green habit, with the lapels, cuffs and turnbacks of the facing colour, a dark green collar and dark green three-pointed cuff flaps piped with the company facing colour, pockets

THE ARMY OF THE KINGDOM OF ITALY 1805–1814

Facing page: Knötel Plate III/29. Guardia Reale d'Onore 1812. From left: guard, officer, trombettista, guard, officer. Colouring as in the text. (Author's collection)

were piped in the company facing colour. The collar and cuffs both had two narrow white horizontal bars of lace batons. There were similar lace bars on the lapel buttonholes. Red contra-epaulettes were worn on both shoulders with brass-scaled straps, and with a white aiguillette on the right shoulder. All buttons were pewter.

The undress uniform, also worn on campaign for everyday wear (although the regiment would have worn full dress coats into action), was a dark green surtout coat with collar, cuffs, turnbacks and piping as for the habit coat. Epaulettes, etc were the same as those worn on the full dress coat and were probably simply transferred from that coat.

Company facings and distinctive colour:

1st Company 'Milano': Pink
2nd Company 'Bologna': Yellow
3rd Company 'Brescia': Buff
4th Company 'Romagna': Red
5th Company 'Venezia': Orange

Breeches etc.
Breeches and waistcoats were white and boots were of the cuffed, heavy cavalry pattern with blackened iron spurs. White overall trousers were worn with the fatigue coat and after 1810 heavy grey cloth overall trousers with black leather inserts and cuffs and a single row of cloth covered buttons on the outer seam were worn with the surtout coat in campaign dress order.

The dark green greatcoat had a facing colour lining and trim to the edge of the collar and cape, and white metal buttons. Gauntlets were whitened leather.

Equipment
The cartridge box was worn on a white leather belt over the left shoulder and had a large, open brass buckle behind the left shoulder. The cartridge box lid was decorated with a brass crowned eagle badge. The waist belt was white with a closed brass buckle, embossed with a grenade badge. The regiment's sabres were of a unique pattern having a brass, three bar hilt with the Iron Crown in pierced relief at the side of the basket and had white sword straps and knots. Scabbards were polished steel.

Officers and NCOs
An NCO's rank was indicated by diagonal bars worn above the cuff in the same way as those worn throughout the Army:

Trombetta-maggiori: two silver bars, piped red
Maresciallo d'alloggio capo: two silver bars, piped red
Marescialli d'alloggio: a single silver bar, piped red
Brigadieri: two white woollen bars piped red
The aiguillette was mixed silver and red for the senior grades.

THE GUARDIA REALE

Italien.

Reiter.   Offizier.   Trompeter.   Reiter.   Offizier.

Ehrengarden.
Das Italienische Heer unter Vicekönig Eugen.
1812.

Die Ehrengarden (Guardie d'onore) wurden 1805 in der Stärke von 4 Kompagnien errichtet. 1806 kam eine 5. Komp. dazu. Die Kompagnien waren durch die Farbe der Kragen, Aufschläge, Rabatten und Schoossumschläge unterschieden. Die Bezeichnungen und Abzeichenfarben waren folgende: 1. Komp. Mailand — rosa —, 2. Komp. Bologna — gelb —, 3. Komp. Brescia — chamois —, 4. Komp. Romagna — scharlachroth —, 5. Komp. Venedig — orange —. Die Ehrengarden begleiteten als Stabswache den Vicekönig Eugen in's Feld. Nach den Verlusten im Russischen Feldzuge 1812 wurde die Stärke der Truppe auf eine Kompagnie herabgesetzt.

Knötel, Uniformenkunde. Band III. No. 29.   Verlag von Max Babenzien in Rathenow.

Trooper's sword, Guardia Reale d'Onore. Buff hilt bound with brass wire. Steel guard and scabbard. Red cloth 'pad' below the hilt where it rests against the scabbard. (Private Collection, photo © and courtesy of Laurent Claudet)

Officers' helmets were gilt with a silver-plated base, the crowned 'N' was also in gilt. The coat was the same cut as the rank and file but of finer cloth and with silver rank epaulettes and aiguillettes. All lace was silver. Senior officers used the silver oak leaf design on the collar, cuffs and lapels. Surtouts and stable jackets were as for the men with officers' rank distinctions. Breeches and waistcoats were white. Belts were white in full dress and black leather for campaign. The cartridge box was decorated with silver lace. The sabre was of the same pattern as the troopers with a gilded hilt and the brass scabbard had black leather inserts. Officers' greatcoats were dark green with wide silver lace trim to the cape and silver piping on the body.

Musicanti

Initially at least *trombettieri* probably wore coats of reversed colours with white lace on the collar and cuffs and white aiguillettes, although it should be pointed out that this is based on very slight information. The helmet was the same as that for the troopers with a red crest and a plume of either red or facing colour.

Trumpets were brass with silver cords (mixed sky blue and silver for the 2nd and 5th Companies). Trumpet banners were of a 'swallow-tail' design of the troop facing colour with silver fringes. On the obverse the banners had the Iron Crown and laurels all in silver; on the reverse was a laurel wreath encircling the motto 'GUARDIE REALI / D'ONORE', again all in silver.

By 1810/early 1811 however the *trombettieri* had adopted a new uniform. Although this was broadly similar to the above and the new uniform coat was still in 'reversed colours', it had sky blue facings and plain white aiguillettes, the helmet had a white crest (one illustration shows a *trombettista* of the 5th Company 'Venezia' with an orange crest) and a white plume.

THE GUARDIA REALE

Bivouac of the Guardia Reale d'Onore, Marienpol 26 June 1812. Engraving after a contemporary sketch by Albrecht Adam et al., from *Voyage Pittoresque Et Militaire De Willenberg En Prusse Jusqu'à Moscou Fait En 1812: Pris Sur Le Terrain Même* (Munich: Hermann & Barth, 1828). Note the mixture of practical service dress and the full dress of the guard, who has obviously just come off duty. (Public domain)

The *tamburi* were uniformed the same as *trombettieri* although a contemporary illustration shows the *tamburo* of the Modena company wearing below-knee black gaiters. It appears likely that this was repeated across the other companies.

Horse Furniture

Troopers' shabraques were of the 1805 pattern as used by both the Guard and the line dragoons. These were dark green with a wide outer lace inside which was narrow white piping. The rear corners were decorated with white crowns. The dark green square valise and the double pistol holsters were both trimmed the same as the shabraque. When not in use, the greatcoat was strapped to the top of the portmanteau with the red lining uppermost, except on full dress parades when it seems not to have been carried.

Trombettieri' shabraques were either of the same pattern as the troop or, as some contemporary illustrations show, facing colour; both edged white with an outer piping of facing colour.

Officers' shabraques were dark green with a double wide silver lace stripe along the edge, with narrow dark green piping along the edges of each stripe. The crowns in the rear corners were of silver embroidery. The pistol holster covers were triple layer and dark green, trimmed in the same manner as the shabraque.

Each company rode a distinctive colour of horse:

1st Company:	blacks
2nd Company:	bays
3rd Company:	blacks
4th Company:	bays
5th Company:	chestnuts with white socks

Trombettieri of all companies rode the customary greys

THE ARMY OF THE KINGDOM OF ITALY 1805–1814

Bivouac of the Guardia Reale d'Onore. Note the unique pattern of the fatigue cap. Contemporary engraving from Albrecht Adan et al., *Voyage Pittoresque Et Militaire De Willenberg En Prusse Jusqu'à Moscou Fait En 1812: Pris Sur Le Terrain Même* (Munich: Hermann & Barth, 1828). (Public domain)

Dragoni Della Guardia Reale (Dragoons of the Royal Guard)

History and Organisation

The Dragoni Della Guardia Reale was actually raised by the merging of the two existing cavalry units of the Presidential Guard, the Horse Grenadiers (who formed the first two companies of the Dragoni) and the Chasseurs a Cheval (who formed the second two), although the decree[7] that created the regiment ordered that it was to be recruited from men of the line cavalry of at least five year's service and an unblemished record.

The constituent units of the regiment were in France when Napoleon was crowned Emperor (then organised as a single squadron of four companies) and when they returned to Italy in late 1805 they were organised with a small regimental staff and two squadrons each of two companies. The formal establishment of the regiment was, however, not laid down until 21 May 1808, although it may actually have been similar, if not identical, since 1805. See Appendix II for actual strength return in July 1807, which is illustrative of some part of the establishment.

The May 1808 order set out the regiment's establishment as:

Regimental Staff
1 *colonnello*   1 *capo-squadrone*
1 *aiutante maggiore*   1 *quartiermastro tesoriere*

---

7   Dated 20 June 1805.

1 *sottoaiutante maggiore*
2 *ufficiali di sanita*
1 *veterinario*
1 *trombetta-maggiori*
1 *portastendardo*
1 *sottotenente istruttore*
1 *vammastro*
1 *brigadiere trombetta*
6 *maestro-artigiani* (master craftsmen: bootmaker, tailor, breeches maker, armourer, saddler, (?[8])

Company Establishment
1 *capitano*
2 *sottotenente*
4 *marescialli d'alloggio*
8 *brigadieri*
2 *trombettieri*
82 *dragoni*
2 *tenente* (1 1° *classe*, 1 2° *classe*)
1 *maresciallo d'alloggio capo*
1 *ottantadue dragoni*
1 *maniscalo*
1 *tambure*

Initially the *maniscalo* on the staff, and the *tambure* and 22 dragoni of each company, were to be dismounted. By August 1811 the dismounted section had disappeared at which time all ranks are recorded as being mounted and a fifth company was added to the establishment in that month to act as a depot (although the author has not found the exact date). On 18 November of the same year the company establishment for all companies was raised to 140, including 40 *dragoni 2° classe*.

In 1813, after returning from the Russian campaign, the regiment was reformed with a reduced establishment of four companies.

An order of 11 August 1808 set out that the regiment should be mounted on bay horses, except for the *trombettieri* who were to ride greys.

Service

1809		Joined the Army after the Battle of Sacile on 16 April
	8 May	Battle of the Piave
	14 Jun	Battle of Raab (1 *capitano* wounded)
	5 Jul	Battle of Wagram (248 officers and men)
1812	7 Sep	Battle of Borodino
	24 Oct	Battle of Maloyaroslavetz
	16 Nov	Battle of Krasnoi
	28 Nov	Battle of the Beresina?
		During the campaign Martinien records 'Killed or Disappeared': 2 *capitani* 5 *tenenti* 1 *chirurge*
	13 Dec	Skirmish near Kowne (1 *tenente* wounded)

---

8   The author has not found the profession of this sixth individual, although all records of the establishment agree that there were six.

Facing page: Knötel Plate III/18. Dragoons of the Royal Guard, 1812. Colouring as in the text. (Author's collection)

1813–1814		Defence of the Kingdom of Italy
1813	16 Sep	Skirmish at Weisselburg (1 captain, 2 *tenenti* wounded)
1813	27 Nov	Skirmish at Leguano (2 *tenenti* wounded)
1814	8 Feb	Battle of the Mincio (289 officers and men; 2 *capitani*, 2 *tenenti* wounded)

Uniform

The uniform of the Dragoni Della Guardia Reale was formally laid down in a decree dated 15 April 1806, prior to which they had worn the uniform of their old units of the Presidential Guard, but as items needed replacement these were of the new Dragoni Della Guardia Reale patterns when the older was not in store. The resultant appearance must have been somewhat 'untidy' to say the least. A single contemporary painting records an otherwise unrecorded simplification of the uniform in 1813 but, in the absence of any other confirmation it is not repeated here.

Headwear

The helmet worn by the Dragoni Della Guardia Reale was of the same pattern as that of the French and Italian line dragoon regiments. The helmet was brass, with a brass crest embossed with a 'shell' design at the side and embossed on the front with an Italian eagle bearing a star, with an 'N' surmounted by the Crown of Lombardy at its centre. The horsehair tail and houpette were black and the turban was leopard skin, extending over the peak which was trimmed with a narrow brass edging. Chin scales were brass and the full dress plume was red. Fatigue caps were dark green with red piping and grenade badge. Although usually of the Pokalem pattern the older line pattern is also illustrated suggesting that, as so often, older stocks continued to be used and issued.

Coat

The dark green coat was the usual pattern in the Army and of the same cut as that worn by the two line dragoon regiments. It had a dark green collar without piping, white lapels and red 'Brandenburg cuffs' with white three-pointed cuff flaps.[9] The turnbacks were red with white grenade badges mounted on a green cloth backing that showed as a narrow edge to the badge, but by 1812 however (and the present author has been unable to find a date for the change) the turnback badges were a white 'Iron Crown'. Red contra-epaulettes were worn on both shoulders with brass-scaled straps and with a white aiguillette on the right shoulder. All buttons were pewter and embossed with a crowned 'N' (the crown was, of course, the Iron Crown of Lombardy).

---

9 A surviving coat has dark green cuffs and cuff flaps, both unpiped. This variation is not recorded anywhere except for this coat.

THE GUARDIA REALE

Italien.

Dragoner.   **Offizier.**   **Trompeter.**
Dragoner.
Dragoner-Regiment der Königlichen Garde.
Das Italienische Heer unter Vice-König Eugen.
1812.

Das Garde-Dragoner-Regiment war ganz nach dem Muster der Französischen Dragoner der Kaisergarde (Dragons de l'Imperatrice) uniformirt. Der augenfälligste Unterschied bestand darin, dass die Italienischen Garde-Dragoner weisse Knöpfe, die Französischen gelbe trugen. Die ersteren hatten in den hinteren Schabraken-Ecken eine Granate, letztere eine Krone. Der Schabraken-Besatz entsprach in der Farbe den Knöpfen. Ganz abweichend aber waren der Farbe nach die Trompeter uniformirt. Während die Trompeter-Montur der Französischen Garde-Dragoner weiss mit hellblau und Gold zeigte, erschienen die Italienischen in hellblau mit roth und Silber.

Knötel, Uniformenkunde. Band III. No. 18.   Verlag von Max Babenzien in Rathenow.

To protect and preserve the expensive full dress coat, on campaign the regiment wore a dark green surtout coat with a green collar piped red, all other facings and details were as for the habit.

Breeches etc.
The breeches and waistcoat were white with pewter buttons (smaller versions of those on the coat). The boots were of the cuffed heavy cavalry pattern with steel spurs. Greatcoats were dark green, with a dark green collar, all lined red. The greatcoats are sometimes shown with red piping at the edges and along the edge of the collar, although this could be simply the lining showing. Buttons were white metal. Gauntlets were whitened leather.

Equipment
A whitened leather pouch belt was worn over the left shoulder supporting a black leather cartridge box; the belt had a large, open, brass buckle behind the shoulder. The cartridge box lid was decorated with a brass crowned eagle badge. The waist belt was white with a closed brass buckle, embossed with a grenade badge. The straight heavy cavalry sword had a three bar hilt and a white sword knot and tassel; it was carried in a brass scabbard with black inserts on double slings from the waistbelt. On campaign the belt was often worn over the right shoulder, and with the pouch belt, thus gave the appearance of cross belts.

The musket was simply a shorter version of the same weapon as that carried by the infantry, and was of the same bore, thus it was a true musket and not a cavalry carbine. The infantry musket was bound and fitted in steel but it appears that the Dragoni Della Guardia Reale had a variant bound and fitted with brass, it had a whitened leather sling with a brass buckle. When mounted, the Dragoni carried their muskets in a bucket, butt downwards, on the right side of the saddle.

Officers and NCOs
An NCO's rank was indicated by diagonal bars worn above the cuff in the same way as those worn throughout the Army:

Trombetta-maggiori: two silver bars, piped red
Maresciallo d'alloggio capo: two silver bars, piped red
Marescialli d'aloggio: a single silver bar, piped red
Brigadieri: two white woollen bars piped red
The aiguillette was mixed silver and red for the senior grades.

The officer's helmet was the same pattern as the troopers' but all brass was gilded.

The coat was of the same cut as the rest of the unit with silver epaulettes of rank, silver aiguillettes and turnback badges and silver cords worn on the right shoulder. Belts were white for full dress and black leather for campaign wear. Officers' greatcoats were dark green, double breasted and trimmed with silver lace on the collar and edge.

Officers wore silver epaulettes to show ranks in a sequence identical throughout the Army:

Colonello/colonello-sotto: two silver bullion-fringed epaulettes
Maggiore: as above but with gold straps
Capo di battaglione: silver bullion-fringed epaulette on the right shoulder, contre-epaulette on the left
Capitano: as above but fine-fringed epaulette
Tenente: as above but with a narrow red stripe along the straps
Sottotenente: as above but with two red stripes
The *aiutante*, usually (although not necessarily) a *capitano*, wore the *capitano* epaulettes of rank but on opposite shoulders

Trombettieri
The *trombettieri*' helmets were the same pattern as that of other ranks but with a red mane, black houpette and sky blue plume. Fatigue caps were sky blue with white piping and white grenade badge.

The *trombettieri* wore a sky blue habit with red collar, lapels, turnbacks, cuffs and cuff flaps. The epaulettes were the same as worn by the troopers with a mixed red and white aiguillette. The collar, lapels and cuffs were trimmed with 3 cm of silver lace and the buttonholes were edged with silver lace with small tassels on the inside ends. The pockets were piped red. The two buttons at the rear waist of the coat had a silver lace 'trefoil' pattern around them. The pockets were piped red. The turnbacks badge was a white grenade. All buttons were pewter.

For campaign dress *trombettieri* used a sky blue surtout with all facings as for the habit and narrow silver lace on the collar and cuffs.

Breeches and boots were as for the other ranks, waistcoats were white with pewter buttons

The trumpets were brass with white or mixed white and crimson cords, and the crimson trumpet banner was square with silver fringes at all four edges embroidered with an Imperial eagle surrounded by a laurel, all in silver.

Belts and swords were the same as those used by the troopers but the sword knot was red. Greatcoats were sky blue with a white lining.

Horse Furniture
The dark green shabraque was the 1805 pattern used by the line *dragoni*, with double pistol holster covers and black leather saddle. The shabraque had white lace piped in dark green, and the pistol holsters were decorated the same. The rear corners of the shabraque had a white grenade badge. The valise was dark green with white lace, and when not in use, the greatcoat was strapped to the top of the portmanteau with the red lining uppermost.

Officers' shabraques were dark green with a double silver lace edging each piped red, the outer twice the width of the inner.

Trombettieri' shabraques were the same as those of the officers but with white lace in place of the silver. The valise was sky blue trimmed with white.

By an order of 11 August 1808 the regiment was to be mounted on bays with *trombettieri* on the traditional greys.

Gendarmeria Scelta Della Guardia Reale (Elite Gendarmes of the Royal Guard)

History and Organisation
The Gendarmeria Scelta was organised as only a single, very weak, company and was formally raised by a decree of 6 September 1808 for police and security duties within the Royal Palace, and the Royal Guard's Camp when on campaign. From the creation of the Kingdom until 1807 the unit's duties had been carried out by a detachment of the Gendarmerie d'Elite of the French Imperial Guard but when these were recalled to France at the end of 1807, Eugène retained two officers and 25 gendarmes in Italy and these became the nucleus of the Gendarmeria Scelta.

The Gendarmeria's full establishment was three officers (sources vary as to the commander's rank, either a *capo di squadrone* or a *capitano*), three *sergenti*,[10] four *brigadieri*, one *trombettista*, one *maniscalo* and 55 *gendarmi*.[11] For administrative purposes the Gendarmeria Scelta were attached to the Guard Dragoons as a 'sub-division'.

Service
The Gendarmeria Scelta was not a field combat unit although it was present with the army at most, if not all, of its actions even if it generally served at Headquarters. However *Tenente* Durand of the Gendarmeria was wounded at Raab on 14 June 1809, but this is the only recorded officer casualty during any of the Army's campaigns.

Uniform
The uniform of the company of Gendarmeria was not laid down in the 1808 decree and, almost by default, they were initially uniformed almost identically to their counterparts of French Garde Impériale, whose men had provided the original cadre of the unit.

Headwear
The headwear was a black-peaked bearskin without front plate; the chin scales were brass and the shiny leather peak was bound in brass. The patch at the rear was crimson with a white grenade. The full dress cords were white and the plume, worn above the national cockade on the left of the cap, was red.

For service on foot the Gendarmeria Scelta wore the black bicorne with national cockade and red carrot-shaped pompom. Fatigue caps were dark blue with crimson piping and tassels.

Coat
The dark blue habit had crimson collar, lapels, cuffs, cuff flaps and turnbacks, all piped dark blue. The pockets were piped in crimson and the turnback devices were white grenades. A white, fringed epaulette was worn on the

---
10 Literally 'deputy marshals', equivalent in effect to sergeants.
11 Originally recruited one from each of the 30 departments, plus the 25 French gendarmes.

right shoulder and a trefoil epaulette and an aiguillette on the left. All buttons were pewter. Before 1813 (perhaps when the unit was reformed after the campaign in Russia?) the coat had changed to dark green in place of the blue but all other details remained the same.

Breeches etc.
Waistcoats were buff coloured cloth but the breeches were soft buff leather. Boots were of the high, heavy cavalry pattern with steel spurs. On foot the Gendarmeria Scelta wore high, black gaiters with cloth covered buttons.

Greatcoats were dark blue with white metal buttons and crimson lining. The author has not come across any confirmation that the greatcoats changed to dark green in line with the coat, but given the longevity of such items, even if intended it is unlikely that it came into effect before the fall of the Kingdom. Gauntlets were white with buff cuffs.

Equipment
Equipment was of the same pattern as that in use by the Dragoni Della Guardia except that the Gendarmeria wore the light cavalry pattern waist belt and carried the light cavalry pattern sabre, with a white sword knot and tassel. All belts were buff leather edged white, again in the same manner as the Gendarmes of the French Imperial Guard.

Officers and NCOs
All rank distinctions and badges were the same as those used by the Royal Guard's infantry. Officers' belts were buff leather edged silver and their dark blue greatcoats were trimmed silver along the edge of the cape and perhaps on the cuffs. Officers carried the light cavalry pattern sabre with a silver sword knot and tassel. The sub-division's commander wore a white plume in his bearskin.

Musicanti
The trumpeter's uniform was generally of the same appearance as that of the rest of the unit although of a different colouring. The cords of the bearskin were mixed crimson and white and the plume was crimson tipped white. The coat was crimson with crimson collar, light blue cuffs, lapels, turnbacks and piping on the pockets and silver lace on the collar lapels and turnbacks. The aiguillette and epaulette were mixed light blue and white. The trumpeter's cloak was light blue lined crimson. Trumpets were brass with mixed crimson and white cords.

Horse Furniture
The dark blue shabraques were of the Dragoni Della Guardia pattern with triple holster covers; both holster covers and shabraque were edged with a wide white lace piped crimson and the shabraque had white grenades at the rear corners. The valise was dark blue with white trim. The *trombettieri'* shabraques were of the same pattern and were crimson with white edging piped dark blue. Officers had silver lace piped dark blue in place of the white

Facing page: Knötel Plate III/59. Infantry of the Royal Guard, 1812. Colouring as in the text. (Author's collection)

piped crimson and silver grenades in the rear corners. It is *possible*[12] that the dark blue changed to dark green at the same time as the regiment's coat colour changed.

Infantry of the Royal Guard

Reggimento di Fanteria della Guardia Reale (The Infantry Regiment of the Royal Guard)

History and Organisation

The senior regiment of infantry of the Royal Guard was created by the decree of 26 June 1805 and was created from and absorbed the units of Granatieri and Cacciatori della Guardia del Presidente[13] (Presidential Guard) of the defunct Italian Republic.

Although often considered as two units the Granatieri and Cacciatori were officially the 1st and 2nd battalions respectively of the same regiment and shared a single regimental staff.

The regimental strength was laid down as a regimental staff and two battalions, each of five companies, and an order of 14 March 1808 confirmed the establishments as:

Regimental Staff

1 *colonnello*	1 *maggiore*
2 *capo di battaglione*	2 *aiutanti-maggiori*
2 *sottoaiutanti-maggiori*	1 *quartiermastro*
2 *ufficialo di santa*	2 *aquile-alfiori*
1 *vammastro*[14]	1 *tamburo-maggiore*
1 *caporale-tamburo*	30 *musicanti*

4 *maestro-artigiani* (master craftsmen: bootmaker, tailor, breeches maker, armourer)

Company Establishment

1 *capitano*	1 *tenente 1° classe*
1 *tenente 2° classe*	1 *sottotenente*
1 *sergente-maggiore*	4 *sergenti*
1 *quartiermastro*	8 *caporali*
3 *tamburi*	2 *zappatori*
82 *soldati*	

A decree of 16 October 1808 increased the company establishment to 140 officers and men.

12　Aesthetically it would seem more pleasing to the eye, and that was often important, particularly in elite units.
13　These two battalions each had an establishment of eight companies totalling 546 men, making them somewhat larger than the new Royal Guard units, and provided an excess of officers and NCOs.
14　Apparently unique to the Guard, this was an NCO in charge of the regimental wagons.

THE GUARDIA REALE

Italien.

Garde-Jäger. Veliten-Offizier. Velit (Karabinier).
  Velit (Grenadier) Garde-Grenadier. Garde-Karabinier.

Das Italienische Heer unter Vice-König Eugen.
1812.

Das Blatt bringt eine Zusammenstellung der Infanterie-Uniformen der Königlichen Garde. Der Garde-Grenadier und Garde-Karabinier gehören dem Garde-Infanterie-Regiment an (Reggimento d'infanteria della guardia reale). Der Karabinier unterscheidet sich vom Grenadier durch die spitzzulaufenden Rabatten, durch das Fehlen des Blechschildes an der Pelzmütze und die Farbe des Stutzes. Das Regiment trug, wie ersichtlich eine Uniform, die derjenigen der Grenadiere der alten Garde Napoleon I. fast genau entsprach, nur die grüne Grundfarbe, die weissen Knöpfe und das weisse Mützenblech erscheinen abweichend. Die Grenadiere und Karabiniers der Veliten unterscheiden sich durch dieselben Stücke, wie sie oben beim Garde-Regiment angeführt sind. Der Jäger gehört vermuthlich einer der Elite-Kompagnien des Rekruten-Regiments an (Reggimento coscritti della guardia), da ein besonderes Garde-Jäger-Regiment in der ordre de bataille von 1812 nicht angeführt wird.

Knötel, Uniformenkunde. Band III. No. 59.   Verlag von Max Babenzien in Rathenow.

On 12 April 1811, an artillery company was added to the regiment, with two 3-pdr pieces, drawn by eight horses each.

In the rebuilding and reorganisation of the Royal Guard in 1813 following its near-complete destruction in Russia the Carabinieri battalion (ex Cacciatori) was disbanded. The survivors were drafted into the Granatieri and the Carabinieri battalion itself was replaced in the establishment with a second battalion of Granatieri, the regiment then formally became Granatieri a Pieda della Guardia Reale.

Throughout the regiment's existence the 5th Company appears to have existed as essentially a depot company, rather than a field company.

It is perhaps worth noting that the uniform of this regiment was not laid down in the initial decrees and at first it continued to wear the uniform of the old Presidential Guards although the uniform quickly evolved into a copy of that worn by the French Imperial Guard. Most of the differences, particularly for the Granatieri, could have been achieved simply by altering current equipment rather than the expense of issuing new. The old Presidential Guard uniform of the Cacciatori was replaced by one resembling that of the Granatieri by an Order dated 15 April 1806.

Granatieri a Piedi Della Guardi Reale (Foot Grenadiers of the Royal Guard)

Service

1805	14 Oct	Surrender at Ulm
	2 Dec	Battle of Austerlitz
1809		Joined the Army after the Battle of Sacile on 16 April
	27–30 Apr	Battle of Caldiero
	8 May	Battle of the Piave
	14 Jun	Battle of Raab
	5 Jul	Battle of Wagram (343 officers and men)
1812	7 Sep	Battle of Borodino
	24 Oct	Battle of Maloyaroslavetz
	16 Nov	Battle of Krasnoi
	28 Nov	Battle of the Beresina?
		During the campaign Martinien records 'Killed or Disappeared': 1 *capitano* 11 *tenenti* 2 *chirurgi*
1813–1814		Defence of the Kingdom of Italy
1813	5 May	Skirmish at Gesdorf (1 *capitano* wounded)
1814	8 Feb	Battle of the Mincio (522 officers and men)
	16 Feb	Skirmish at Salo (2 *capitani* and 2 *tenenti* wounded)

Uniform

Headwear

From at least mid 1806 the Granatieri wore a black bearskin of a pattern identical to that of the grenadiers of French Imperial Guard but with a white metal plate embossed with the Imperial eagle with the letters R and I on either side. The patch at the rear of the bonnet was red with a white cross, replaced from 1809–10 with a white grenade. The full dress cords and flounders were white. The national cockade was worn on the left side of the bearskin and, in full dress, this was surmounted by a tall red plume.

When the regiment was created in 1805 it continued to wear the bearskin of the previous Presidential Guard, which was similar to the above but had a shiny black leather peak, a brass plate embossed with a grenade and double cords. Given the usual contemporary habit of the re-use of obsolete equipment, so far as it was possible, it is probable that many of these bearskins were 'adapted' to reflect the new pattern and continued in use until they were worn out or lost. Perhaps it would not be unrealistic to have seen some companies with the peakless bearskin and others wearing bearskins with peaks throughout 1805 and early 1806 as the 'updating' of these proceeded throughout the regiment until eventually everyone had the new version, or something that equated to it closely. The Weiland Manuscript, dated to c. 1806, shows a grenadier of the Royal Guard[15] in the new pattern of bearskin, the single cords of the new regulations but the Presidential Guard pattern plate – suggesting it was an old pattern bearskin which had been 'adapted'.

Fatigue caps, of the French pattern, were dark green with red piping and tassels and had a red grenade on the front.

Coat

The dark green habit[16] was of the same pattern as that worn by the French Army and the majority of the Italian Army, although if the French Guard is a guide it was made from a finer cloth. It had a red collar, cuffs and turnbacks, white lapels and three-pointed cuff flaps, all unpiped. The turnback device was a white grenade and the vertical pockets were piped red. The full-fringed epaulettes were red and all buttons were pewter. For campaign wear the regiment wore a dark green surtout with all details the same as the full dress coat.[17]

---

15 Alain Pigeard (ed.), *Le Manuscrit de Weiland: Uniformes de l'Armée Français et de ses Alliés de 1806 à 1815* (Paris: Tradition, 1998), p. 28.

16 It is worth noting that Weiland's work, published in 1807, although probably compiled the previous year, shows a grenadier of the Italian Guard still wearing what was probably a coat of the previous Presidential Guard pattern with white fringed epaulettes and red lapels piped white. Alain Pigeard (ed.), *Le Manuscrit de Weiland: Uniformes de l'Armée Français et de ses Alliés de 1806 à 1815* (Paris: Tradition, 1998), p. 28. As with all such things, coats would be issued from the depot until stocks were exhausted whatever new regulations were promulagated since they had been made.

17 The French Imperial Guard infantry famously donned their full dress uniform before battle, and there is some evidence that the Royal Guard did the same.

Coat button of the pattern used throughout the Royal Guard. Note the design of the breast of the Eagle (compare to the pouch badge below). (Private Collection, photo © and courtesy of Laurent Claudet)

Breeches etc.

Breeches and waistcoats were white, with pewter buttons; the over-the-knee gaiters were white for full dress and black for campaign wear, both had white metal buttons. Dark green overall trousers were also issued for campaign wear with the surtout coat and bicorne hat. The greatcoat was dark blue, possibly surplus from the French Guard, double breasted with two rows of white metal buttons and worn with epaulettes transferred from the coat.

Equipment

All equipment was of the same design as that of the elite companies of the line infantry with whitened leather belting and brass buckles and fittings. Cartridge boxes were black leather with a white metal royal eagle[18] surmounted by the Iron Crown on the flap and a small grenade in each corner. In 1805 the flap is often shown as decorated with a simple brass grenade, presumably the older pattern from the Presidential Guard. The sabre-briquet was of the usual pattern with a brass hilt and carried in a black scabbard fitted in brass, the sword strap was white with a red knot and tassel. The bayonet was carried in a brown leather scabbard fitted in either iron or brass.

NCOs

Unsurprisingly the Italian Army followed the French system of rank distinctions; the senior grades of non-commissioned officers having silver or gold thread worked through the bearskin cords and epaulette fringes. The knot of the sabre-briquet was mixed silver and red.

Rank was indicated by diagonal bars worn above the cuff, in exactly the same form as those of the French Army:

Sergente-maggiore: two diagonal silver bars, piped with the regimental colour
Sergente: a single bar as above
Caporale: two white woollen bars piped with the regimental piping colour
Caporale-furiere: as above, with the addition of a silver lace inverted chevron on the upper right sleeve

The *aiutante-sottufficiale* wore the uniform of a *sottotenente* with the epaulettes reversed, although without a gorget plate and with the sabre strap as for an NCO.

Corporali were uniformed, armed and equipped identically to the remainder of their company, their rank indicated only by their rank stripes.

---

18 The Italian royal eagle faced to its right while the French Imperial eagle customarily faced to its left.

THE GUARDIA REALE

Large eagle badge of the pattern used throughout the Royal Guard, probably from the lid of a cartridge box. Note the design of the breast of the eagle. (Private Collection, photo © and courtesy of Laurent Claudet)

Officers
Officers' bearskins were of the same pattern as that of the other ranks but the cords were silver.[19] The plate was also often silvered.

Staff officers, *capo di battaglione* and all field officers wore white plumes, company officers wore plumes of the same colour as the rank and file of their company.

As with the line infantry (see below), in undress and for campaign officers are often shown with dark green waistcoats and breeches with the surtout.

Officers' rank was indicated by their epaulettes, viz.

Colonello/colonello-sotto: two silver bullion-fringed epaulettes
Maggiore: as above but with gold straps
Capo di battaglione: silver bullion fringe epaulette on the right shoulder, contre-epaulette on the left
Capitano: as above but fine fringed epaulette
Tenente: as above but with a narrow red stripe along the straps
Sottotenente: as above but with two red stripes

---

19 If the Army of Italy followed the formula of other nations (and of the British and Danish Guards even today) then officers' bearskins were made of a finer fur than that of the men's. The officers' bearskins used the fur of the female bear, those of the rank and file used the fur of the male.

The *aiutante*, usually a *capitano*, wore the same uniform with the epaulettes of rank on opposite shoulders

Musicanti

Tamburi wore the uniform of the other ranks but two variations of the coat are recorded. The first is the same as the rank and file with the addition of red and white *tamburi* lace on the collar, cuffs, lapels and pockets. The second has silver lace in place of the red and white and also has silver lace on the buttons and buttonholes. Other details of equipment, etc. were as for the *tamburi* of the line infantry. The brass barrel of the drums was embossed with steel grenade badges and is often shown with blue in place of red and white hoops.

Tamburo-maggiori c. 1809: black bicorne with white feather edging trimmed with a silver scallop-edged lace and tassels, a tall white plume with two red and one green ostrich feathers at the base, national cockade. The coat was dark green with a dark green collar, but otherwise the same colouring as the rank and file. The collar, lapels, cuffs, cuff flaps and turnbacks were all edged with silver lace, and the buttons and buttonholes had silver lace trim. The fringed epaulettes were silver and the rank stripes were silver piped in red (the turnback badges, not visible in the illustration, were silver). The waistcoat had silver trim to the pockets and edge. All buttons were silver. The breeches had silver spearheads on the thighs and the short black ankle-boots had silver fringing around the top. The drum major's baldric was red edged with silver and with a silver drumstick plate on the chest, the waist belt was the same colour with a silver buckle plate embossed with the Imperial eagle. The sword was the infantry officer's sabre with silver hilt, sword knot and tassel, carried in a black leather scabbard fitted in silver. The gauntlets were white with silver scallop-edge lace on the cuffs. The baton was brown wood, fitted in silver with silver cords.

Musicanti c. 1809: Similar uniform to the *tamburo-maggiore* but with silver trefoil epaulettes in place of the full-fringed ones, no shoulder belt, a plain white waist belt supporting an infantry officer's epée and English pattern boots.

Zappatori

The sappers wore the same basic uniform as the rank and file but with the addition of a red badge on the upper of both sleeves. This badge was in the form of crossed axes with a red grenade above. Sappers had the usual white leather apron, and the smaller cartridge box worn on the right hip. The musket was of the same calibre as those of the rank and file but of a shorter, lighter pattern. In all Guard regiments muskets were bound and fitted with brass. The axe had a black wooden shaft and a brass heel. All other details and equipment were as for the line regiments.

THE GUARDIA REALE

Regimental Artillery Company
Very little information survives on the dress of the regimental artillery companies of the Guard beyond a brief note by Prince Eugène of 27 April 1811 which states that they were to have a bearskin, dark green coat with dark green collar, cuffs and lapels piped red, red turnbacks and cuff flaps. The company probably had dark green breeches and a mid to dark grey greatcoat.

Eugène ordered that this uniform was also to be that of the artillery companies of the other foot regiments of the Guard, although probably with the shako replacing the bearskin as appropriate.

Cacciatori/Carabinieri a Piedi Della Guardia (Foot Chasseurs/Carabiniers of the Royal Guard)

History and Organisation
Originally titled Cacciatori, the battalion's title was changed to Carabinieri Della Guardi Reale in 1810. As mentioned above the battalion was disbanded in 1813 following the 1812 campaign in Russia. The survivors were drafted into the grenadiers.

Service

1805	14 Oct	Surrender at Ulm
	2 Dec	Battle of Austerlitz
1806	20 Mar–2 Jun	Siege of Colberg
1807	15 Jan–20 Aug	Siege of Stralsund
1808		Dalmatia
1809	27–30 Apr	Battle of Caldiero
	14 Jun	Battle of Raab
	5 Jul	Battle of Wagram (349 officers and men)
1812	7 Sep	Battle of Borodino
	24 Oct	Battle of Maloyaroslavets
	16 Nov	Battle of Krasnoi
	28 Nov	Battle of the Beresina?

Martinien records no casualties from this battalion at any action although it is more than possible that some of its casualties are recorded under the Granatieri and perhaps in 1812 are recorded under the Coscritti (who from 1813 carried the same regimental name).

Uniform Until April 1806
Before it was changed by the Order of 15 April 1806 the battalion continued to wear the uniform it had been using at its raising in May 1804, and had worn as part of the Presidential Guard. This consisted of a leather helmet, similar to that worn by the Austrian Army of the period although without the crest, a red coat, with all facings in green, white waistcoat and breeches

and short black gaiters. The only known illustration of this uniform is by Hoffmann when the battalion was in Paris for the Imperial coronation in 1804, he shows the red coat but with a green waistcoat and a shako.

The new uniform of 1806 appears to have come into use fairly swiftly however and no vestiges of this uniform remain by the time painter/compiler of the 'Otto Manuscript' made his observations in 1807.[20]

Uniform from the 1806 Regulations

Headwear

The bearskin was of the line light infantry pattern; black fur without a front plate and with a red patch decorated with either a white hunting horn or possibly a simple white cross. The full dress cords were white and the plume was dark green tipped red, above the national cockade. Fatigue caps were dark green with red piping and tassel with a red bugle horn at the front.

Coat

The dark green habit coat had pointed lapels and cuffs. The lapels were white and the collar, turnbacks and cuffs red. Turnbacks were decorated with white bugle horn patches and the pockets were piped red. The epaulettes were originally yellow with a green fringe and crescent but this was swiftly altered (by 1806) to green straps with red crescents and fringes. All buttons were pewter. The surtout was the same pattern as that of the grenadiers but with pointed cuffs and bugle horn badges on the turnbacks.

Breeches etc.

The same details as for the grenadiers. When the greatcoat was worn, as was customary, the epaulettes were transferred from the coat and worn on it.

Equipment

Of the same pattern as used by the grenadiers but with a green sword knot with red tassel on the sword.

Officers and NCOs

NCO rank stripes were in the form of chevrons, in keeping with the pointed 'Polish' cuffs. All other details and variations were as used in the Granatieri a Piedi Della Guardi Reale (see above).

Musicanti

Tamburo-maggiori c. 1809:[21] black bicorne with short white feather edging trimmed with silver edged lace, figured with a zigzag pattern along the edge, and silver tassels. national cockade secured with a silver strap and button. The coat was dark green with a red collar, green (pointed) lapels, green cuffs and

---

20 The best modern version of the manuscript is that edited by Guy C. Dempsey Jr, *Napoleon's Soldiers: The Grande Armée of 1807 as Depicted in the Paintings of the Otto Manuscript* (London: Arms and Armour, 1994). This is an absolutely invaluable guide to the actual appearance of the Grande Armée as opposed to what it was supposed to look like.

21 This description is based upon a plate that appeared in 'Le Briquet 3/88'.

red cuff flaps. The turnbacks cannot be seen but as the coat has a red lining it may be assumed that they are red with silver devices. The collar, lapels, cuffs, and turnbacks(?) are all edged with a wide silver lace, the cuff flaps with a narrow silver piping. The fringed epaulettes are silver but noteably no rank stripes are shown. The waistcoat and breeches are white without decoration. All buttons are silver. The drum major's baldric is red edged with wide silver lace and, outside that, a short silver fringing. A zigzag pattern of wide silver lace runs along the complete length of the baldric. The sword is the infantry officer's straight sword with a gilt hilt, but no sword knot or tassel, carried in a black leather scabbard fitted gilt. No waistbelt is visible. The gauntlets are white and the officer wears standard pattern 'jockey boots'. The baton is brown wood, fitted in silver with silver cords.

Tamburi of the Carabinieri had the same distinctions as the Granatieri but with the brass drum barrels embossed with bugle horns in place of the grenades of the latter.

Zappatori
Zappatore distinctions were the same as those for the grenadiers.

Veliti Della Guardia Reale (Velites of the Royal Guard)

History and Organisation
The decree which created the Royal Guard specified that recruits for the Veliti should be at least 5ft 2in (Paris = 5 ft 5 in Imperial or 1.65 m metric), between 18 and 25, be able to read and write, and have an annual income of 200 Milanese Lira to be paid to the State for their training and maintenance. After two years service Velites could be transferred to the line with the rank of *sergente*.

Initially it was planned to raise three battalions of Veliti, one of Veliti Granatieri and two of velite Cacciatori, each of four companies. The initial plan for there to be departmental recruiting areas was abandoned by the formal regulations of 19 August 1805, and this regulation set out the establishments as:

Regimental Staff
1 *colonnello*   1 *maggiore*
3 *capo di battaglione*   3 *aiutanti-maggiori*
2 *sottoaiutanti-maggiori*   1 *quartiermastro*
2 *chirurge-maggiori*   1 *vammastro*
1 *tamburo-maggiore*   2 *caporale-tamburo*
30 *musicanti*[22]
2 *maestro-artigiani* (master craftsmen: bootmaker, armourer)

---

[22] Including a Head of Music and two deputies.

Company Establishment

1 *capitano*	2 *tenenti*
1 *sergente-maggiore*	4 *sergenti*
1 *quartiermastro*	1 *furiere*
8 *caporali*	3 *tamburi*
80 *soldati*	

In the autumn of 1806[23] a fifth cacciatore company was raised. Then on 10 June 1807 a sixth cacciatore company and a fifth granatiere company were added to the regiment, at the same time a *sottotenente* was added to the establishment of each company. By 1813 the establishment was back to five companies per battalion with the 5th company essentially working as a depot company.

On 14 March 1808 the establishment was increased again when one sub-adjutant, one medical officer and two craftsmen were added to the staff, each company formally gained two sappers and the rank-and-file strength was increased to 97. On 16 October of the same year the rank and file was further increased to 122.

When, in 1809, the senior regiment changed its designation from Cacciatori to Carabinieri, the Velites followed suit and the battalion became Velite Carabinieri.

From 17 January 1811 it was decided that veliti with five years' service who had not been transferred to the line would no longer have to pay the annual fees.

Problems with recruitment meant that the 3rd Battalion was not actually raised until 9 March 1808 and even then only with an establishment of one granatiere and one cacciatore company. On 15 November 1810, however, the lack of recruits caused the 3rd Battalion to be disbanded and its personnel transferred into the two other battalions. Thereafter the regiment constituted only two battalions.

In 1813 the majority of the men who returned from Russia were passed into the line as NCOs and the regiment took the field as a single battalion, almost all new recruits.

During the 10 years of its existence 3,679 men passed through the regiment, a large percentage of whom actually did progress into the line as NCOs.

Service

1806	29 Sep	Skirmish at Cattaro: 1 *capitano* killed, 1 wounded
1807	15 Jan–20 Aug	Siege of Stralsund
1808 (Dalmatia)		1 battalion
1808 (Spain)		1 battalion

---

23 The author has not found the exact date for this increase.

THE GUARDIA REALE

	18 Jun	Skirmish at St Paul (1 *tenente* wounded)
	2 Sep	Skirmish at San-Roy (1 *capitano*, 3 *tenenti* killed)
	12 Oct	Skirmish at St-Golgat (1 *tenente* wounded)
1809 (Germany)		1 battalion
	16 Apr	Battle of Sacile (1 *capitano* killed)
	30 Apr	Skirmish at Illasi: 1 *capo di battaglione* killed 1 *tenente* died of wounds 3 *capitani* and 3 *tenenti* wounded
	8 May	Battle of the Piave
	14 Jun	Battle of Raab (1 *tenente* wounded)
	5 Jul	Battle of Wagram (610 officers and men)
1809 (Spain)		1 battalion
	5 May	1 officer wounded on advance guard duty at Caldiero
	Jun	Siege of Gerona (610 officers and men)
	8 Jul	Storm of Mountjoie: 1 *tenente* killed 1 *capo di battaglione* wounded 1 *tenente* died of wounds 1 *capitano* and 2 *tenenti* wounded
1810 (Spain)		1 battalion
1811 (Spain)		1 battalion
1812 (Spain)		1 battalion
1813 (Spain)		1 battalion
1812	7 Sep	Battle of Borodino
	24 Oct	Battle of Maloyaroslavetz: 2 *capo di battaglione* killed 2 *capitani* killed 2 *chirurgi* killed 1 *capo di battaglione* wounded 3 *capitani* wounded, 2 subsequently died 11 *tenenti* wounded, 3 subsequently died
	14 Nov	Smolensk (1 *tenente* wounded)
	16 Nov	Battle of Krasnoi
	28 Nov	Battle of the Beresina (1 *capitano* killed, 1 *tenente* wounded)
1813–1814		Defence of the Kingdom of Italy
1813	8 Sep	Skirmish at Leybach (1 *capitano*, 3 *tenenti* wounded)
1813	12 Sep	Skirmish at San-Marein (1 *capitano* killed, 2 *tenenti* wounded)
1814	8 Feb	Battle of the Mincio (638 officers and men)

Uniform

Headwear
In full dress the velite battalions wore the grenadier or chasseur pattern bearskin as appropriate, as used by the senior regiments, except that by at least 1808, and possibly even from 1805, the velite grenadiers' plate was brass in place of white metal. On campaign the regiment often wore the infantry pattern shako with a white metal crown and Imperial eagle plate on the front and the usual national cockade secured by a white cockade strap. The shako cords were white and plumes followed the pattern of those worn on the bearskin. The white fatigue caps had grass green piping and either the grenade or bugle horn badge as appropriate on the front.

Coat
The white habit coats of the 1st Battalion, the Veliti Granatieri, had square grass green lapels, and grass green collars, cuffs[24] and three-pointed cuff flaps, all piped white. The turnbacks were grass green, unpiped, and the turnback ornaments were white grenades (changed to yellow by 1808/9). Pockets were piped in grass green. All buttons were initially pewter but by 1808/9 had changed to brass, and full-fringed red epaulettes were worn. By 1811 the cuffs of the coats had been changed to white piped in grass green.

The coats of the 2nd Battalion, Veliti Carabinieri, had pointed lapels, Polish cuffs and bugle horn insignia but were otherwise the same as those of the 1st Battalion. Epaulettes were the same pattern as worn by the Guard Carabinieri.

Breeches etc.
Breeches and waistcoats were white and the high gaiters were black with white metal buttons. White overall trousers were issued for campaign. The dark grey greatcoats were of the 'guard double breasted pattern', with white metal buttons and were worn with the epaulettes transferred from the coat.

Equipment
All equipment was identical to that of the appropriate Granatieri and Cacciatori companies of the senior guard regiment although the cartouche box crowned eagle badge was brass.

Officers and NCOs
All distinctions and rank badges were the same as those of the Granatieri and Carabinieri except with gold differencing in place of silver, and a surviving officer's coat has gold grenades on red cloth backing on the turnbacks.[25] The Officer's gorget was gold with silver details (an Imperial eagle or a crowned 'N').

On campaign officers frequently wore a dark green surtout with grass green collar and cuffs, piped white, white cuff flaps, grass green piping to the pockets and grass green turnbacks with the same badges as on the habit.

---

24 When first formed the cuffs were white piped green, but these had been replaced by green piped white before the end of 1806.
25 Museo del Risorgimento in Bologna.

THE GUARDIA REALE

The regimental *colonnello* is shown *c.* 1810 wearing a regulation uniform with the square lapels of the 1st Battalion. His headwear is a black bicorne with silver scalloped-edge lace and cords and a silver cockade strap, no plume. He carries a straight infantry-style epée with silver hilt and a gold sword knot and tassel in a plain black scabbard. Unusually he does not appear to be wearing a waist belt. His boots are black heavy cavalry pattern and his horse furniture is a dark green shabraque edged with a broad silver (outer) and a narrow silver (inner) lace, with silver grenades in the outer corners. The dark green double pistol holster covers are edged with two rows of wide silver lace.

Musicanti
Tamburi wore a coat of the same pattern and colour as the rank and file but with the addition of gold lace on the collar, lapels, buttonholes and cuffs. The drums had the customary brass barrel with blue hoops decorated with white grenades between the cords.

One source for 1812 gives the lace as red and white and only on the collar and cuffs and with all other details as for the senior guard regiments.

In 1812 a contemporary illustration of *tamburi* on campaign shows exactly the same uniform as the rank and file without differencing in any way.

Tamburo-maggiori, Veliti Granatieri *c.* 1809: black bicorne with white feather edging trimmed with a gold scallop-edged lace and tassels, a tall white plume with two red and one grass green ostrich feathers at the base, national cockade with a gold cockade strap. White coat with a grass green collar, lapels and turnbacks, all laced with gold and with gold lace around the buttons and buttonholes, gold fringed epaulettes, gold rank stripes and gold lace on the seams of the sleeves and back of the coat. The waistcoat had gold trim to the pockets and edge. All buttons were gold. The breeches had gold Hungarian knots and the boots were the cuffed English pattern. The baldric worn by the *tamburo-maggiore* was red edged with gold with gold grenades and embroidery along its length and with a gold drumstick plate on the chest, the waist belt was the same colour with a gilt buckle plate. The sword was the infantry officer's sabre with gilt hilt, sword knot and tassel, carried in a black leather scabbard fitted in gold. The gauntlets were white with gold scallop-edge lace on the cuffs. The baton was brown wood, fitted in gold with gold cords.

Musicanti, Veliti Granatieri *c.* 1809: The same uniform as above but with gold trefoil epaulettes, plain waist belt with brass buckle, straight-bladed epée, and plain breeches. No baldric.

Zappatori
All distinctions were the same as those in use in the Granatieri and Carabinieri battalions, although Boisselier shows the *zappatore* with a red collar.

An axe sold at auction in 1916 had its head engraved 'Reggimento Veliti' and must have been from this regiment.[26]

Regimental Artillery Company

See the notes above for the senior regiment.

Marinai Della Guardia Reale (Sailors[27] of the Royal Guard)

History and Organisation
Although the Marinai Della Guardia Reale (Sailors of the Royal Guard) traditionally date from 1806 when Venice was absorbed into the Kingdom[28] there is no firm evidence for their existence before an order of August 1807, and they were only formally attached to the Guard by an Order of 13 June 1808.

The Order of 13 June 1808, by which the sailors became a part of the Guard, set out an establishment for the unit of

1 *comandante tenente*	1 *luogoenente*
1 *primo mastro*	1 *secondo mastro*
1 *quartiermastro*	1 *mapo timoniere*
2 *aiutante timonieri*	1 *mastro cannoniere*
2 *cannonieri*	1 *pilota*
40 *marinai*	

On 14 February 1811, the establishment was increased by the addition of 14 NCOs, 60 *marinai 1° classe*, 60 *marinai 2° classe* and six 'boys', two of whom were listed as *tamburi* (presumably in training since European armies have never customarily used 'drummer boys'). It is doubtful if the unit ever reached its full establishment strength.

The unit was raised mainly in the Venetian provinces and throughout its existence remained in garrison in that locality.

Service
Carmignani gives no campaign service for the sailors except that they were with the Grande Armée in the campaigns of 1806–1807 and thus almost certainly at the Siege of Colberg (20 March to 2 June 1806) and the Siege of Stralsund (15 January to 20 August 1807). In 1809 they remained in Venice but in 1812 a detachment of three officers and 103 NCOs and other ranks were with the Grande Armée in Russia. Additionally it is almost certain that the unit would

---

26 Piero Crociano, Massimo Fiorentino and Alfred Umhey, 'À Propos de l'Esponton des "Dragoni Napoleone…"', *Soldats Napoleoniens: Les Troupes Françaises, Alliés et Coalisées. Hors-série No. 1, Avril 2003* (Paris: Éditions de la Revue Napoléon, 2003), pp. 78–84.
27 As with the French unit this is often translated as 'marines', correctly it should be sailors and indeed they were naval personnel, *not* combat marines.
28 Piero Crociano, *L'Esercito Italico 1805–1814: Guardia Reale* (Parma: Albertelli, 2005), p. 42.

have been involved in the defence of the Kingdom in 1813–1814, probably alongside larger units such as the Reggimento Guardia Alla Città di Venezia. Martinien records no casualties, wounded or killed, amongst the unit's officers at any point.

Uniform
The unit wore two distinctly different uniforms, the earlier one is not recorded officially but illustrations[29] show it to have essentially been a dark green version of the full dress uniform of the Sailors of the French Imperial Guard, with red cuffs and all piping, braid and frogging in white and a 'top hat' as worn with the post-1810 uniform. The later, simpler version was ordered by Eugène in a letter dated 6 March 1810.

Post-March 1810[30]
Headwear
Post-1810 the regiment wore a hat that resembled a top hat with a wide, curled-up brim; the same pattern as the hat worn by the navy. This top hat had a brass lozenge plate embossed with an anchor at the front. Above the plate was the national cockade secured with a white cockade strap, in turn surmounted by an elongated carrot-shaped plume; the plume was red for 1st class sailors and green for 2nd class. The dark green fatigue cap was piped red and almost certainly had a red anchor badge at the front, although this is not always shown on illustrations.

Coat
The short-tailed coat was of a similar cut to the surtout and was dark green with red collar and cuffs, and dark green turnbacks piped red. The fringed epaulettes were red or dark green, following the pompom colour. All buttons were white metal.

Breeches etc.
The unique pattern of waistcoat was double breasted and either red or dark green, as appropriate for 1st or 2nd class sailors, with white metal buttons. Breeches were dark green, with 'Hungarian' pattern gaiters trimmed with red or green lace and tassels, and with white metal buttons. For campaign wear dark green overall trousers were issued with a red or dark green stripe on the outer seam. The dark green infantry pattern greatcoats had a red collar and white metal buttons and the epaulettes from the coat.

Equipment
All equipment was of the same pattern used by the line infantry elite companies, the sword strap was white with a red tassel, and the cartridge box flap had a white metal lozenge-shaped plate bearing an anchor beneath the Iron Crown.

---

29 Including an unpublished watercolour by Boisselier, regrettably without a source given on it.
30 There is a superb study of sailors in this uniform in the Collection of HM The Queen and reproduced (sadly in monochrome) in *Napoleon's Italian and Neapolitan Troops*: Otto von Pivka (Digby Smith) (London: Osprey, 1979), p.15.

Officers and NCOs

An NCO's distinctions and rank stripes were the same as those used by the rest of the Royal Guard infantry regiments. In addition senior NCOs added silver lace to the brim and edge of the crown of the hat.

Officers wore the same hat as the rank and file with any metalwork silvered and silver lace on the brim and upper edge of the crown of the hat. The carrot-shaped pompom was red over white over green but in full dress officers used a red over white plume with a green ball pompom at the base. Officers' coats were the long-tailed surtout pattern, with silver epaulettes of rank in the same system as those of the Granatieri a Piedi. Waistcoats were red with silver lacing on the front. Breeches were dark green with silver Hungarian knots on the front thigh and silver piping on the outer seam, although on campaign it appears that officers wore plain dark green breeches. Boots were Hungarian pattern with silver lace and tassels. All officers carried the curved, light cavalry pattern sabre suspended from a black leather light cavalry pattern waist belt.

Tamburi

The uniform was that of the rank and file with the addition of red and white lace on the collar and cuffs. All other variations of uniforms, equipment, etc. were the same as those of the tamburi of the line infantry regiments.

Coscritti Della Guardia Reale (Conscripts of the Royal Guard); from 1813, Cacciatori Della Guardi Reale (Cacciatori of the Royal Guard)

History and Organisation

The Coscritti Della Guardia Reale were raised in 1810 following an initiative by Eugène to increase the size of the Guard[31] along the same lines as the increase in the strength of the French Imperial Guard effected by the raising of the 'Young Guard' regiments.[32] Like these latter French Regiments the Coscritti Della Guardia Reale was to be recruited from the best of the conscripts, with a height of at least 5ft 5in.[33] The intention was, as in the French Imperial Guard, that suitable candidates from the rank and file would, after two years, be transferred into the line regiments as NCOs.

The regiment was raised at a strength of two battalions, each of five companies, and a regimental staff. Companies were to be of the same establishment as those of the Velites.

---

[31] The first mention of the raising of the unit is in a letter from Eugène to Napoleon dated 13 September 1810. Napoleon gave his approval in a reply of 4 October.

[32] Piero Crociano actually refers to the Conscriti as 'the Italian Young Guard', in 'Napoleon's Italian Army, Part V', *Tradition No. 46* (London: Belmont Maitland, 197?), pp. 29–32; and *No. 47, No. 48* (London, Belmont-Maitland 197?)

[33] This is 5ft 5in Paris, equal to 5ft 8in Imperial (1.72 m metric). These were most definitely the tallest of the recruits.

On 4 February 1811 the regiment was augmented with an artillery and support company comprising two 3-pdr guns and caissons, a four horse ambulance, 4 six-horse caissons for supplies, two caissons for ammunition of musket cartridges, a four-horse wagon for the administrative papers etc. and a field forge to be drawn by three horses.

As with the other foot regiments of the Guard, the 5th company of each battalion appears to have performed as a depot company forwarding trained personnel to the regiment, rather than serving as a field company in itself.

In the re-establishment and reorganisation of the Guard in 1813, a decree from Eugène, dated 26 February, abolished the title 'Coscritti' and retitled the regiment as Cacciatori Della Guardi Reale (Cacciatori of the Royal Guard), traditionally in recognition of the regiment's service in Russia. By the same decree the regiment was reformed as four battalions, each of five companies, as previously.

The regiment's depot was, throughout its existence, at Milan.

Service

1812	7 Sep	Battle of Borodino
	24 Oct	Battle of Maloyaroslavets: 1 *colonnello* wounded 1 *major* wounded 1 *capitano* subsequently died of wounds, 4 others wounded 2 *tenenti* killed, 27 others wounded of whom 7 subsequently died of wounds
1813	6 Sep	Skirmish at Laybach (3 *capitani* wounded)
	12 Sep	Skirmish at St Marein (3 *tenenti* killed)
	13 Sep	Skirmish at St Marein
	16 Sep	Skirmish at St Marein (2 *capitani* and 5 *tenenti* wounded)
	19 Sep	Skirmish at Tchernütz
	25 Sep	Skirmish at Tchernütz (4 *capitani* wounded, 4 *tenenti* wounded, 1 subsequently died of wounds)
	27 Sep	Skirmish at Tchernütz
1814	8 Feb	Battle of the Mincio
	16 Feb	Skirmish at Salo (1 *capo di battaglione* wounded, 3 *capitani* killed, 1 wounded, 4 *tenenti* wounded)

Uniform

Headwear

The Coscritti wore the infantry pattern shako with a white upper band and a brass Italian Imperial eagle plate. The national cockade at the front was secured with white cockade strap. Shako cords were white and the full dress plume was green with a black tip; on campaign the plume was replaced with a black over green ball pompom. Chin scales were brass. The dark green fatigue caps had white piping and tassel and white Imperial eagle badge at the front.

Coat
The habit was dark green with square lapels, dark green lapels, cuffs, and turnbacks, all piped white. The collar and three-pointed cuff flaps were red piped white, and the pockets were also piped white. The turnbacks were red piped white, with a white Imperial eagle turnback badge. Full-fringed epaulettes were green with a red crescent (although Boisselier in his 1955 study shows green shoulder straps piped white). All buttons were white metal.

The two additional battalions raised in 1813 wore the short-tailed habit-veste with square lapels but all facings and other details were as for the 1810 pattern habit. Some illustrations show green shoulder straps piped white in place of the full epaulettes, and red cuffs with white cuff flaps are also sometimes shown on this coat.

Breeches etc.
Breeches and waistcoats were white, with white metal buttons. Gaiters were black over-knee pattern, also with white metal buttons. On campaign white overall trousers were issued. Greatcoats were the same pattern as worn by the Velites and worn with the fringed epaulettes of the coat when these were used. By 1812 the regiment had adopted the short, below-knee pattern gaiters, as always these were black with either white metal, or black cloth covered, buttons.

Equipment
Equipment was of the same pattern as that used by the senior regiments. The sword strap was red with white knot and tassel, or white with a red knot and tassel.

Officers and NCOs
All distinctions and rank badges were the same as those used by the Granatieri a Piedi Della Guardi Reale (as above). The officers' turnback devices were in silver. A print dated to 1812 shows an officer in service dress wearing a green surtout and green breeches with silver Hungarian knots on the thighs.

Musicanti
All distinctions and equipment was as used by the Veliti. Musicians were also uniformed the same as those of the Veliti but with silver distinctions in place of gold.

Zappatori
All distinctions and equipment was as used by the Veliti but one contemporary source shows the bearskin with a brass plate, red cords and tassels and a green plume.

Regimental Artillery Company

There is little information on the regimental artillery beyond that recorded for the senior regiment, except that the coat turnbacks had a white eagle badge and the company wore a shako with red cords, in place of the bearskin.

Artigliera Della Guardia Reale (Artillery of the Royal Guard)

History and Organisation

The decree of 20 June 1805 that raised the Royal Guard also disbanded the majority of the artillery of the Presidential Guard retaining only a 64-strong Horse Artillery Company commanded by *Capitano Comandante* Raspi.

However the need for logistical support forced the raising of a train company on 30 June 1806 with a strength of:

1 *tenente*	1 *sottotenente*
1 *maresciallo d'alloggio capo*	2 *marescialli d'alloggio*
1 *brigadiere furiere*	2 *brigadieri*
1 *tromba*	2 *maniscachi*
1 *sellaio*	
21 *1° classe soldati*	53 *2° classe soldati*

A decree of 1808 set out a new establishment to the Horse Artillery (although the train establishment remained unchanged):

1 *capitano comandante*	1 *capitano*
1 *1° tenente*	2 *2° tenenti*
1 *veterinario*	1 *custode d'artiglieria*[34]
1 *operaio*[35]	1 *maresciallo d'alloggio capo*
6 *marescialli d'alloggio*	1 *brigadiere furiere*
6 *brigadieri*	2 *tromba*
1 *maniscalco*	
24 *1° classe cannonieri*	36 *2° classe cannonieri*

By a decree of 4 February 1811 the Guard's artillery arm was strengthened again with the addition of a company of foot artillery of:

1 *capitano comandante*	1 *capitano*
1 *1° tenente*	2 *2° tenenti*
1 *sergente-maggiore*	4 *sergenti*
1 *caporale-furiere*	8 *caporali*
6 *artificieri*	2 *tamburi*
40 *1° classe cannonieri*	60 *2° classe cannonieri*

A second train company, with each company with an increased establishment of:

1 *tenente*	1 *sottotenente*
1 *maresciallo d'alloggio capo*	4 *marescialli d'alloggio*
1 *brigadiere furiere*	4 *brigadieri*

---

[34] Literally a 'warder of artillery'.
[35] Literally 'worker' but obviously a professional artisan.

THE ARMY OF THE KINGDOM OF ITALY 1805–1814

Italien.

Reitende Garde-Artillerie.   Offizier der reit. Artillerie.   Artillerie-Train der Garde.
Offizier der reit. Garde-Artillerie.   Garde-Fuss-Artilleristen.
Offizier der Garde-Fuss-Artillerie.

Das Italienische Heer unter Vice-König Eugen.
1812.

Die Uniform der Garde-Artillerie war derjenigen der entsprechenden Waffe des französischen Heeres sehr ähnlich. Fast übereinstimmend erscheint namentlich die reitende Artillerie der Garde. Die Garde-Füss-Artillerie zeigt dagegen ganz andere Uniformfarben. Bei der reitenden Artillerie der Linie und beim Garde-Artillerie-Train scheint für die Uniformirung die Waffenbrüderschaft mit dem Polnischen Hülfscorps, das eine Zeit lang einen Bestandtheil des Italienischen Heeres ausmachte, von Einfluss gewesen zu sein. Wenigstens gemahnt die Kopfbedeckung an Polnische Vorbilder. Sie hat die Form einer Czapka, mit dem Unterschiede, dass nicht eine Ecke des oberen, viereckigen Theiles nach vorn gerichtet ist, sondern eine der Breitseiten Infolgedessen ist auch der Stutz nicht, wie sonst üblich, links seitlich angebracht, sondern gerade vorn in der Mitte. Hier konnte aus Mangel an Raum nur ein Offizier der reitenden Artillerie dargestellt werden. Die Mannschaften trugen die Litzen auf der Brust, die beim Offizier silbern sind, in Roth, ferner rothe Epauletten. Als Beinbekleidung dienten grüne enganliegende Hosen mit rothen Seitenstreifen und Stiefeln „à la Suwarow" mit rother Einfassung.

Knötel, Uniformenkunde. Band III. No. 17.   Verlag von Max Babenzien in Rathenow.

THE GUARDIA REALE

1 *tromba*
1 *sellaio*
40 *1° classe soldati*

2 *maniscachi*
60 *2° classe soldati*

Facing page: Knötel Plate III/17. Horse and Foot Artillery and train of the Royal Guard, 1812. (Author's collection)

And a staff for the whole artillery arm of:

1 *capo di battaglione*
1 *sotto aiutante maggiore*
1 *ufficiale di santa*
1 *guardia d'artiglieria*

1 *tenente aiutante maggiore*
1 *quartiermastro*
1 *veterinario*
4 *capi operai*

In Moscow, on 4 October 1812, Napoleon brought together the artillery companies of the Guard's infantry regiments into a second, provisional, foot artillery company and a captain, a *brigadiere trombettista* and 14 *bracciante* were added to the Staff.

Artiglieria a Cavallo (Horse Artillery)

Headwear
The uniform was modelled on, and almost identical to, that worn by the French Guard Horse Artillery. The headwear was a black colpack but without a bag, and at the left side the national cockade surmounted by a red plume. A number of contemporary drawings show a red bag to the colpack but the decree of 15 April 1806 is definite in stating 'without bag'.[36] By 1811, however, it appears that the colpack had, regulations or not, gained a red bag. Cords were red and the chin scales brass. Fatigue caps were as for the foot battery but blue.

Coat
For full dress uniform was a dark blue hussar-style dolman and pelisse with dark blue collar and cuffs, both edged red, 18 rows of red frogging and five rows of brass buttons. The pelisse was edged with black fur. The hussar-style barrel sash was red and blue.

On campaign the dolman and pelisse were replaced with a dark blue surtout, or a habit with pointed lapels, the sources are unclear. The coat (whichever pattern it was) had a black collar piped red, red Polish cuffs and red turnbacks with a dark blue grenade badge. A red, fringed epaulette was worn at the right shoulder and red trefoil epaulette and aiguillette on the left. All buttons were brass.

In 1811 a basic uniform colour change from dark blue to dark green was projected and this *was* in use by 1813 but when the actual changeover was actually effected is unknown, perhaps in the rebuilding of the Army after the 1812 campaign. The dark green surtout/habit coat was certainly issued and in use in 1813–14 but whether the dark green hussar-style full dress

---

36 Cf. Piero Crociani's *L'Esercito Italico 1805–14: Guardia Reale* (Parma: Albertelli, 2005), p. 95.

uniform ever got further than the projected stage and some officers' privately purchased versions is unknown.

Breeches etc.
Breeches were dark blue with red Hungarian knots on the thighs and a red stripe on the outer seam and were worn with Hungarian boots with red lace and tassel. The waistcoat worn with the surtout was dark blue with brass buttons. Greatcoats were of the cavalry pattern with red lining and piping at the edge of the collar and cape and white metal buttons. A red and dark blue barrel sash with red cords was worn with the dolman and pelisse.

In the 'new' uniform of 1813 all of the dark blue items were replaced with green and the barrel sash became green and red.

Equipment
The basic equipment was the same as that used by the senior infantry regiments of the Guard, with a brass grenade badge on the cartridge box lid. The sword strap was white with a red knot and tassel. Additionally the sabretaches were blue edged red with a brass crossed cannon badge below an Imperial eagle, also in brass. From 1813, after the return from Russia, the rebuilt unit adopted a green field to their sabretaches but all other details of the design were unchanged.

Officers and NCOs
The officers and NCOs rank badges and distinctions worn on the surtout were the same as those used by the foot regiments of the Guard, with all lace, epaulettes, etc. in gold or yellow.

Officers' rank badges on the hussar-style dolman were in the form of chevrons above the cuffs; the first chevron trimmed the upper edge of the cuff and was 14 mm wide.

> *Capitano comandante*: four gold chevrons alternately 14 mm and 23 mm[37]
> *Capitano*: three gold chevrons, two of 14 mm with one of 23 mm in between
> *Tenente*: two gold 14 mm chevrons
> *Sottotenente*: one gold 14 mm chevron

The same sequence and colouring was used for the spearheads on the breeches.

All officers' lace and braid were gold, the barrel sash was blue and gold, and belts were red leather with gold edging and fittings (at least in full dress, whether such finery was much used in the field is debatable). Sabretaches were dark blue edged gold and with a gilt design of crossed cannon surmounted by the Imperial eagle. With the undress uniform all belts were black leather with gilt fittings.

As with the rank and file after 1812 green replaced the dark blue.

---

[37] The author has not seen the *capitano comandante*'s rank badges laid down anywhere. As the Horse Artillery had a *capitano* as second in command it is likely that the commander used the rank badges of a squadron commander in the cavalry.

Musicanti

There are two recorded variations of the *trombettieri*' uniforms, both from contemporary illustrations. Given that a new uniform might expect to be issued each year there is no reason why both cannot have been worn at different time periods.

A variant, dated to *c.* 1806, shows a white colpack with a white plume tipped sky blue, gold cords and a sky blue bag piped red, with a gold tassel. Red dolman and pelisse with sky blue collar and cuffs, both piped gold. Black fur on the pelisse. Mixed gold and sky blue frogging and aiguillette. Red and sky blue barrel sash. Sky blue breeches with red and gold lace and decorations. Hungarian boots edged red and gold. The sabretache has a sky blue face with the usual gold lace border and brass badges. Brass trumpet with mixed red and gold cords.

The second illustration repeats the white colpack but with a red bag piped dark blue, white plume and mixed red and white cords. Red dolman and pelisse with dark blue facings, white lace and frogging, and brass buttons. White fur on the pelisse. White cords for the trumpet and a red sabretache edged yellow. The trumpet is brass with red cords.

The surtout was red with black (possibly dark blue) collar piped red and red cuffs and turnbacks piped dark blue. Epaulettes and aiguillettes were mixed red and white.

Horse Furniture

Gunners' shabraques were of the same pattern as those of the line in dark blue with a wide red edge and red grenades in the rear corners. *Trombettieri*' shabraques were of reversed colours and the officers had a double gold edging with red piping at the extreme edge.

Artiglieria a Piedi (Foot Artillery)

The 1811 decree that ordered the raising of the Regiment of Foot Artillery made no mention of a uniform for it. However there is a letter in the State Archives of Milan asking for information about the new regiment's uniform, and the same document packet contains the following answer:

> The Foot Artillery will have the same uniform as the Artillery of the Line, except for having vertical pockets [to the coat] as in the other Guard Corps. Officers and Artiglieri will have the bearskin of the Gendarmerie.[38]

Headwear

Unsurprisingly the foot artillery of the Royal Guard had a uniform similar to that of their French counterparts. Headwear was a black bearskin of the same model as that of the Gendarmerie (although a contemporary illustration shows it without the peak) with a white grenade on the red rear patch. In full

---

38 Piero Crociano, *L'Esercito Italico 1805–1814: Guardia Reale* (Parma: Albertelli, 2005), p. 74.

dress this cap had red cords and a red plume above the national cockade; on campaign the cap's only decoration was the cockade. The fatigue caps were dark green with red piping and tassel and a red grenade badge at the front.

Coat
As laid down in the Milan Archives document mentioned above the dark green habit was of the same pattern as that of the line artillery, with black collar and lapels piped red and red cuffs, turnbacks and cuff flaps piped dark green. Turnbacks were decorated with dark green grenade badges and the vertical pockets were piped red. All buttons were white metal. All rank and file wore red full-fringed epaulettes.

In 1813 a dark green surtout was ordered for the artillery but it seems unlikely that this was issued before the fall of the Kingdom the following year.

Breeches etc.
Breeches and waistcoats were dark green with white metal buttons and the black over-the-knee gaiters had white metal buttons for parade dress and cloth covered buttons on campaign. The dark green greatcoats were of the Guard infantry pattern and worn with the epaulettes from the coat.

Equipment
As with the Horse Artillery the equipment was of the same basic pattern as that used by senior infantry regiments of the Royal Guard, with either a brass grenade badge or a brass badge of crossed cannon barrels on the cartridge box lid. The sword strap was white with red knot and tassels.

Officers and NCOs
Officers' and NCOs' distinctions and rank insignia were the same as those of the rest of the Guard's foot regiments. Officers' bearskins had the grenade badge in silver and silver cords for parade dress. Officers' belts were white for full dress and a more practical black leather for campaign, and all dismounted officers wore English pattern boots, mounted officers wore the high-cuffed heavy cavalry pattern boots.

Musicanti
The *tamburi* of the Foot Artillery wore the basic uniform prescribed for their company but with the addition of broad white lace trim, inside the piping, to the lapels, collar and cuffs.

Drum aprons and the drum carriage belts were white leather with brass buckles and the carriage belt was decorated with a brass drumstick plate on the upper front. The drums had brass barrels and the hoops were painted with diagonal stripes of green–white–red–white.

Treno d'Artiglieria di Guardia (Artillery Train of the Guard)

Headwear
The Guards train of artillery wore the czapska similar, if not essentially identical, to that originally issued to the line horse artillery. This had a black

upper part, piped black at the top and red down the vertical edges. The lower part was a black fur turban with a brass lozenge plate at the front bearing a device of crowned crossed cannon barrels over a pyramid of cannonballs. The national cockade had a white cockade strap and was surmounted by a light green carrot-shaped pompom.

There is one interesting and notable aspect of the czapska as it was worn throughout the Kingdom's army: in most armies, including the French and Polish, the czapska was designed in such a way that, when worn, a corner of the flat top was central at the front. In the Army of Italy all illustrations of the czapska show it designed and manufactured in a different way, so that when worn the corners of the top were square to the front and the flat top parallel to the peak. This peculiarity is shown throughout the Army wherever the czapska was in use.

In 1811 the shako was introduced to replace the czapska, whilst some illustrations show this as the line artillery peakless pattern others show the more traditional style worn throughout much of the army. The latter certainly seems the more likely of the two. It had the same plate, cockade and pompom as the czapska but, for parade dress, had light green cords and plume.

Fatigue caps were mid-grey with light green piping and tassels.

Coat
The mid-grey coat was of the surtout style with short tails. The collar, Polish cuffs and turnbacks were light green and the vertical pockets and front of the coat leading down into the turnbacks were piped in the same colour. The front of the coat had lace batons in the same form as the coats of the Horse Artillery and there were two similar batons on the cuffs. The coat had light green, fringed epaulettes. All buttons were white metal. In 1811 the battalion serving the Foot Artillery made changes to their coats (how far, if at all, these changes were reflected by the Horse Artillery battalion is unknown): the epaulettes were replaced by mid-grey shoulder straps piped in light green and the cuffs were changed to the Brandenburg pattern with cuff flaps, all still in light green, with two light green batons, worn one above the other but both on the cuff, although a painting in the collection of HM The Queen shows the cuffs without these lace batons.

When the Army was reformed after the 1812 campaign the regiment was given coats of the same cut as above but in green with red facings and red lace batons.

Breeches etc.
Waistcoats were mid-grey with white metal buttons and breeches were soft buff leather with white metal buttons on the outer seams and were worn with high, cuffed riding boots with steel spurs. Members of the regiment who were not mounted wore mid-grey breeches and black gaiters as for the infantry. Whitened leather gauntlets were worn for parade and buff gauntlets on campaign. The light grey greatcoats were of light cavalry pattern, with a light green collar and lining.

In 1813, when the regiment was reformed after the disastrous Russian campaign, the breeches and waistcoats were changed to dark green.

Equipment

The drivers wore a pouch belt and cartridge box of the line light cavalry pattern, with a brass crossed cannon badge on the cartridge box lid. The second shoulder belt supported an infantry pattern sabre-briquet in a black leather scabbard with light green sword strap and a white knot with light green tassel. Short, dragoon pattern muskets were carried on the saddle.

Officers and NCOs

Insignia was the same as that used by the light cavalry and *brigadiere* were equipped as for the drivers. Senior NCOs and all officers carried the light cavalry sabre worn from a waist belt, and on campaign both favoured the bicorne hat with silver lace and tassels, although the official headwear after 1811 was the shako like the troop. An illustration by Brandani shows an officer *c.* 1811 with a shako with a silver upper band and a triple inverted chevron of silver lace at the sides, the point of the chevron just touching the upper band.[39] After 1813 officers' uniforms followed the pattern of the officers of the Horse Artillery. Greatcoats were dark grey with a light green collar.

Musicanti

The regiment's *trombettieri* were uniformed as for the rank and file with the addition of white lace to the edges of the collar and cuffs and red cords and plume to both the czapska and shako. *Trombettieri* carried the light cavalry sabre with a red sword strap and tassel. Trumpets were brass with green or red cords.

Tamburi had the same distinctions as the *trombettieri* but wore mid-grey breeches and black gaiters and all equipment was as for the *tamburi* of the line infantry.

Horse Furniture

All draft horse harness was plain mid-brown leather with brass buckles and fittings. The outriders' saddles were brown leather with a plain grey saddle blanket and a round mid-grey valise, piped light green at the ends.

Sergenti and other senior NCOs were mounted and used a mid-grey version of the 1805 pattern dragoon shabraque, with wide light green lace at the edge, piped mid-grey. The pistol holsters were light green laced white and piped light green.

In 1811 the half-shabraque was introduced; the cloth was the same colouring as the 1805 pattern and the dogtooth edging to the white sheepskin was light green. The valise was changed to a square pattern and was mid-grey with light green lace on the ends.

---

39 Piero Crociani, *L'Esercito Italico 1805–14: Guardia Reale* (Parma: Albertelli, 2005), p. 75. Neither Crociani nor his artist give the source for this, but with Crociani's reputation the present author is loathe to discount it.

THE GUARDIA REALE

Trombettieri' shabraques were mid-grey (possibly green from 1813) with red trim, the sheepskin was black with a red dogtooth edging.

Officers' shabraques were of the 1805 dragoon officers' pattern in mid-grey with silver lace decorations and grenades, the silver lace was piped with light green. This pattern continued in use by officers after the half-shabraque was introduced for other ranks.

All ordnance, halter collars, etc. were painted dark green (not the olive green of the French artillery but a true dark green).

Elements of the Army of Italy moving past a small group of Italian and/or French general officers. The unit leading is, as with many of Adam's drawings, the Guardia Reale d'Onore

Engraving after a contemporary sketch by Albrecht Adam from *Voyage Pittoresque Et Militaire De Willenberg En Prusse Jusqu'à Moscou Fait En 1812: Pris Sur Le Terrain Même*. Albrecht Adam et al, Munich: Hermann & Barth, 1828. (Public Domain). The illustration bears the date 27 June 1812

3

The Cavalleria di Linea (Cavalry of the Line)

Organisation

When the Kingdom of Italy was created in 1805 the new Kingdom's mounted arm comprised only two regiments of *dragoni* (dragoons, converted from the two regiments of hussars of the former Cisalpine Republic by an Order of 5 February 1805) and a single regiment of Cacciatori a cavallo ('chasseurs a cheval'/light horse).[1] Subsequently a further three regiments of Cacciatori a cavallo were raised in 1806, 1810 and 1811 and numbered consecutively as the 2nd, 3rd and 4th Regiments.

The internal organisation of all cavalry regiments, both heavy and light, was broadly similar. A regiment consisted of a regimental staff, four field squadrons and a depot. A squadron comprised of two companies and, as with much of the Kingdom's army, was organised along the lines of the French cavalry regiments.

Regimental Staff

1 *colonnello*
1 *maggiore*
2 *aiutante*
1 *capo di battaglione*
8 *aiutante-sottoufficiale*
1 *tromba-maggiori*
1 *furiere*
2 *colonnello sotto*
2 *capo-squadrone*
1 *quartiermastro*
2 *chirurgo-sotto*
1 *aquile-alfiori*
1 *veterinario*[2]

5 *maestro-artigiani* (master craftsmen: bootmaker, tailor, breeches maker, armourer, saddler)

---

1 The term Cacciatori a cavallo in Italian or 'chasseurs à cheval' in French is literally 'hunters on horseback', and it is found in the military of many European nations of the era. Light horse is the nearest English-language equivalent, although not quite conveying the same 'feel'.
2 A second *veterinario* was added to the wartime establishment of the regiment by an order of 11 April 1812.

THE CAVALLERIA DI LINEA (CAVALRY OF THE LINE)

Company Establishment
1 *capitano*
2 *sottotenente*
2 *sergente*
4 *caporali*
2 *tromba*
75 *soldati*
1 *tenente*
1 *sergente-maggiore*
1 *caporale-furiere*
1 *maniscalo*
1 *tamburo*[3]

Additionally all regiments had a ninth depot company with a permanent establishment of officers and NCOs and varying numbers of rank and file as they came in, were trained, and were forwarded to the regiment.

Reggimenti de Dragoni (Regiments of Dragoons)

Service

1st Regiment 'Regina'		
1805 Italy	Nov	'Venice Observation Corps'
1806 Naples		Conquest of the Kingdom of Naples
1809 Austria	5–6 Jul	Battle of Wagram (*Capo-Squadrone* Charpentier wounded)
1812 Russia	1 Nov	Battle of Wiasma (4 officers killed)
	1 Nov	Battle of Krasnoi (1 officer killed)
	1 Nov	Battle of the Beresina (4 officers mortally wounded; *Capitano* Pessina killed near the Beresina the following day)
	10 Dec	Skirmish at Wilna (1 officer killed)
1813 Germany	16 Sep	1 *capitano* killed on reconnaissance near Laibach
1814	8 Feb	Battle of Mincio (7 officers wounded, including *Colonello* Narboni and *Colonello Sotto* Charpentier)
2nd Regiment 'Napoleone'		
1805 Italy	Nov	'Venice Observation Corps'
1806 Naples		Conquest of the Kingdom of Naples
1808 Spain	Oct	One *tenente* wounded 'escorting a courier to the frontier'
	6 Dec	'Skirmish in Catalonia' (1 officer wounded)
1809 Italy/Austria	18 Apr	Battle of Sacile (2 officers wounded)
	14 Jun	Battle of Raab (2 officers wounded)

---

3   Only in the dragoon regiments.

	5 Nov	Skirmish at Brixen in the Tyrol (1 officer wounded)
1810 Spain	28 Feb	Skirmish in Catalonia (1 officer killed, 1 wounded)
	30 Dec	Skirmish at Boria-Blancas, Catalonia (1 officer killed, 6 wounded)
1811 Spain	3 Jan	Two officers wounded while 'on a reconnaissance'
	29 Sep	Skirmish at Tarrés (1 officer wounded)
	25 Oct	Battle of Sagunto: strength of 466 officers and men (1 officer wounded)
1812 Spain	11 Aug	Skirmish at Guadarrama (1 officer wounded)
1813 Spain	24 Mar	Skirmish at Castro-Cordiala (1 officer killed, 6 wounded)
Germany	2 May	Battle of Lützen (3 officers wounded)
	21 May	Battle of Würschen (1 officer wounded)
	27 May	1 officer killed, 10 wounded (one mortally) 'on reconnaissance near Goldberg'
	26 Aug	Battle of Dresden (1 officer wounded)
	12 Sep	Skirmish at Weissenfeld (1 officer wounded)
	16–18 Oct	Battle of Leipzig (3 officers killed, 9 wounded)
	30 Oct	Battle of Hanau (1 officer wounded)
1813 Italy	9 Nov	Skirmish at Roveredo (1 officer wounded)
		On 23 December 1813 the regiment mustered only 10 officers and 111 men with a total of 82 horses at its depot in Milan

Uniform

Headwear

The Italian dragoon regiments wore the French pattern of heavy cavalry helmet, brass with a high brass comb crest and a black horsehair tail and houpette. The front of the crest was embossed with a stylised head of Medusa at the top directly below the houpette. The helmet was trimmed with a turban of black-brown fur, except in the 1st Squadron of the 'Regina' regiment where the turban was leopard skin, the upper and lower edges of the turban appear as being trimmed with a narrow line of brass, although actually this was a part of the helmet and the turban sat between these two lines of brass. The peak was of shiny black leather trimmed with brass. From 1808 the regiment 'Napoleone' wore a brass metal crowned 'N' at the front of the fur turban.[4] The chin scales were brass. In full dress the small brass socket at the left side above the chin-scale boss held a tall, dark green plume with a facing colour tip or plain dark

---

4 This 'N' is sometimes shown as being white metal, although this seems unlikely and is probably no more than an error of observation.

green in the 1st Squadron of the 'Regina'. A variation of a facing colour plume with a green tip is shown by André Jouineau for the 'Regina' in 1812.[5]

Fatigue caps were of the same pattern as used by the infantry but from about 1811 the cavalry regiments began to use the 'Pokalem'-style cap, a round cloth cap with soft top. Both patterns of cap were dark green with facing colour piping.

Following the form of French dragoon regiments (indeed, all French line and light mounted regiments),[6] the first company of the first squadron was designated as an elite company and wore the bearskin in place of the helmet, again in the same manner as the French dragoons (and the grenadier companies of the infantry). The bearskin was of black-brown fur, with a red cloth patch at the rear with a white cross, from around 1808–09 the cross was replaced with a white grenade. Two patterns of bearskin were in use, the first was of the infantry style without front plate and the other, apparently more common and of an older pattern, had a black leather peak bound in brass and a brass front plate embossed with a grenade. Given the extreme longevity of bearskins it is unlikely that the older pattern totally disappeared until perhaps 1810 or even 1812/1813. The cords on the bearskin were either white (1st Regiment) or red (2nd Regiment) and the plume, worn at the left side of the bearskin, was red with a national cockade at its base. There is some evidence that from *c.* 1809 the elite companies replaced their bearskin on campaign with the dragoon helmet with either a red, or a dark green tipped red, plume.

Coat
The dark green habit had the collar,[7] lapels, turnbacks and cuffs in the regimental facing colour, and dark green three-pointed cuff flaps piped in the regimental facing colour. The vertical pockets were piped with the regimental facing colour. The turnbacks had dark green grenade badges. The elite company wore red, fringed epaulettes with brass-scaled straps; the centre companies had dark green shoulder straps piped in the facing colour. All buttons were of white metal and two designs are known, both have a crowned 'N' but the crown could be either the Iron Crown or the French-style Imperial Crown.[8]

Facing Colours:
1st Regiment 'Regina': Pink
2nd Regiment 'Napoleone': Crimson (red from 1812?)

---

5 *Borodino The Moskova: The Battle for the Redoubts*: F. G. Hourtoulle (Paris: Histoire & Collections, 2000), p. 91.
6 The French Army designated the regiments of chasseurs à cheval and hussars as 'light', the regiments of dragoons (and later the chevau-léger-lanciers) as 'line', and the carabinier and cuirassier regiments as 'heavy'.
7 A contemporary painting in Castel St Angelo in Rome is recorded by Rene North in the notes to his 'Paint Your Own Cards, set 106' as showing the 2nd with green collar and cuffs. All other sources however record these as of the facing colour, an option that the author would favour.
8 The author's feeling, and it is emphatically no more than that, is that the latter are French 'stocks' perhaps sent to Italy to cover a shortage for whatever reason.

THE ARMY OF THE KINGDOM OF ITALY 1805–1814

Dragoons of the Kingdom of Italy *c.* 1812. Drawings by René North from various contemporary sources. (Author's collection)

THE CAVALLERIA DI LINEA (CAVALRY OF THE LINE)

Set 106　　Italian Dragoons　　1812
No. 6.　　Trooper　　2nd. Regt.

Set 106　　Italian Dragoons　　1812
No. 4.　　Drummer　　2nd. Regt.

Set 106　　Italian Dragoons　　1812
No. 5　　Elite Coy.

Given the state of dyes in the early nineteenth century there may have been little actual difference between 'crimson' and 'red', and any such 'change' could possibly have been no more than a change in dye batch or the interpretation of the individual observer.

In 1813 the dragoons adopted the 'Spencer' habit-veste with short tails and lapels closed to the waist, the same cut as that adopted by the French Army under the so-called 'Bardin Regulations'. With the new coat the facing colours remained unchanged, as did their placement on the coat. On this new pattern of coat however the regulations gave the elite companies' standard cloth shoulder straps although the previous fringed epaulettes may well have been retained at the discretion of the *colonnello* – certainly such things were usual in most contemporary armies. It should perhaps be noted that given the stocks of coats held in the depots it is possible that the new coat may not have actually been evident in the Army until late 1813, or even 1814 (something that applies throughout the Army).

During the campaign in Spain the exigencies of war, and the problems of supply, forced the regiment 'Napoleone' to have coats made in the locally available dark brown, or mid red-brown, cloth. These coats were nonetheless made to the regulation cut and retained their original facings although of a colour nearer claret than the original crimson, buttons were transferred from the original coats, as were elite company epaulettes.

An unusual button in a private collection is traditionally from the 2nd Regiment 'Napoleone' and is embossed with a cursive 'N' below an Imperial or royal crown (not the Iron Crown). It is possible that this pattern of button was the first used by the dragoon regiments. Given the longevity of such items, these buttons could have remained in use in many cases throughout the life of the regiments.

Breeches etc.
Breeches were white, and the regiments wore the high-cuffed heavy cavalry boots with steel spurs. On campaign the breeches were replaced with, or worn underneath, grey overall trousers with cloth covered buttons at the outer seam (these were also made in the local brown cloth when the regiments were in Spain). Waistcoats were white with white metal buttons. White leather gauntlets were worn for parade, replaced by gauntlets of buff leather on campaign. In Spain there is some evidence of the use of brown trousers in place of grey.

Greatcoats were very light grey, almost white, with a lining of the regimental facing colour, and with a light grey shoulder length cape at the shoulders. The front of the greatcoats and the capes were closed with large, cloth covered buttons, and they had deep, turned back cuffs.

Equipment
The whitened leather pouch belt was worn over the left shoulder and supported a black leather cartridge box against the right hip; the belt had a large, open, brass buckle behind the shoulder. The cartridge box lid was decorated with a brass grenade for the elite company, but was plain for all other companies. The waist belt was white with a closed brass buckle and

supported the straight heavy cavalry sword on double slings. On campaign the belt was often worn over the right shoulder, and with the pouch belt it thus gave the appearance of cross belts. Swords had a brass three bar hilt and the scabbards were black leather with brass fittings. The sword knot was red in the elite company and white for the centre companies.

The musket was a shorter version of the same weapon as that carried by the infantry, and was of the same calibre, thus it was a true musket and not a cavalry carbine. Like the infantry musket it was bound and fitted in steel and had a whitened leather sling with a brass buckle. When mounted, dragoons carried their muskets in a bucket, butt downwards, on the right side of the saddle.

Officers and NCOs

As might be expected, the NCOs' insignia and rank badges were the same as those of the infantry, in silver or white and with a narrow regimental facing colour piping along the edge. Senior NCOs of the elite companies had mixed silver and red fringes on their epaulettes and mixed silver and red cords on the bearskin. The sword knots were mixed silver and company colour, or mixed silver and red in the elite company.

Officers' helmets were gilded brass with gilded brass chin scales and leopard skin turbans. Field officers' helmets had the leopard skin extended down to cover the peak. On campaign, and when not in action, many officers wore the bicorne with silver lace trim to the upper edges and national cockade with silver lace cockade strap. Field officers used white plumes while those of the company officers were white with a tip of the regimental facing colour. Officers of the elite company wore the bearskin with silver cords, white plumes tipped red and the grenade on the rear patch was in silver.

Officers' coats were of the same cut as those of the rank and file but of a finer cloth, all buttons silver-plated, and the turnback badges were silver. The epaulettes of rank, which followed the same sequence as the infantry, were silver. On campaign officers customarily wore a dark green surtout coat with collar, cuffs, turnbacks and piping as on the habit.

Breeches and waistcoats were white, gauntlets were whitened leather and spurs were usually silvered. Greatcoats were dark green and of the same pattern as those of the troopers with white metal, sometimes silvered, buttons.

Officers' pouch-belts and waist belts were white leather for parade and black leather for campaign, all buckles and fittings were silvered. Swords were of essentially the same pattern as those of the other ranks but had gilded hilts, and were carried in a black leather scabbard with gilt fittings and silver sword knot and tassel.

Musicanti

The *trombettieri* of dragoons wore the same pattern of helmet as the other ranks with a white horsehair tail and houpette and a facing colour plume with dark green tip. The coat was of reversed colours, that is either pink or crimson, with dark green facings. The *trombettieri* of the elite companies had white full-fringed epaulettes. The collar, cuffs and lapels were trimmed with either plain white or mixed white and facing colour lace. Trumpets were brass and had either green or mixed green and facing colour cords.

The tamburo wore the same uniform as the *trombettieri* but with black gaiters instead of the riding boots of his mounted colleague. The drummer's apron and drum carriage belt were whitened leather with brass buckles, the carriage belt was decorated with a brass drumstick plate on the breast. The drums had brass barrels and the hoops were painted with diagonal stripes of green–white–red–white. Sword knots and tassels were of the regimental facing colour.

The *tromba-maggiori* wore the same uniform as the rest of the *musicanti* with the addition of the usual rank insignia and the silver, or mixed silver and facing colour lace to the collar, cuffs, and lapels. The bicorne had silver lace edging silver tassels and the plume was of the regimental facing colour tipped green.

1º Reggimentto
Trombettista, 1806–1807: a sky blue coat of the same cut as that worn by the light horse regiments with white lace batons on the breast, a crimson collar and crimson Polish cuffs, both edged with a wide white lace. White fringed epaulettes with brass-scaled straps and crescents. Usual dragoon pattern helmet with white mane and houpette. Light grey overalls with crimson lace to the seams and pockets. Black leather sword scabbard fitted with brass.

Trombettista, elite company, 1810–1812: pink habit with pink collar and dark green lapels, both edged with wide white lace. White fringed epaulettes with brass-scaled straps and crescents. White gauntlets. Black-peaked bearskin with brass chin scales, peak binding and plate embossed with a grenade badge, white plume tipped pink. Dark green early pattern shabraque with white laced edging, edged again with a narrow pink lace, and a white grenade badge in the rear corners, dark green double-holster covers with the same lace as the shabraque and a dark green square portmanteau again with the same lace. Plain white trumpet cords.

2º Regimentto
Trombettista, 1810: crimson habit coat with dark green collar, lapels and turnbacks, all edged with wide white lace. White fringed epaulettes with brass-scaled straps and crescents. Usual dragoon pattern helmet with brown fur turban, white houpette and white plume tipped crimson, and white mane. Buff gauntlets with white cuffs. Dark green half-shabraque with white lace edging piped dark green and a white grenade badge in the rear corners, brown sheepskin with crimson dogtooth edging. Plain white trumpet cords.

Tamburo, 1810: coat as above but with crimson collar, laced white, crimson Brandenburg cuffs piped dark green and plain green cuff flaps. Plain white fringed epaulettes. Dragoon pattern helmet with black fur turban with brass crowned 'N' on the front, black houpette, crimson mane, white plume tipped crimson. Black gaiters. Brass drum with the hoops diagonally striped in red–white–green–white–red–etc. Brown wooden drumsticks and brass drumstick plate on the cross-belt.

THE CAVALLERIA DI LINEA (CAVALRY OF THE LINE)

Zappatori
Two regimental *zappatori* were attached to the elite company and wore the regulation uniform of that company with the addition of the usual *zappatore* insignia and equipment. The buff leather apron was slightly shorter than that of the infantry sappers and when mounted the apron was rolled up and held at the waist by a wide waist belt with brass buckle plate, embossed with a grenade. The *zappatori* may have carried the lance after the fashion of the French dragoon sappeurs, possibly with a facing colour over white pennon – this is shown in some modern illustrations (e.g. those of Lucien Rousselot) but no contemporary sources are given.

In the Museum der Bundeswehr in Dresden is a halberd identified as being from the 2º Regimentto 'Napoleone' and taken at the Battle of Dresden on 27 August 1813. Dr Gerhard Bauer has suggested that this is from the Eagle Guard of the regiment. The head is similar in style and size to that of the *zappatore* axe but on a shaft approximately six feet 11 inches in length. It seems an incredibly impractical weapon to carry on horseback, and assuming that the head has not been remounted onto a longer shaft (for which there is no evidence), it may be simply a parade item.[9]

Horse Furniture
In 1805 the shabraque used by the dragoon regiments was dark green with squared rear corners and a brown leather saddle with black leather rubbing patches. The shabraque and pistol covers had a wide white band around the outer edge and white grenades decorated the rear corners of the shabraque. The dark green valise was square and dark green with white edging at the ends. When not worn the cloak was folded with the facing colour lining on the outside and strapped on top of the valise.

Trombettieri' shabraques were of the same pattern with white trim and were of the regimental facing colour.

Officers' shabraques were of a similar pattern; dark green but with triple holster covers and a double silver stripe, the outer stripe twice the width of the inner, in place of the white. The rear corners of the shabraque were devoid of the grenade decoration.

In 1808 the dragoon troopers and *trombettieri* adopted the French-style half-shabraque with white sheepskin saddle cover edged with a dark green dogtooth cloth. The dark green cloth was decorated the same as the 1805 pattern. As in the French Army the officers continued to use the 1805 pattern shabraque.

---

[9] For a full discussion of this item see 'Comme Les Licteurs Romains', in Dr Gerhard Bauer, *Soldats Napoleoniens: Les Troupes Françaises, Alliés et Coalisées. Hors-série No. 1, Avril 2003* (Paris: Éditions de la Revue Napoléon, 2003), pp. 60–62.

THE ARMY OF THE KINGDOM OF ITALY 1805–1814

Italien.

Regiment Königin-Dragoner
(Dragoni Regina).

Regiment Napoleon-Dragoner
(Dragoni Napoleone).

Das Italienische Heer unter Vize-König Eugen.

1812.

Die Uniform der Italienischen Dragoner hielt sich streng an das Französische Vorbild. Die Uniform der Italienischen Garde-Dragoner haben wir bereits gebracht. Auffallend ist nur der schwarze Pelzbrähm auf dem Helme des Napoleon-Dragoners nach Art des französischen Kürassierhelmes. Die Abbildung in dem Zanolischen Werke ist ziemlich ungenau.

Knötel, Uniformenkunde. Band VI. No. 42.   Verlag von Max Babenzien in Rathenow.

THE CAVALLERIA DI LINEA (CAVALRY OF THE LINE)

Cacciatori a Cavallo (Light Horse Regiments)

Service

Facing page: Knötel Plate VI/42. The two regiments of dragoons of the Kingdom of Italy, 1812. (Author's collection)

1º Regimentto, 'Reale Italiano' ('Royal Italian')		
1805 Italy	Nov–Dec	Venice Observation and then Blockade Corps
1807 Germany	1 Jun	Engagement on the Passarge (7 officers killed, including *Colonnello* Zapetti, and six more wounded)
	7 Jun	Storm of Guttstadt. After this engagement the regiment left the Army to return to Italy.
1808 Spain		No engagements of note although one officer was wounded in June (location and exact date unrecorded)
1809 Austria	6 Jul	Battle of Wagram (1 officer wounded)
1809 Spain	3 Dec	Skirmish at Girona (1 officer wounded)
1810 Spain	10 Apr	Skirmish at Mora (*Colonnello* Villeta wounded)
	10 Dec	One officer wounded on patrol in Catalonia
1811 Spain	4 Jan	Action near Lerida (1 officer mortally wounded)
	26 Oct	Combat at Daroca (1 officer killed, 2 wounded)
1812 Spain		No memorable actions recorded
1813 Germany	26 Aug	Battle of Dresden (2 officers wounded)
	29 Aug	Battle of Culm (11 officers wounded, 1 mortally)
	3 Oct	One officer wounded on patrol in Saxony
	30 Oct	Battle of Hanau (1 officer wounded)
1814 Italy	3 Mar	Battle of Parma (7 officers wounded)
	5 Mar	Battle of the St-Maurice Bridge (1 officer wounded)
2º Regimentto, 'Reale Prince' ('Royal Prince')		
1808 Spain	8 Nov	Skirmish at Sana (1 officer wounded)
1809 Austria	6 Jun	Skirmish at Klagenfurt (1 officer wounded)
1812 Russia	22 Jul	Skirmish at Rechenkevitchi (3 officers wounded)
	29 Jul	Skirmish at Welissa (3 officers killed, 7 wounded, 1 mortally)
	9 Aug	Skirmish at Janoyotschi (1 officer wounded)
	7 Sep	Battle of Borodino (1 officer killed, 2 wounded)

	22 Sep	One officer wounded on outpost duty 'near Moscow'
	24 Oct	Battle of Maloyaroslavets (1 officer wounded)
	3 Nov	Skirmish at Wiasna (*colonnello* killed, 2 other officers wounded)
	10 Dec	Skirmish before Wilna (3 officers missing, 2 wounded)
	13–14 Dec	Skirmishing at Kowno (2 officers wounded, 1 mortally)
1813 Germany	4 Mar	One officer wounded during the retreat from Berlin
	26–27 Aug	Battle of Dresden (3 officers wounded)
		Two further officers were killed and 10 wounded, 1 mortally, during the defence of Dresden up to 13 October
1813 Italy	15 Nov	Battle of Caldiero (1 officer wounded)
1814 Italy	8 Feb	Battle of the Mincio (1 officer killed, 1 wounded)
3° Regimentto		
1812 Russia	7 Sep	Battle of Borodino (1 officer killed, 2 wounded)
	7 Oct	1 officer killed in a nameless skirmish 'near Moscow'
	24 Oct	Battle of Maloyaroslavets (1 officer killed, 2 wounded)
	3 Nov	Skirmish at Wiasna (1 officer killed, 5 wounded, 2 mortally)
	9 Nov	One officer killed in a minor skirmish near Smolensk
	4 Mar	One officer wounded in a skirmish 'near Berlin'.
1813 Germany	5 Apr	Skirmish on the Elbe (1 officer wounded)
1813 Italy	3 Sep	One officer killed while on reconnaissance 'in Italy'.
	21 Oct	Skirmish at Ceneda (1 officer killed)
	22 Oct	One officer wounded while on outpost duty near Ceneda
	3 Dec	Battle of Rovige (10 officers wounded, including *Colonnello* Ramboure)
1814 Italy	8 Feb	Battle of the Mincio (6 officers wounded)
	23 Feb	Skirmish near Mantua (1 officer wounded)
	3 Mar	Battle of Parma (1 officer wounded)
	11 Mar	Skirmish near Guestalla (1 officer wounded)

	31 Mar	One officer wounded on reconnaissance near Milan
4° Regimentto		
1813 Germany		(began the campaign with a strength of 433 officers and men)
	22 Feb	Skirmish at Münchberg (9 officers wounded)
	20 May	Battle of Bautzen (2 officers wounded)
	26 Aug	Skirmish of Liegnitz (2 officers wounded)
	13 Oct	1 officer wounded while on outpost duty near Leipzig
1813 Italy	10 Nov	1 officer wounded while on patrol 'in Italy'
	13 Nov	Skirmish at Caldiero (1 officer wounded)
1814 Italy	8 Feb	Battle of the Mincio (strength of 261 officers and men, 12 officers wounded in the battle)
	10 Mar	Skirmish at Roverbella (1 officer wounded)

Uniform

Headwear

Although the regiment was formed in 1805 the new regulation uniforms were not issued to the 1° Regimentto until the following year, until then the regiment continued its earlier uniform from the Cisalpine Republic.[10] Even with the 1806 issue, although the regiment should then have been equipped with the shako it seems that the older Polish-style czapska remained in use. The box of the cap was black trimmed at the edges with black cord and with a black fur turban. The national cockade with white cockade strap was worn at the front left upper edge and was surmounted by a dark green over yellow plume or ball pompom. The peak was black leather with brass edging and the chin scales were also brass. Some companies of the regiment may have continued wearing the czapska until as late as 1808 or 1809 (this could simply have been because such things take a decade to wear out and replacement was thus not a priority).

The 2° Regimentto *may* also have been issued with the czapska but it is more likely that it received the shako of black felt with black leather reinforcement to the upper and lower edges and a white metal lozenge plate embossed with regimental number within a bugle horn. The shako had white metal chin

---

10 This may be for no other reason than that there was already supply still in stores. A similar delay happens in any change of uniform, military prudence always dictates that whatever is in store is used first, thus contemporary illustrations often show a mix of old and new patterns of equipment. Modern research has shown that even after the disaster of 1812, much of the new Grande Armée of 1813 were issued with the older style of coat, so great was the number of coats in store. Records for the French Army indicate that the depot may have held enough coats at the end of any year to re-equip the whole regiment.

scales and a national cockade, with white cockade strap, surmounted by a green ball pompom or plume. By 1810 both the 1° and 2° Regimentti were definitely wearing the shako and the 3° and 4° Regimentti were issued the shako from their raising in 1811 (see below for notes on the headwear of the 3° Regimentto however). For parades the centre companies wore white shako cords and a dark green plume with a pompom of regimental colour at the base and a tip of the same colour.

A variation to the above known to have been worn by the 1° Regimentto was that the shako had a large national cockade with long white cockade strap at the front in place of the lozenge plate. Knötel shows this shako with a white inverted 'V' of lace at the sides.

The elite companies[11] of all regiments wore the black fur hussar-style colpack with facing colour bag piped white for the 1° Regimentto, dark green for the 2° and 4° Regimentti, and probably also for the 3°. Cords were white for the 1° Regimentto and red for the 2°, 3° and 4° Regimentti, with red pompoms or plumes in all four regiments.

It has been suggested that all companies of the 3° Regimentto initially wore the black fur colpack, without the customary bag, with white metal chin scales, white cords and regimental colour pompom, or plume as above. However in his article on the 3° Regimentto[12] Ricardo Papi presented definitive arguments that this is simply a misinterpretation of the sources and that the centre companies wore the shako, with the colpack reserved for the elite company, the same as the other three regiments.

In 1814 the regiments officially adopted the cylindrical shako as regulated for the French light cavalry in the 'Bardin Regulations'. This was of black felt with the national cockade at the front upper edge, white cords and the upper edge trimmed with yellow. Chin scales were white metal and the peak and rear cuff of black leather. Whether this was ever issued in any quantity before the dissolution of the Kingdom at the end of 1814 is open to doubt.

The fatigue caps of the chasseurs were dark green with facing colour piping and tassel and may, in some cases, have been decorated with the bugle horn insignia at the front of the headband.

Coat

The first coat pattern of the 1° and 2° Regimentti was a dark green surtout with the collar, pointed cuffs and turnbacks of the regimental colour and the vertical pockets piped in the regimental facing colour. The coat was closed with a single row of eight white metal buttons and each button and buttonhole had a broad white lace baton with pointed end. Each side of the collar was decorated with a similar baton of white lace and there were two similar batons on the lower sleeves, one above and one below the cuff edge. The 3° were initially issued with the same pattern of coat as the 1° and 2° Regimentti.

---

11 As in the dragoon regiments the 1st Company of the 1st Squadron was designated as the elite company.

12 'Le 3e Régiment de Chasseurs à Cheval Italiens', Ricardo Papi, *Soldats Napoleoniens: Les Troupes Françaises, Alliés et Coalisées. No. 26, Juin 2010* (Paris: Éditions de la Revue Napoléon, 2010), pp. 58–63.

THE CAVALLERIA DI LINEA (CAVALRY OF THE LINE)

The 4° Regimentto wore a 'a la Kinski' pattern coat, which was similar in cut to the surtout but with short tails (with horizontal pockets?), all other details as for the first three regiments although this coat did not have the lace batons. This pattern of coat was adopted by the other three regiments in 1812, apparently before the Russian campaign.

For service dress all regiments wore the surtout or habit-a-Kinski. In most respects this appeared the same as the full dress coat but was without the lace batons on the breast or cuffs.

The regimental facing colours were:

1° Regimentto 'Reale Italiano', yellow
2° Regimentto 'Reale Principale', red
3° Regimentto (untitled), orange
4° Regimentto (untitled), crimson

Before 1810 the centre companies of the 1° and 2° Regimentti wore facing colour contre-epaulettes with white metal scales on the straps, the elite companies wore full-fringed versions of the same epaulettes with white fringes. From 1810 dark green bastion ended shoulder straps with facing colour piping were adopted by the centre companies; the elite companies continued the fringed epaulettes of the previous pattern but now with red crescents and fringes; note, this pattern may never have been taken into use in the 1° Regimentto the sources are somewhat contradictory.

The 3° Regimentto, although wearing a Kinski pattern coat as above for campaign wear, is recorded as having equipped its elite company with an hussar-style full dress uniform. The hussar-style dolman and pelisse were dark green with white lace trim to the edge, white lace 'trees' on the rear seam and orange collar and pointed cuffs edged with white lace. The pelisse was trimmed with black fur. Braiding on both dolman and pelisse was white and all buttons on both dolman and pelisse were white metal.

By 1814, shortly before the dissolution of the Kingdom, the 1° Regimentto, and possibly the 2° Regimentto as well, also appear to have adopted the full hussar-style uniform for their elite companies with 16 rows of white braid on the breast of the pelisse and dolman and three rows of small white metal buttons, the collar and cuffs were of facing colour and the barrel sash was red and white for all regiments.

Breeches etc.
Breeches and waistcoats were dark green, the former having facing colour spearheads on the thighs and a wide facing colour stripe (white in the 2° Regimentto) on the outer seam.

Boots were of the 'Hungarian' pattern with shaped tops and white, red for the elite companies, lace trim and tassel.

Dark green or grey overall trousers with black leather inserts and cuffs were issued for campaign wear in 1811. These had a wide facing colour stripe on the outer seam, a double stripe in the 3° Regimentto, and a single row of either white metal or cloth covered buttons.

Greatcoats were dark green greatcoats, of the same pattern as those of the dragoons and with facing colour lining and collar as on the coat, all buttons were white metal.

On full dress parades all ranks wore white wrist gloves but these were replaced by white leather gauntlets on campaign.

Equipment

The pouch belt was whitened leather and the cartridge box was black leather with a plain lid in the centre companies but with a brass bugle horn badge for the elite companies. The narrow white waist belt fastened with a brass 'S' clasp/buckle, all other fittings were also brass.

The sabre was of the curved light cavalry pattern, with brass hilt (both single bar and triple-bar hilt variants were in use)[13] and a white sword knot and tassel, or red in the elite companies. The sabre was carried in a black leather scabbard, fitted in brass, suspended from twin white leather slings.

Pistols, carried in holsters at the front of the saddle and hidden beneath the shabraque, were copies of the French Year IX light cavalry model, but made within the Kingdom, not in France.

In 1809 the French light cavalry carbine of Year IX pattern, fitted in brass, was issued to all regiments. This was suspended from a whitened leather carbine bandolier fitted with brass, with a steel carbine clip, and worn over the pouch belt. Although of French pattern the carbine was again actually manufactured in arsenals within the Kingdom.

The 3° Regimentto wore a facing colour sabretache suspended from the waist belt on white slings. The face of the sabretache had a white edging and bore the regimental number in white at its centre.

Officers and NCOs

The NCOs had the same basic distinctions as the infantry with the sleeve insignia in the form of lace chevrons above each cuff. *Sergenti* and senior NCOs did not carry the carbine.

Officers' headwear followed the pattern worn by the regiment and was trimmed with the normal silver lace and had silvered cords. The sword knots were silver. Plumes were white for field and staff officers and white with a tip of the facing colour for company officers.

As with so much in the Kingdom's army many officers imitated their French counterparts and, even when serving in the centre companies, wore the black fur colpack. Elite company officers and senior field and company officers are also sometimes recorded wearing variants of the hussar-style uniform with facings of the regimental colour, silver braid and black or white fur on the pelisse. Many of these 'fantasies' were quite individual, particularly for the field officers.

The officers' surtouts and Kinski coats had silver lace batons, and breeches were decorated with silver lace Hungarian knots or spearheads on the thighs

---

13 The author has not found confirmation as to whether the two variants were issued differently to different regiments, different companies within the same regiments, or even entirely randomly as stocks were available.

THE CAVALLERIA DI LINEA (CAVALRY OF THE LINE)

Officer, Cacciatori a cavallo c. 1807. Colours as in the text. (Courtesy General Research Division, The New York Public Library. 'Italy, 1805–1808' The New York Public Library Digital Collections, 1910)

Dessin colorié de Quinto Cenni.

and silver stripes on the outside seams. Boots had silver lace and tassels and, at least on parade, silver-plated spurs were worn. Silver epaulettes were worn on the surtout and Kinski coat and followed the same sequence as that of the dragoon regiments.

Officers' rank badges on the hussar-style dolman were in the form of chevrons above the cuffs; the first chevron trimmed the upper edge of the cuff and was 14 mm wide.

Colonello: five silver chevrons, three of 14 mm alternating with two of 23 mm
Maggiori: as for the *colonello* but with the centre 14 mm chevron in gold
Capo di squadrone: four silver chevrons alternately 14 mm and 23 mm

Capitano: three silver chevrons, two of 14 mm with one of 23 mm in between
Tenente: two silver 14 mm chevrons
Sottotenente: one silver 14 mm chevron

The same sequence and colouring was used for the spearhead-shaped lace on the front of the breeches.

A plate by Guglielmo Aimaretti for Luca Cristini's study of the Army[14] shows an officer, dated 1813, wearing the cylindrical shako that was introduced into the French Army by the 'Bardin Regulations'. The shako is scarlet with a black leather peak, upper and lower bands. The upper band has a silver 'chain effect' braid and below the band is a wide band of silver lace. The plume is a white feather 'falling' style. The same plate shows the officer wearing a green pelisse with silver braid and brown fur and scarlet lancer-style trousers with a broad silver stripe down the seam. He is armed with a heavily curved 'Mameluke' sword in place of the normal sabre (again a highly-fashionable affectation in the French and British Armies as well as the Italian).

Musicanti

Trombettieri generally wore the same pattern coat as the troop but in reversed colours, that is a facing colour coat with green facings, but with white lace as for the regiment. The fringed epaulettes were white and trumpet cords either white or mixed white and facing colour. Headwear was as for the rest of the regiment with a facing colour plume, tipped white. Swords etc. were the same as for the troop although *trombettieri* were not issued with carbines.

1° Regimentto

Trombettista, elite company, *c.* 1811: yellow hussar-style dolman and pelisse with white braid and yellow collar and cuffs, both trimmed with white lace. A black colpack with yellow bag, laced white with a white tassel, and a green plume with yellow tip. The breeches were green with white lace and a red sabretache edged white with a central white wreath encircling a white 'R'. Saddlery was a white sheepskin with yellow dogtooth edging.

Note, Boisselier illustrates an almost identically dressed trumpeter under the date of 1805. The only noticeable difference is that the colpack is more noticeably brown-black, the thigh decorations on the breeches are Hungarian knots, and, unusually, the trumpet cords are mixed red and yellow.[15]

Trombettista, 1812: a yellow coat of the same pattern as in use by the rank and file, with green collar and cuffs, both trimmed with white lace. Plain black shako with national cockade but no plate, brass chin scales and a white over yellow plume. Green breeches with white Hungarian knots and lace to the outer seam. Green cloth covered cartridge box belt trimmed with white

---

14 Luca Stefano Cristini and Guglielmo Aimaretti, *L'Esercito Del Regno Italico 1805–1814. Volume 2: La Cavalleria* (Lodigliano: Soldiershop, 2011), plate A.
15 Plate 5 by Henri Boisselier published in *Le Sabretache*, Paris 1957.

THE CAVALLERIA DI LINEA (CAVALRY OF THE LINE)

lace. Mixed green and yellow trumpet cords.

Trombettista, 1813: a sky blue uniform as for the rank and file, with yellow collar, cuff-flaps and turnbacks, white lace and blue cuffs piped yellow. Red epaulettes with brass-scaled straps. Breeches were sky blue with yellow Hungarian knots and stripes. A white colpack with red bag piped yellow, and yellow cords and plume. Black sheepskin shabraque with yellow dogtooth edging. Mixed green and yellow trumpet cords.

2º Regimentto

Trombettista, 1812: red coat of the same pattern as the rank and file with green collar and cuffs, both trimmed with white lace, white lace batons on the breast collar and cuffs and a wide piping of green down the front seam of the coat continuing into the green turnbacks. White full-fringed epaulettes. Plain black shako with national cockade but no plate, brass chin scales and a white over red plume above a white over red ball. Green breeches with white lace and Hungarian knots. Black Hungarian boots trimmed silver. Plain white trumpet cords.

Boisselier shows a (undated) variant of this uniform with red decorations on the breeches and a plain red ball at the base of the plume.

Officer's belt buckle, 3º Cacciatori a Cavallo. Date unknown. Brass with eagle, cornet and number in steel. (Private Collection, photo © and courtesy of Laurent Claudet)

Trombettista, 1812–13: white colpack with red plume and red bag piped white, white tassel. Sky blue coat with red collar, turnbacks and Polish cuffs all piped white. White breast lace and white metal buttons. Brass covering on the epaulette straps with white crescent and fringe. Buff yellow gauntlets. Grey overalls fitted and cuffed in black leather and with a broad red stripe at the outer seam. Black sheepskin shabraque with red dogtooth edging. Dark green portmanteau with red lace and a red '2' on the ends. Brass trumpet with red cords.

3º Regimentto

Tromba-maggiori, 1810: orange coat of the same cut as the rank and file, with green facings, white epaulettes with mixed orange and white fringes, white lace and six white lace chevrons on each sleeve. Buff breeches with orange stripe and spearheads and an orange czapska with white fur turban, piping and cordon, with tricolour plume, red, over white, over green surmounting a white pompom. Orange cloth shabraque with a wide dark green lace piped orange and with a white horn below the Iron Crown in the rear corners. Green portmanteau with orange lace at the ends and a white horn badge. White cords on the brass trumpet.

Trombettista, elite company, 1810: orange coat of the same cut as the rank and file, with green facings edged with white lace, epaulettes with green

Facing page: Knötel Plate II/45. Mounted Chasseurs, Gendarmes, etc of the Army, 1812. (Author's collection)

straps and white fringing. Dark green breeches with orange stripe on the outer seam. Black colpack, with white cords and a white over orange plume. Trumpet and shabraque as above except for the omission of the badge on the shabraque and portmanteau.

Trombettista, elite company, 1810: orange surtout coat with orange collar and Polish cuffs and plain green turnbacks. Both the collar and cuffs had a wide white lace edge, itself in turn trimmed with a wide dark green lace. The collar had a single dark green bastion tipped baton from the front edge. White fringed epaulettes. Black colpack without a bag, brass chin scales, and a white over orange plume above a white over orange ball. Dark green overalls with orange lace trim. Black sheepskin shabraque trimmed orange, orange portmanteau with green lace. Brass trumpet with white cords.

Trombettista, elite company, 1813: orange pelisse[16] with white lace batons, as worn on the rank and files' coats, and white fur trim, orange cuffs laced white, and white lace at the rear seams. White colpack with orange bag and a red ball pompom. Dark green overalls with a double orange stripe. Orange cloth shabraque with green lace edge and a white horn badge in the rear corners. Orange portmanteau, laced green and with white '3' on the ends. The black leather sabretache is plain except for a large white horn badge below a white iron crown. Brass trumpet with white cords. See also the colour plates in this work.

4° Regimentto

1811–1812: crimson coat of the same pattern and style as the rank and file with dark green collar and Polish cuffs, both trimmed in wide white lace, itself trimmed with wide dark green lace and a wide dark green piping down the front of the coat, dark green turnbacks piped crimson. White fringed epaulettes with mixed white and crimson fringes. Plain shako with national cockade but no plate and a white over crimson plume with a crimson ball pompom base. Dark green breeches with crimson Hungarian knots and lace. White sheepskin with crimson dog's tooth edging. Dark green portmanteau with the ends laced in the appearance of a cockade of crimson (outer) then white then dark green. Brass trumpet with white cords.

Zappatori

The two *zappatori* attached to the regiment's elite company wore the uniform of the company with red epaulettes and white crossed axe badges on the sleeves of the coat, but they did not wear the traditional *zappatore* apron. They wore the hussar-style colpack of the same pattern as the regiment's elite company.

---

16 The *trombettista* is illustrated wearing the pelisse, presumably over the dolman but this is speculation.

THE CAVALLERIA DI LINEA (CAVALRY OF THE LINE)

Italien.

Jäger zu Pferd.   Reitender Gensdarm der Königl. Garde.
Pompier. Zögling des Waisenhauses.   Fuss-Gensdarm.

Das Italienische Heer unter Vicekönig Eugen.
1812.

Die Uniform der reitenden Gensdarmen der Königl. Garde entspricht fast genau derjenigen der Französ. Elite-Gensdarmen derselben Epoche. Letztere trugen für gewöhnlich roten, zur Parade weissen Stutz an der Pelzmütze. Ob dasselbe bei den Italien. Gensdarmen der Fall war, liess sich nicht ermitteln. Unsere Vorlage hat weiss. Auch die Uniform des Fussgendarmen hat ihr Vorbild in Frankreich, nur dass an Stelle der blauen Grundfarbe, die in Italien bevorzugte grüne tritt. Auffällig erscheint der Sitz der Bajonetscheide beim Pompier. Das Bajonet wurde damals gewöhnlich dicht neben dem Säbel getragen, während es hier an der Patrontasche befestigt scheint. Die Uniform des Jägers zu Pferde erscheint eigenartig durch die Brustlitzen. Die Uniform des Waisenhauszöglings zeigt noch starke Anklänge an die Uniform der Lombardischen und Cisalpinischen Legion von 1797 (vergl. Blatt 11, Band III.)

Knötel, Uniformenkunde. Band III. No. 45.   Verlag von Max Babenzien in Rathenow.

1º Regimentto, 1807: Cacciatori-style infantry bearskin with white cords and red plume.[17] Dark green hussar-style dolman with white lace and braid and white crossed axe badges on the sleeves. The *zappatore* of the 1º had worn this uniform at least as early as 1801 and it is recorded again in 1807.

3º Regimentto, 1807: Essentially the same uniform as that described for the 1º but with the colpack of their regiment with white cords, red plume and a yellow patch with a green cross, similar to that on the bearskins of the infantry grenadiers, in place of the more usual bag.

1812: Coat of the same cut as the rank and file but with a dark green collar with an orange 'patch' at the front edge, at the rear of which is a single white button, and the sapper's crossed axes badge in white on the upper arms. Red epaulettes with brass-scaled straps. Black colpack without bag but with an orange patch in the manner of the bearskin, with a green cross; and a red ball pompom. Green overalls with orange stripe and white buttons. Buff gauntlets with black leather cuffs. White sheepskin shabraque with orange dog's tooth edging, dark green portmanteau with white lace ends, trimmed orange, and a white '3' at the centre.

Horse Furniture

The full dress shabraque was dark green with rounded front and pointed rear corners and trimmed with a wide white band piped at the outer edge with the regimental distinctive colour. The rear corners may have been decorated with a white bugle horn in some regiments. The rubbing patch, girth strap and all leatherwork were of black leather. On campaign the above was replaced with a plain white sheepskin saddle cover with dogtooth edging of the regimental facing colour. From 1811 this shabraque replaced the cloth one described above for all orders of dress. The round portmanteau was dark green with a broad white band, piped in the facing colour, around each end.

Trombettieri' cloth shabraques were of the same pattern as the rank and file but of facing colour edged and piped green. On campaign, like the men, they used white sheepskin shabraques with facing colour dog's tooth edging. However, the sheepskins of *trombettieri* of the 2º Regimentto were black.

Officers' shabraques were as for the men with silver lace trim and piping and a silver bugle horn badge. Officers used the full cloth shabraque for campaign as well as for parades, although officers of the elite companies of the both the 1º and 4º Reggimenti are recorded using a leopard skin shabraque trimmed yellow and crimson respectively, of the same pattern as the rank and file's sheepskins, although these were almost certainly for parade use only.

---

17 Around 1803–1804 this had a yellow rear patch with a green cross.

Plate A

Eugène de Beauharnais, Viceroy of Italy, Duke of Leuchtenberg (1781-1824)
(Illustration by Henri Boisselier (1881–1959))
See Colour Plate Commentaries for further information.

Plate B

Dragoni Della Guardia Reale, 1812
L–R: Officer in full dress; trumpeter in full dress; dragoon in stable dress
(Illustration by Henri Boisselier (1881–1959))
See Colour Plate Commentaries for further information.

Plate C

2° Dragoni, Napoleone, 1811–1812
L–R: colonel; officer; dragoon
(Illustration by Henri Boisselier (1881–1959))
See Colour Plate Commentaries for further information.

Plate D

2° Dragoni, Napoleone, *c*. 1810
L–R: Drummer; trumpeter of the elite company
(Illustration by Henri Boisselier (1881–1959))
See Colour Plate Commentaries for further information.

Plate E

**1° Cacciatoria a Cavallo 'Reale Italiano'
Senior officer, full dress, *c.* 1808**

(Illustration by Henri Boisselier (1881–1959))

See Colour Plate Commentaries for further information.

Plate F

**1º Cacciatoria a Cavallo 'Reale Italiano'
Colonel (left) and troopers, *c.* 1810**
(Illustration by Henri Boisselier (1881–1959))
See Colour Plate Commentaries for further information.

Plate G

**2° Cacciatoria a Cavallo 'Reale Principale'
Trumpeter (centre) and troopers, *c.* 1812**
(Illustration by Henri Boisselier (1881–1959))
See Colour Plate Commentaries for further information.

Plate H

**2º Cacciatoria a Cavallo 'Reale Principale'
Elite company trooper, campaign dress, Russia 1812**
(Illustration by Henri Boisselier (1881–1959))
See Colour Plate Commentaries for further information.

Plate I

3° Cacciatoria a Cavallo
Elite company trumpeters full dress *c.* 1806 (top left), campaign dress *c.* 1810 (top right), campaign dress *c.* 1813 (bottom)
(Illustration by Henri Boisselier (1881–1959))
See Colour Plate Commentaries for further information.

Plate J

**3° Cacciatoria a Cavallo
Sapper (top) and trooper, campaign dress, 1812**
(Illustration by Henri Boisselier (1881–1959))
See Colour Plate Commentaries for further information.

Plate K

4° Cacciatoria a Cavallo
L–R: Trooper, campaign dress, Russia 1812; colonel in full dress 1813–14; trooper in full dress 1813

(Illustration by Henri Boisselier (1881–1959))
See Colour Plate Commentaries for further information.

Plate L

1° Fanteria di Linea. Mounted colonel and fusilier, full dress 1811–1812
(Illustration by Henri Boisselier (1881–1959))
See Colour Plate Commentaries for further information.

Plate M

2° Fanteria di Linea. Grenadier (rear view), grenadier (front view), sapper, grenadier company drummer, full dress c. 1808–09

(Illustration by Henri Boisselier (1881–1959))

See Colour Plate Commentaries for further information.

Plate N

4° Fanteria Leggera. Drum major, drummer, cornet, *c.* 1810
(Illustration by Henri Boisselier (1881–1959))
See Colour Plate Commentaries for further information.

Plate O

3° Fanteria Leggera. Officer of chasseurs and chasseurs, *c.* 1806–07
(Illustration by Henri Boisselier (1881–1959))
See Colour Plate Commentaries for further information.

Plate P

Guardia d'onore Milano 1809 (top); Guardia Reale Dragon 1809 (bottom)
Typical of the series of plates by 'CM' in the Anne S. K. Brown Collection in Providence, Rhode Island.
Reproduced with their kind permission.
See Colour Plate Commentaries for further information.

THE CAVALLERIA DI LINEA (CAVALRY OF THE LINE)

Gendarmerie Legione (Gendarme Legion)

The Gendarmerie was originally raised in 1806 as a single legion,[18] but by 1808 it had increased to three legions; each with a strength of two mounted squadrons and two foot companies. The squadrons were of two company strength, each with the normal cavalry establishment. The companies of dismounted Gendarmeri had a similar establishment to the line infantry but with only 100 rank and file.

The Gendarmerie Legione were charged with policing the borders of the Kingdom as well as apprehending deserters and 'draft dodgers' and although not designated as a part of the field army certainly experienced combat in the fighting within the Kingdom in 1813 and 1814.

Headwear
The Gendarmerie wore the black felt bicorne trimmed with white lace at the upper edge and with white tassels at the outer tips. The bicorne had the national cockade with a white cockade strap and white metal buttons and a tall red plume for parades, this latter replaced by a carrot-shaped pompom for all other orders of dress. Fatigue caps were dark green with crimson piping and tassel.

Coat
The coat was the regulation pattern habit in dark green with crimson collar, cuffs, turnbacks and lapels, and dark green three-pointed cuff flaps and pockets piped crimson. The turnbacks were decorated with white grenade badges and all buttons were white metal. A white, fringed epaulette was worn on the right shoulder and a white trefoil epaulette and aiguillette on the left.

Breeches etc.
For the mounted companies breeches were initially of buff leather, later replaced with cloth, with white waistcoats and buff leather gauntlets. The boots were of the same heavy cavalry pattern as worn by the dragoons. Greatcoats were light grey with crimson lining and collar.

In the foot companies the breeches and waistcoats were white, gaiters were black over-the-knee pattern with white metal buttons and from 1810 white overall trousers were issued for everyday wear. Greatcoats were again as issued to the line infantry.

Equipment
The equipment of the mounted companies was of the same pattern as that used by the dragoon regiments but with the light cavalry waist belt and sabre with a white sword knot and tassel.

The dismounted companies used equipment of the same pattern as that issued to the elite companies of the line infantry, although the flap of the

---

18 The term 'legion' for a military unit had re-emerged during the eighteenth century to designate a unit which was composed of both horse and foot – and sometimes artillery.

THE ARMY OF THE KINGDOM OF ITALY 1805–1814

Italien.

Soldat einer Reserve-Kompagnie.

Scharfschütz	Füsilier und Voltigeur	Grenadiere	Karabinier
von Brescia.	der Linien-Infanterie.	der Linien-Infanterie.	der leichten-Infanterie.

Das Italienische Heer unter Vice-König Eugen.
1812.

Bei den Fusstruppen dieser Armee ist wieder deutlich das Französisce Vorbild zu erkennen. Bei der Linien-Infanterie trugen die Grenadiere (Granatieri) und Füsiliere (Fucilieri) weisse Uniformen mit regimenterweis verschiedenfarbigen Abzeichen, welche letztere roth, grün und weiss in verschiedener Zusammenstellung waren. Weisse Abzeichen hatten, um sie von der gleichfarbigen Uniform loszuheben, grünen oder rothen Vorstoss. Umgekehrt hatten die grünen und rothen Abzeichen weissen Vorstoss. Die Grenadiermütze hatte unter dem Blechschilde einen kleinen, nach innen klappbaren, ledernen Augenschirm. Die Voltigeure (Volteggiatori) waren grün uniformirt. Die Reserve-Kompagnien (Compagnie di riserva) trugen fast dieselbe Uniform ohne die Voltigeurepaulettes. Der Scharfschütz von Brescia (Bersagliere Bresciano) zeigt in seiner Uniform keine Anlehnung an französisches Muster. Bei der leichten Infant. (Fanteria legiera) trugen wie in Frankreich, die an Stelle der Grenadiere errichteten Karabiniers (Carabinieri) als Auszeichnung die Pelzmütze und die Grenadierepaulettes, die Voltigeure den Czako und die grünen Voltigeurepaulettes.

Knötel, Uniformenkunde. Band III. No. 25.   Verlag von Max Babenzien in Rathenow

cartridge box was undecorated. The sabre-briquet had a white sword knot and tassel.

Officers and NCOs

An NCO's rank distinctions were as for the dragoons and the line infantry, senior NCOs had silver trim on the bicorne.

Officers had white plumes and silver trim to the bicorne and plume. Buttons and turnback badges were silvered. Rank epaulettes were the same as those worn in the line infantry and dragoons. All belts were of buff leather edged with silver and the light cavalry sabre had a silver sword strap and tassel.

Musicanti

Trombettieri and *tamburi* were uniformed essentially the same as the Gendarmerie but with the addition of red and white lace on collars and cuffs. *Trombettieri* had crimson plumes and are shown, as sometimes are the *tamburi*, with mixed red and white fringing on the epaulette.

Trumpets were brass with mixed crimson and white cords. Drums were of the same pattern as used by the line infantry. *Trombettieri*' and *tamburi*' equipment was the same as that of the dragoons and the line infantry respectively.

Tamburo, 1812–1814:[19] Black bicorne trimmed with white scalloped lace, pink plume with a green tip above the national cockade. Pink coat with green collar, lapels, and cuffs all trimmed white, green turnbacks, green epaulettes with white fringes. Breeches, gaiters, equipment, etc. as above. Brass drum with red–white–green–white, diagonally striped hoops.

Musicante, 1812–1814: The same plate shows a musician in a uniform differing only in the sabre-briquet being worn on a waist belt.

Zappatori

The same source as mentioned above shows a *zappatore* of the Legion in a regulation coat with crimson crossed axes on the upper arms. Black bearskin, without plate, with white cords and a red plume, and the usual *zappatore* equipment of apron, axe, etc.

Horse Furniture

The Gendarmerie used the 1805 pattern of horse furniture described for the dragoon regiments. The shabraque had white trim and grenade badge, or silver for officers.

Facing page: Knötel Plate III/25. Infantry of the Army of Italy. From left: Brescia Rifle Battalion, Departmental Reserve Battalion, fusilier and voltigeur of the line infantry, line infantry grenadier, light infantry carabiner. Colouring as in the text. (Author's collection)

---

[19] Unpublished watercolour by Henri Boisselier

4

The Fanteria di Linea (Infantry of the Line)

History and Organisation
When the Kingdom of Italy was created in 1805, it had five regiments of line infantry inherited from the dissolved Cisalpine Republic. A sixth regiment was raised in July 1806, and in June 1808 a seventh regiment was created from troops of the disbanded Papal Army.[1] Napoleon had entrusted Eugène, as viceroy, with the organisation of the Army, and he had planned an eventual establishment of 12 line infantry regiments, however the continuing recruitment difficulties for even the existing seven regiments meant that there was never an expansion beyond these seven.

In 1805 the regimental establishment was two battalions, each with an establishment of seven fuciliere (fusilier or centre companies) and two elite companies, one granatiere (grenadier) company and one Volteggiatore (voltigeur/light) company. In 1808, in line with the changes to the French establishment, the battalions were reorganised as four centre and two elite companies. At the same time a third battalion was authorised for each regiment and the disbanded companies were used as the cadre for this battalion – by 1809 all regiments had raised the third battalion. In 1811 the strength of the infantry regiments was further increased to four field battalions, a regimental artillery company (again in line with the French establishment) and a depot battalion of four fusilier companies only. The establishment of a regiment was identical to that of the French line infantry and conformed to the Order of 18 February 1808:

Regimental Staff
1 *colonnello*   1 *colonnello sotto*
1 *maggiore*   3 *capo di battaglione*
5 *aiutanti*   10 *aiutanti-sottufficiale*
2 *quartiermastri*   1 *chirurge-maggiore*

---

1   Initially this regiment continued to wear the uniforms of its constituent units but by the beginning of 1809 the records indicate that it had been re-uniformed and re-equipped in line with the rest of the Kingdom's infantry regiments.

THE FANTERIA DI LINEA (INFANTRY OF THE LINE)

4 *chirurgo-sotto*
1 *tamburo-maggiore*
8 *musicanti*
4 *maestro-artigiani* (master craftsmen: bootmaker, tailor, breeches maker, armourer)

1 *aquile-alfiore*[2]
1 *caporale-tamburo*

Additionally, from June 1808, two '*sergente porta aquila*' (*secondo portatore d'aquila* and *terzo portatore d'aquila*)[3] were added to the staff. They carried the rank of *sergente* but were paid as a *sergente-maggiore* – as with so much of the Kingdom's army this is a direct reflection of the French Army's practice.

Company Establishment

1 *capitano*
1 *cottotenente*
4 *sergenti*
8 *caporali*
121 *soldati*

1 *tenente*
1 *sergente-maggiore*
1 *caporale-furiere*
2 *tamburi/cornette*

Regimental Artillery Company Establishment

1 *capitano*
1 *sottotenente*
4 *caporali*
58 *soldati*

1 *tenente*
4 *sergenti*
1 *tamburo*

The company was armed with two 4-pdr guns. This company was also responsible for the transportation of the regimental baggage and supplies.

Service
(If no location is given for a regiment/battalion it was in the Kingdom)

1° Regimentto		
1807 Germany	1 Feb	Skirmish at Neugarten (4 officers wounded)
	Mid Mar–2 Jul	Siege of Colberg (5 officers killed, all on 18 May, and 14 officers wounded)
1809 Italy/Austria	16 Apr	Battle of Sacile (2 officers killed, 15 wounded)
	30 Apr	Battle of Castel-Cerino (4 officers wounded)
	8 May	Battle of the Piave
	21 May	Battle of Pressburg

---

2 Initially a sergeant or a *sergente-maggiore*, from a decree of 27 June 1808 he was to be a tenente or *sottotenente* and was termed 'Primo Portatore d'Aquila'.
3 These were added to the regiments by a decree of 27 June 1808 to guard the regimental eagle. At the same time the battalion eagles were withdrawn to be replaced with a single regimental eagle – as so often, this is a reflection of the changes in the French Army.

THE ARMY OF THE KINGDOM OF ITALY 1805–1814

	13 Jun	2 officers wounded on outpost duty near Raab
	14 Jun	Battle of Raab (4 officers wounded)
	4 Nov	Skirmish at Nieder-Basen, Tyrol (1 officer wounded)
1810 Spain		No actions of note
1811 Spain	7 Oct	One officer wounded at an unknown location
	25 Oct	Battle of Sagunto (1 officer killed, 7 wounded)
	Oct	Siege of Sagunto (2 officers killed, 2 wounded)
	7 Nov	Battle near Valencia (2 officers killed, 7 wounded)
1812 Spain	25 Dec–9 Jan	Siege of Valencia (1 officer killed, 2 wounded)

2° Regimentto

1805 Italy	30 Oct	Battle of Caldiero (3 officers wounded)
	Nov–Dec	Venice Observation and Blockade Corps
1806 Naples	26 Feb–18 Jul	Siege of Gaeta (2 officers wounded; strength of 533 men at the start of the siege)
	22 Jul	Storm of Capua (1 officer wounded)
1809 Italy/Austria	16 Apr	Battle of Sacile (1 officer wounded)
	8 May	Battle of the Piave (1 officer wounded)
	21 May	Battle of Pressburg
	14 Jun	Battle of Raab
	Oct	One *capitano* was killed at an undated and unnamed engagement in Croatia
1810 Ionian Islands	Apr	One officer was killed and another wounded in the defence of the islands against a British raid
1812 Russia	24 Oct	Battle of Maloyaroslavets (*Capo di Battaglione* Zampa and 6 other officers killed, 19 officers wounded including the colonel, 4 of whom subsequently died of their wounds)
	30 Nov	*Capitano* Reugeot wounded in skirmishing near Borisov
1813 Germany	27 Feb	*Tenente* Vigaud wounded on the roads between Magdeburg and Berlin
	7 Sep	Battle of Lippa (3 officers killed and 4 wounded, one mortally)

THE FANTERIA DI LINEA (INFANTRY OF THE LINE)

	15 Sep	Skirmish near Lippa (2 officers killed and 11 officers wounded)
1813 Italy	7–8 Nov	4 officers wounded in skirmishes in North Italy
	9 Nov	Skirmish near Goriza (1 *capitano* mortally wounded)
1814 Italy	Jan	Siege of Ancona, 2nd Battalion was part of the garrison

3° Regimentto

1805 Italy	Nov	Venice Observation Corps
1806 Naples	26 Feb–18 Jul	Siege of Gaeta (strength of 531 men at the start of the siege)

4° Regimentto

1805, Italy	Nov–Dec	Venice Observation and Blockade Corps
1808 (1st Bn), Spain		
1808 (2nd and 4th Bns), Germany		
1808 (3rd Bn), Italy		
1809, Spain		
1810, Spain		
1811, Spain		
1812 (1st and 3rd Bns), Germany		
(2nd Bn), Spain		
1813 (2nd Bn), Germany		Returned to Italy to join the other battalions of the regiment during the Armistice (2 June to 10 August)
1814, Italy	8 Feb	Battle of the Mincio

5° Regimentto

1805 Italy	Nov–Dec	Venice Observation and Blockade Corps
1807 (1st Bn), Spain		
1808 (1st and 2nd Bns), Spain		
1808 (3rd and 4th Bns), Germany		
1809 (1st and 2nd Bns), Spain		
1810 (1st and 2nd Bns), Spain		

THE ARMY OF THE KINGDOM OF ITALY 1805–1814

1811 (1st and 2nd Bns), Spain		
1812 (1st Bn), Germany		
(2nd Bn), Spain		
1813 (2nd Bn), Germany		Returned to Italy to join the other battalions of the regiment during the Armistice (2 June to 10 August)
1814 Italy	8 Feb	Battle of the Mincio

6° Regimentto

1805 (1st Bn), Spain		
1806 (1st and 2nd Bns), Spain		
1807 (1st and 2nd Bns), Spain		
1808 (1st, 2nd and 3rd Bns), Spain		
(4th Bn), Germany		
1809 (1st, 2nd and 3rd Bns), Spain		
1810 (2nd Bn), Spain		
(3rd Bn), Germany		
1811 (2nd Bn), Spain		
(3rd Bn), Germany		

7° Regimentto

1805 (1st Bn), Spain		
1806 (1st Bn), Spain		
1807 (1st Bn), Spain		
1808, Spain		
1809, Italy/Austria	8 May	Battle of the Piave
	14 Jun	Battle of Raab
	8 Jul	Skirmish at Pressburg (503 men present, 2 officers wounded)
1810, Italy	2 Jan	A *capitano* was mortally wounded at an otherwise unrecorded skirmish or action 'near Mantua' (he died on the 7th)
1811, Spain	17 Oct	Fight at Ayerbe during the Siege of Sagunto (3 officers killed, 4 wounded)
1812, Spain	6 Jan	*Capo di Battaglione* Ruse wounded while on patrol

THE FANTERIA DI LINEA (INFANTRY OF THE LINE)

	8 Feb	2 officers killed, 3 wounded in an unnamed action
	5 May	*Capo di Battaglione* Ruse wounded in an action against guerrillas
	26 May	Battle of Molino Del Rey (2 officers wounded)
1813, Germany	19 May	Battle of Königswartha (*Capo di Battaglione* Ventura and 5 other officers killed, 8 wounded)
	18 Aug	Assault on Lahn (1 officer killed)
	6 Sep	Battle of Jutterboek (1 officer killed, 12 wounded)
	16 Oct	Battle of Leipzig (1 officer wounded)
1813, Spain (probably only one bn or perhaps a provisional bn)	7 Jun	Defence of Tarragona (1 officer wounded)
1814, Italy	8 Feb	Battle of the Mincio (1 officer wounded)
	2 Mar	Attack on Parma (1 officer wounded)
	6 Mar	Skirmish near Reggio (3 officers wounded)

Uniforms

Headwear

In 1805 all companies wore supposed to wear the black felt bicorne, with the national cockade of (from the outside) white, red and green at the upper left held in place by a white cockade strap, fastened with a white metal button. The regulations laid down that the bicorne was to have a carrot-shaped pompom above the cockade; green over white for the *Fucilieri*, red for the Granatieri and green for the Volteggiatori. Interestingly however, a series of contemporary illustrations of the 1° to 5° Fanteria di Linea in the Anne S. K. Brown collection show the *Fucilieri* of all five regiments with white disc pompoms edged red. The same illustrations also show the grenadier companies to have been wearing black bearskins with red cords and plume and a brass plate embossed with a grenade device. The author senses that these illustrations are probably correct as to what the grenadier companies were actually wearing, even in 1805, despite the regulations…

Note: even after the introduction of the shako, all companies continued to wear the bicorne in undress uniform and on the march.

By 1808 the Fuciliere and Volteggiatore companies should have received the French-style shako, of black felt with black leather peak and top, reinforcing trim at the upper and lower edges, and a wide V of reinforcing leather at the sides. The front of the shako was decorated with a white metal lozenge-shaped plate (brass in the 1° Regimentto until at least 1809/10) embossed with the regimental number surmounted by the 'Iron Crown of Lombardy'. The national cockade, as above, was worn above the plate and fastened with a white cockade strap and white metal button. The chin scales were of white metal with plain round bosses.

A surviving plate of the 2° Regimentto from *c.* 1808 recently sold by Bertrand Malvaux of Paris is of the regulation lozenge pattern, showing a hunting horn with '2' in the loop of the horn and the Iron Crown above. The horn almost certainly indicates that the plate is from the Volteggiatore company. However, interestingly the plate is brass not the regulation white metal. There is currently no evidence as to whether this pattern was repeated across the other companies or even other regiments.

The grenadier companies wore bearskins of the same pattern as the French elite companies with a brass plate at the front embossed with the traditional flaming grenade motif, again as used in the French Army. The red cloth patch at the back of the bearskin bore a white cross, later probably replaced with a white grenade. On campaign, grenadiers sometimes wore a shako of the same pattern as those of the fusiliers, with a lozenge-shaped plate embossed with a grenade above the regimental number. In 1811 the bearskins were formally withdrawn from all line regiments, although as in the French infantry, the evidence suggests that this order was widely ignored.

Fatigue caps were of the French 'bonnet-de-police' pattern and were white (green prior to 1808) with piping and tassel of the regimental facing colour and the front of the headband decorated with the regimental number for the fusilier, and a grenade or bugle horn for the elite companies. When not worn the cap was rolled and strapped beneath the cartridge pouch.

During inclement weather both the shako and the bearskin could be fitted with a black cloth or oilskin cover with a neck-flap at the rear, often with the regimental number painted in white on the front. Contemporary illustrations also show white cloth covers in use on the shako with the regimental number stencilled in black on the front.

Coat

In 1805 the coat was a dark green habit, of the same pattern as used in the French Army, with either white piped red or red piped white tails and white square-cut lapels piped white. The upright red collar, sometimes shown with white piping, was open in a 'V' at the throat to expose the black stock. The coat's red piped white 'Brandenburg' pattern cuff had a dark green three button cuff-flap piped white, both square and three-pointed variants are recorded (although it is possible that square cuff flaps are simply poor observation by the artists). Suhr shows a fusilier of the 1st Regiment *c.* 1807, in a green coat without cuff flaps but with three buttons, in a vertical row, on the cuff. The lapels were fastened each side with six white metal buttons plus a further button at each shoulder point. The red-piped vertical pockets had three white metal buttons.

In 1808 the green coats were replaced with almost identical coats of white with regimental facings, as below. As with all such things with the level

THE FANTERIA DI LINEA (INFANTRY OF THE LINE)

Coat buttons of the 1st and 6th Infantry. Although the example from the 6th Infantry is fairly crude, the author has seen examples that are quite delicately made. (Author's collection)

of stock of coats at regimental depots it no doubt took some time for this change to work through the army.[4]

Some modern writers have stated that in 1812 infantry regiments which formed part of the Grande Armée for the invasion of Russia were partially re-uniformed with the new style habit-veste or 'Spencer' coat, with lapels closed to the waist and short tails. However the author has not found a contemporary source for this assertion, or a contemporary illustration of it, and very few of these coats were ever issued to the Italian line regiments; at best they were probably worn only by small numbers of the elite companies, and certainly the great majority of the Kingdom's infantry continued to wear the habit until the fall of the Kingdom in 1814. There is no doubt, however, that the 'project of 1812' intended the Army of the Kingdom to be re-uniformed along the lines of the French '1812 Bardin Regulations'.

Regimental Facings 1808–1814[5]

Number	Lapels	Collar	Cuffs	Cuff Flaps	Turnbacks & Pockets
1	White piped Green	Green	White piped Green	Red	White piped Green
2	Red piped White	White piped Red	White piped Red	Green	White piped Red
3	Green	Red piped Green	Green	Red	White piped Green
4	White piped Red	Red	White piped Red	Green	White piped Red

4　In the French Army many regiments were still issuing the pre-1812 pattern coat as late as 1814.
5　A series of manuscript drawings of the Army of the Kingdom of Italy by 'CM' in the Anne S.K. Brown collection, dated to *c.* 1809, agrees with the colours in this table but appears to show no piping on collar, lapels or cuffs for any of the regiments.

5	Red piped Green	Green	Red piped Green	Green	White piped Green
6	Green piped Red	Green piped Red	White piped Red	Red	White piped Red
7	Red piped Green	Red piped Green	Green	Green	White piped Green

The Otto Manuscript's illustration of a grenadier of the 1st Regiment c. 1807/08 shows a green coat with red collar and cuffs, both piped white. Suhr shows the same colourings for the green coat.

Fucilieri Distinctions

The pompom worn on the shakos of the *Fucilieri* was of the ball pattern with a tufted top; usually coloured green over white with a green tuft. Several versions of the pompom are noted giving distinctions between the companies of *Fucilieri* either by the white lower half of the pompom being coloured for the 2nd, 3rd and 4th companies or decorated with a coloured ring; the distinctive colours appear to have followed the French system of green for the 1st company, sky blue for the 2nd, orange for the 3rd and violet for the 4th. The regulations of 14 January 1809 replaced this pompom with a flat disc pompom of green, red and white, the white centre having the company number in black, Faber du Faur shows shakos without pompoms of either type, albeit that he shows the regiments in the field. For full parade dress, white shako cords and flounders were worn. The coat was as described above with bastion tipped shoulder straps of coat colour piped with the lapel colour or lapel piping colour. Turnbacks are recorded both as plain and with a badge of a green star, although Boisselier shows a crowned red 'N' and the 2nd as using a silver crown on a green patch, but unusually does not give his sources.[6]

Granatieri Distinctions

In full dress both the bearskin and the shako had red cords and plume, the Otto Manuscript shows both the line and light 'grenadiers' to have had double cords falling on the right side rather than the more usual left.[7] On campaign the bearskin was worn without decorations, the shako without cords and with the plume replaced with a red carrot-shaped pompom. The habit had red, fringed epaulettes, or red with white crescents, and the turnback badges were red grenades, although one of Suhr's illustrations shows the turnbacks to be undecorated.

---

6 Unpublished watercolours in the author's collection.
7 Guy C. Dempsey Jr, *Napoleon's Soldiers: The Grande Armée of 1807 as Depicted in the Paintings of the Otto Manuscript* (London: Arms & Armour, 1994), various plates.

THE FANTERIA DI LINEA (INFANTRY OF THE LINE)

4° Infanteria di Linea, *c.* 1812. A copy of the contemporary illustration in the Anne S. K. Brown Collection. (General Research Division, The New York Public Library. 'Italy, 1812', *The New York Public Library Digital Collections.* 1910)

Volteggiatore Distinctions
The full dress plume could have been of any of several green/yellow colour combinations; plain green or yellow, green tipped yellow or the reverse and the carrot-shaped pompom worn on campaign could be either green or yellow. Shako cords were green, yellow or a mixture of both and the coat had epaulettes of all green, green with yellow crescents and fringes or the reverse. In all of these there could even be variations in the combinations between battalions of the same regiment although the 1° di Linea is known to have used green epaulettes with a yellow crescent across all of its battalions. The turnbacks were decorated with green bugle horn badges.

Breeches etc.
Breeches and waistcoat were white for all regiments, and for parade dress white cloth, over-the-knee gaiters with white metal buttons were worn; on campaign these were replaced by black gaiters with cloth covered buttons. After 1810 shorter knee-length gaiters were issued with overall trousers of white, grey or brown worn on campaign. Albrecht Adam shows Italian infantry, both officers and men, of Pino's Division in Russia in 1812 wearing linen trousers over their breeches, which was the practice in the French Army and obviously copied in the Italian.

Greatcoats were of French pattern, single-breasted and either grey or brown. The front was closed with six or eight white metal buttons, presumably depending on the height of the wearer.[8] The coat came down to the mid-calf and had an upright collar and deep, turned-back cuffs. The greatcoats of the elite companies were decorated with the epaulettes from the tunic. When not in use the greatcoat was folded and strapped on top of the pack.

Equipment
The equipment of the Italian line infantry was of the same pattern, usually with the same variations, as that used by the French Army. *Fucilieri* wore a single, whitened leather shoulder belt with white metal buckles and fittings, over the left shoulder to support the black leather cartridge pouch. The lid of the pouch was usually plain but on campaign was often covered with a white, or very occasionally black, cloth cover; sometimes with the regimental, battalion and company number, painted on it, for example –

… Rgt di Fanteria
… Battalione
… Compagnia

– or simply the regimental number. Use of such a cover was not in any regulations and, again as in the French Army, was simply a company or battalion convention.

The bayonet scabbard was black leather with brass heel and fittings and was carried in a frog attached to the lower front of the pouch belt.

The elite companies wore twin shoulder belts, the first supporting the cartridge pouch identical to that of the fusiliers but with a brass grenade or bugle horn badge on the lid as appropriate. The second belt supported the French pattern sabre-briquet in a double frog with the bayonet. The sabre-briquet had a brass hilt and its black leather scabbard had brass fittings; sword straps and knots were red for the grenadiers and green, green with a yellow knot, or white with green knot and tassels for the Volteggiatori.

Packs were of brown hide with white leather straps and brass buckles and fittings.

Muskets were Italian-made copies of the French Year IX pattern with iron fittings and whitened leather sling. The Volteggiatore companies were initially armed with the shorter dragoon pattern musket, however, these appear to have been almost entirely replaced with the normal infantry pattern musket by the end of 1811. The author has come across no mention of rifles in use by the Volteggiatori of the Italian Fanteria di Linea, even though they were in use by French voltigeurs during the early Empire.

NCOs
The Italian Army adopted the French system of rank distinctions and the senior grades of non-commissioned officers had silver or gold thread worked through the shako cords and epaulette fringes. NCOs in the elite companies

---

[8] A similar variation in the number of buttons depending on the wearer's height was standard in the uniform coat of the Austrian Army of this period.

had silver epaulette crescents. The Fusiliere NCOs wore the shoulder straps of the company rank and file but had the twin shoulder belts of the elite companies. The knot of the sabre-briquet was mixed silver and white for the fusilier and mixed silver and company colour in the elite companies.

Diagonal bars worn above the cuff, as in the French Army, indicated rank:

Sergente-maggiore: two diagonal silver bars, piped with the regimental colour
Sergente: a single bar as above
Caporale: two white woollen bars piped with the regimental piping colour.
Caporale-furiere: as above, with the addition of a silver lace inverted chevron on the upper right sleeve

The *sergente-maggiore* had silver lace trim to the upper edge of the shako.

The *aiutante-sottufficiale* wore the uniform of a *sottotenente* with the epaulettes reversed, although without a gorget plate and with the sabre strap as for an NCO. Additionally, like the *sergente-maggiore* he had silver lace trim to the upper edge of the shako.

Corporali were uniformed, armed and equipped identically to the remainder of their company, their rank indicated only by their rank stripes.

Officers

Officers' shakos were of the same pattern as that of the other ranks but with all metalwork silvered and the shako cords in silver. The upper edge of the shako, and often the 'V' reinforcing at the sides, was decorated with silver lace, frequently embroidered with stars, oak-leaves or similar fanciful patterns; this lace was of varying widths indicating the rank of the wearer (see below). The lace at the sides of the shako of the senior field officers sometimes formed a solid 'wedge' shape.

After 1810 a prescribed pattern of lace was laid down for the officers of the French Army and this appears to have been adopted by the Italian army, although a number of more 'individual' patterns continued to be used, probably not least because any replacement of existing items was expensive.

Colonello/colonello sotto: gold band of 35 mm above a second 15 mm gold band
Maggiore: silver band of 35 mm above a 15 mm gold band
Capo di battaglione: silver band of 35 mm
Capitano: silver band of 30 mm
Tenente: silver band of 25 mm
Sottotenente: silver band of 20 mm

The field officers and *capo di battaglioni* wore white plumes. Company officers' plumes followed those of the rank and file in the elite companies, or white tipped green in the centre companies, however, fusilier officers often wore only the pompom without the plume.

THE ARMY OF THE KINGDOM OF ITALY 1805–1814

Belt Buckle, probably from an officer of the line infantry. (Private Collection, photo © and courtesy of Laurent Claudet)

On campaign many officers preferred the bicorne with silver lace trim to the upper edges, national cockade, silver lace cockade strap and company colour pompom.

Officers' full dress coats were the same cut and colour as the other ranks but the cloth was of a finer quality and all buttons were silver-plated. The silver epaulettes of rank followed the French system and the silver-plated gorget, worn when on duty, was embossed with a gilt Imperial eagle.

The turnback badges on company officers' coats were the same as those of their men but in silver. Field officers often had Imperial eagle badges on their turnbacks.

For undress and on campaign officers often wore the single-breasted nine-button 'surtout' with long tails and square cuffs, usually without cuff flaps. The collar, turnbacks, and piping were either the same as on the habit coat or were of the colour of the coat. These coats could be either dark green or white (or even dark blue) and were usually worn with epaulettes of rank.

Colonello/colonello-sotto: two silver bullion-fringed epaulettes
Maggiore: as above but with gold straps
Capo di battaglione: silver bullion fringe epaulette on the right shoulder, contre-epaulette on the left
Capitano: as above but fine fringed epaulette
Tenente: as above but with a narrow red stripe along the straps
Sottotenente: As above but with two red stripes

The *aiutante*, who was usually a *capitano*, wore a *capitano*'s epaulettes of rank on opposite shoulders.

Officers' breeches were white and usually worn with boots of the 'English' pattern (also known as jockey pattern) with turned-over tops exposing the buff lining. However, officers of Volteggiatori often wore the 'Hungarian', hussar-style, boots with shaped tops, silver lace and tassels. On campaign officers customarily wore either green breeches or white overall trousers similar to those of their men. The paintings of 'CM' in the Anne S. K. Brown Collection show officers in parade dress wearing white or black gaiters as for the men, thus following the custom in the French Army of the period, where the regulations called for company officers to wear gaiters for full dress parade.

Waist belts were whitened leather for parade and black leather for campaign, both had a large brass buckle plate embossed with either the Imperial eagle[9] or, in the elite companies, the company badge. On campaign

---

9 The fact that the Iron Crown does not appear suggests that such buckles were perhaps imported from France.

the belt was often worn over the right shoulder in emulation of a baldric. The officers of Fusiliere and Granatiere companies carried the straight-bladed epée and those of the Volteggiatore Company the curved sabre. Scabbards were black leather with brass heel and fittings, sword hilts were brass and the sword straps were silver for parade and white leather edged silver on campaign. The gorget, worn when on duty, was silver with a gilt badge.

Officers
1° Regimentto, *c.* 1807. The Otto Manuscript[10] illustrates an officer of the Granatiere company of the 1° Regimentto wearing a green surtout with collar cuffs and cuff flaps all in red, piped white, a bearskin with gold bearskin cords, and gold epaulettes of rank, in place of the expected silver.

Another plate in the same manuscript depicts an officer of Volteggiatori of the same regiment with a 'V' of silver lace, with a third vertical strip of the same running from the point of the 'V' at the sides and both the upper and lower bands of the shako laced silver, the shako plate is a very large lozenge embossed with a '1' below the Iron Crown. The surtout is the same as for the grenadier officer but again the epaulettes and gorget are gold in place of silver.

The mounted field officers' shabraques were dark green with squared front and rear corners. The extreme edge of the shabraque was piped in silver, inside which was a wide silver lace, separated from the piping by a welt of dark green. The knee-patches were black leather. The pistol holster covers were dark green with wide silver lace trim. The girth strap and the horse harness were black with brass buckles and fittings.

Musicanti
The *tamburi* of the Fusiliere and Granatiere companies and the *cornetti* of the Volteggiatori companies wore the uniform prescribed for their company with the addition of broad lace trim to the lapels, collar and cuffs, and sometimes to the cuff flaps, of the coat. This lace was usually of either red and white diagonal stripes or red and white triangles. After 1809, the *tamburi* of the fusilier companies are often shown with 'swallows' nests' of red with the above musicians' lace. The *tamburi* and *cornetti* of the elite companies wore the epaulettes of the company.

Tamburi aprons and drum carriage belts were whitened leather with brass buckles, the carriage belt was decorated with a brass drumstick plate on the breast. The drums themselves had brass barrels and the hoops were painted with diagonal stripes of green–white–red–white or, occasionally simply red and white. The barrels of the drums for the grenadier companies were sometimes embossed with the grenade motif.

The *cornetti* of the Volteggiatori had brass bugle horns with green or mixed green–red–white cords.

The *tamburo-maggiori* of infantry regiments were dressed according to the taste and whim of the regimental colonel, however the Italian Army

---

10   The best published version of the manuscript is that of Guy C. Dempsey Jr, *Napoleon's Soldiers: The Grande Armée of 1807 as Depicted in the Paintings of the Otto Manuscript* (London: Arms & Armour, 1994). Dempsey's text is first class!

developed a greater degree of uniformity than in many other armies of the era (or perhaps simply did not exist long enough for there to be a greater divergence?) Headwear was normally the black bicorne with silver lace trim to the upper edges and a silver cockade strap surmounted by a feather plume of either white, red and white or red, white and green. The coat was identical to that worn by the regiment with the addition of silver lace trim to the collar, cuffs, cuff flaps, turnbacks, lapels, pockets, the seams of the sleeves and the seams at the rear of the coat. The buttonholes were also often decorated with silver lace batons and the coat had heavy silver epaulettes. The *tamburo-maggiore* wore the rank insignia of the *sergente-maggiore* on both sleeves. *Tamburo-maggiore* shoulder belts (sometimes referred to as sashes) were red, often embroidered with a zigzag pattern, and with a heavy silver fringing at the outer edges. The front of the belt carried a silver drumstick plate. The white breeches were normally worn with 'Hungarian'-style boots of either black or red with silver lace trim and tassels. A Boisselier study of the *tamburo-maggiore* of the 4th Infantry shows him with a wide gold lace along the outer seam of his breeches and gold lace trim and tassels on his boots.[11] Waist belts were the same pattern as worn by officers, and supported the straight epée with an NCO's sword strap.

Bandsmen wore a similar uniform, again with silver lace to the collar and cuffs and trefle-knot epaulettes in place of fringed epaulettes. The bicorne was as for the *tamburo-maggiore* without the silver trim and the boots were 'English'-style jockey boots. Bandsmen, in common with company *tamburi* and *cornetti*, wore a single shoulder belt supporting the sabre-briquet with a white sabre strap. Bandsmen are also sometimes shown wearing a single-breasted coat, similar to the officers' surtout, with regimental facings.

Unidentified Regiment
Tamburo-maggiori, 1810:[12] black bicorne with gold lace trim and tassels and a white plume with a green, a white and a red ostrich feathers at the base. White coat, of the same cut as the rank and file, with green lapels, collar, turnbacks, cuffs and cuff flaps, all edged with a double gold lace. Gold rank stripes piped green, gold bullion-fringed epaulettes. All buttons are gold for both coat and the plain white waistcoat. Plain white breeches and English pattern boots. Green *tamburo-maggiore* sash, edged with a broad gold lace and with a brass drumstick badge. The sword is unclear but appears to be a light cavalry pattern sabre with brass hilt and a brass scabbard. Brown mace with silver head and silver cords plaited along its length.

1° Regimentto
Tamburo-maggiori, 1809:[13] brown colpack with a green bag piped in silver and a white plume with a green and a red ostrich feather at the base. Green coat, of the same cut as the rank and file, with white lapels, green collar, and

---

11 Private collection.
12 Study by Boisselier after a contemporary illustration. The figure is positively identified as of a regiment of line infantry even though the overall pattern suggests the Velites of the Royal Guard.
13 Unpublished plate by Boisselier in the author's collection, based on a contemporary illustration.

red cuffs, all piped silver and silver lace on the buttonholes, the silver lace on the collar is piped red at the outer edge and the cuff flaps are plain white. Silver rank stripes and two silver long-service stripes, all piped red, on the left arm and silver bullion-fringed epaulettes. The waistcoat is red with silver lace on the pockets and edges. All buttons are silver for both coat and waistcoat. The breeches are green with silver spearhead lace on the thigh and silver stripes on the outer seam. Boots are hussar-style edged and tasselled silver. The sash is red edged in silver lace, a silver lace zigzag pattern along its length and silver fringe and silver drumstick badge. Light cavalry pattern sabre with silver hilt in a black scabbard fitted silver carried from a red shoulder belt edged with wide silver lace. Brown mace with silver head and silver cords plaited along its length.

A similar unpublished Boisselier watercolour shows the 1808 uniform to be identical except that he wears, in place of the colpack, a black bicorne with a silver lace edging and tassels and three white feathers.

Musicanti, 1809:[14] black bicorne with silver scalloped lace and tassels and white plume. The national cockade has a silver strap. Green surtout style coat with collar as for the *tamburo-maggiore*, red Polish cuffs laced silver, plain white turnbacks, silver piped vertical pockets, wide silver lace on the front buttonholes, and silver trefoil epaulettes. All buttons silver. Waistcoat, breeches and boots as for the *tamburo-maggiore*.

Tamburo of *Fucilieri*, c. 1807:[15] black bicorne as for the rest of the regiment. Dark green coat with red collar and cuffs, and dark green cuff flaps without piping, white lapels piped red. The cuffs are edged with gold braid and the red swallows' nests have three narrow lines of gold piping, around the edges the red cloth of the wings is clearly visible between the two inner lines. All buttons are white metal and the drum plate on the shoulder belt is brass. The drum itself is brass with red and white diagonally striped hoops. All other details are as for the rank and file with white gaiters, even though the fusilier shown alongside the *tamburo* wears black.

Tamburo, c. 1807:[16] shako with a white upper edge, a dark green plume tipped white above a disc pompom of national colours, itself above a national cockade. Mixed red and white cords and racquets. Dark blue coat with red collar and cuffs edged with red and white lace (note, no cuff flaps are apparent, but if present they would have been dark blue with red and white lace), and white lapels with plain red lace, red swallows' nest epaulettes with red and white lace. Brass drum with diagonally striped red–white–blue hoops. All other details as above.

---

14 Unpublished plate by Boisselier in the author's collection.
15 Illustration in the Suhr 'Bourgeois de Hambourg' collection.
16 For the source for both the *tamburo* and the *cornette*, see Luca Stefano Cristini and Guglielmo Aimaretti, *L'Esercito Del Regno Italico 1805–1814, Volume 1: La Fanteria* (Lodigliano, Italy: Soldiershop, 2010).

Cornette of Volteggiatori, c. 1807: bicorne with a national cockade topped by a green tipped yellow carrot-shaped pompom. Dark blue coat with red cuffs, yellow collar and cuff flaps, all edged with red and white lace, and white lapels with plain red lace. Green, fringed epaulettes with yellow crescents. Brass horn with green cords. All other details as above.

4° Regimentto

Tamburo-maggiore, 1809:[17] black bicorne with silver scallop-edged lace, tassels and cockade strap and white feather fringing along the edge, no plume. White coat, of the same cut as the rank and file, with white lapels and red collar, all piped silver and silver lace on the buttonholes, the silver lace on the lapels and collar is piped green at the outer edge. White turnbacks piped green. The cuffs and cuff flaps are hidden under white gauntlets. Silver bullion-fringed epaulettes although no rank badges are in evidence. All buttons are silver for both coat and waistcoat. Waistcoat and breeches plain white. Boots are English pattern. The sash is red edged in silver lace and with a silver zigzag of lace along its length, no drumstick badge. Light cavalry pattern sabre with silver hilt in a black scabbard fitted silver. Brown mace with silver head and without cords.

Tamburo, c. 1807:[18] shako with white cords, a silver lozenge plate and red over white over green carrot-shaped pompom and usual national cockade. White coat with red collar and white cuffs edged with silver lace. White lapels and cuff flaps, both piped green, as was the outer edge of the collar lace. White shoulder straps piped green with red swallows' nests laced silver. All buttons silver. Drumstick plate in brass and brass drum with green hoops.

5° Regimentto

Tamburo-maggiore, c. 1809:[19] black bicorne with wide gold lace, gold tassels and cockade strap, white plume with a red and a green falling ostrich feathers at the base. Red coat, of the same cut as the rank and file, with red cuffs and dark green lapels, collar and cuff flaps. The lapels, collar, buttonholes, cuffs and cuff flaps have a wide gold lace edge and the collar has a single baton of gold lace at the front. White turnbacks with the same wide gold lace as the rest of the coat. White wrist gloves. Mixed dark green and gold, fringed epaulettes. Gold rank stripes on the lower sleeve, possibly piped dark green. All buttons are gilt for both coat and waistcoat. Waistcoat and breeches white, the latter with a broad gold lace trim to the outer seam and a deep gold 'V' of lace on the thighs. Hussar pattern boots with gold lace and tassel. The sash is dark green with a wide gold lace along the edge and gilt drumstick badge. The sword pattern is indiscernible but is worn in a brass scabbard. Brown mace with gilt head and tip and with gold cords twisted along its length.

---

17 Unpublished plate by Boisselier in the author's collection.
18 Unpublished plate by Boisselier in the author's collection.
19 Unpublished plate by Boisselier, private collection.

THE FANTERIA DI LINEA (INFANTRY OF THE LINE)

Tamburo of Granatieri, 1813:[20] shako with white cords, a brass lozenge plate and red pompom with a green tuft and usual national cockade. White coat with red lapels and cuffs and dark green collar and cuff flaps, white turnbacks. The lapels and turnbacks are edged with dark green lace and the collar and cuffs with red and white lace. Red, fringed epaulettes. All buttons gilt. Drumstick plate in brass and brass drum with green/white/red hoops.

Black musician, 1811:[21] a white turban with a brass crescent fastening at the front around a short conical mid-green flat-topped cap with a gold scalloped-edge lace around the edge. White short-sleeve coat with red lapels and turnbacks(?) and a dark green collar, all edged with a broad gold lace and the buttonholes are also gold laced. Gold, fringed epaulettes. The coat sleeves end above the elbow to show the waistcoat sleeves below. The waistcoat was dark green with plain red cuffs and gilt buttons, it had broad gold lace along the cuffs, edges and down the front and gold lace batons at each button, the ends of which are covered by the coat's lapels. The red trousers were of the baggy 'Turkish style', with gold spearhead design lace on the thighs and gold lace on the outer seam. The trousers ended above the ankle to show dark green 'socks' worn with yellow 'Turkish slippers'.

Zappatori

The sappers of the infantry wore the uniform of the grenadier companies and, as was the tradition in most armies of the period, all sappers wore a full beard. The bearskin had white cords and a red plume. Note, the bearskin had no front plate. A red, crossed axe badge was worn on both upper sleeves, sometimes surmounted by a red grenade, similarly the crossed axe badge also appeared on the turnbacks of the coat. The traditional sappers' apron was covered at the waist by a broad white leather belt, fastened with a square brass buckle plate embossed either with a grenade or a crossed axe motif. Aprons were usually whitened leather, although sometimes shown as natural tan-brown colour. Pouch-belts were the same as those of the grenadiers with the addition of a brass grenade or crossed axe badge (or both) on the front. The second belt officially supported either the sabre-briquet or, more often the long sappers' sword, both had a red sabre strap and knot, and the bayonet. The sabre-briquet or sappers' sword (which was the same pattern as carried by the *sergente* – see below) was worn in a black scabbard, the bayonet in a brown scabbard, both were fitted in brass. A wide, whitened leather shoulder belt was worn over the pouch belt to support the axe in a black leather case with a small pouch on the outside to hold the sapper's sharpening tools. Sappers carried muskets of the short dragoon pattern, which were of infantry calibre, with whitened leather slings. From surviving examples the exact design of the axe seems to have varied from regiment to regiment. An axe that was sold at auction in 1916 had its head engraved with '7' surmounted

---

20 Unpublished plate by Boisselier, private collection.
21 Unpublished plate by Louis de Beaufort 'after Boisselier', private collection.

THE ARMY OF THE KINGDOM OF ITALY 1805–1814

Sapper's sword, modern high-quality re-enactment reproduction. (Author's photograph)

by the Iron Crown of Lombardy and must have been from the 7th di Linea.[22]

The *sergente zappatore* wore the same uniform, with the normal rank distinctions but did not carry the axe, and always carried the long heavy sappers' sword with a brass cocks-head pommel and a broad blade with serrated back edge. The sword was carried in a black scabbard fitted in brass.

1° Regimentto

Zappatore, c. 1807: a contemporary illustration in the Otto Manuscript, dated to c. 1807, shows a *zappatore* of the 1st di Linea[23] wearing a tall white colpack with a red bag on the right and double cords and racquets also on the right; on the left is a tall red plume above a national cockade. The coat is white with white lapels and collar but no evidence of piping, red crossed axe badges on the upper arms and red, fringed epaulettes. The waistcoat is white with white metal buttons. The long, almost ankle-length, apron is natural-coloured buff leather, and the gauntlets are a similar colour. The black cartridge box is worn at the centre front on a black waist belt. The musket is fitted in brass and the sword appears to be longer than a sabre-briquet so is probably of the heavy sapper's pattern as carried by *sergenti*. All belts have brass fittings.

Zappatore sergente, c. 1807: Suhr[24] shows the *sergente zappatore* in essentially the same uniform as above but with a red collar on the coat, gold rank stripes piped red on the sleeves and red piping to the edge of the buff leather apron (which extends upwards over the lapels). The cuffs are white piped red and the cuff flaps red piped white. The left shoulder belt has a brass grenade on a red base at the front.

---

22 Piero Crociano, Massimo Fiorentino, and Alfred Umhey, 'À Propos de l'Esponton des "Dragoni Napoleone…"', *Soldats Napoleoniens: Les Troupes Françaises, Alliés et Coalisées*. Hors-série No.1, Avril 2003 (Paris: Éditions de la Revue Napoléon, 2003), pp. 78–84.

23 Guy C. Dempsey Jr, *Napoleon's Soldiers: The Grande Armée of 1807 as Depicted in the Paintings of the Otto Manuscript*: (London: Arms & Armour, 1994), pp. 234–235.

24 Illustration in the 'Bourgeois de Hambourg' collection. The illustrations are by Christian Suhr (1771–1842), although the actual engraving was the work of his younger brothers, Cornelius (1781–1857) and Pierre (1788–1857). The work shows the units that passed through Hamburg between 1806 and 1815 and is known variously as either 'Suhr' or the 'Bourgeois de Hambourg'. The present author has used the term 'Suhr' throughout.

THE FANTERIA DI LINEA (INFANTRY OF THE LINE)

Line infantry, 1809–1812. 'Sketch' watercolour by Henry Boisselier. (Author's collection)

Sapper, *c*. 1808:[25] regulation black-brown bearskin without plate, with white cords and red plume. The bearskin patch is not visible but was presumably red with a white grenade badge. The coat is white with white lapels and a green collar but again with no evidence of piping, red crossed axe badges on the upper arms and red, fringed epaulettes, the cuffs and cuff flaps are hidden by the white gauntlets. White apron and standard black gaiters.

5º Regimentto
Zappatore, *c*. 1809: bearskin without plate and with white cords and a red plume with the national cockade at its base. White coat with red lapels and collar, both without piping, the cuffs are hidden by white gauntlets. Red fringed epaulettes but no rank badges or *zappatore* badges are shown on the sleeve. All buttons are brass. Plain white breeches and sapper's apron.

Regimental Artillery Companies
The artillery companies attached to each regiment of line infantry from 1811 were divided into 24 *artiglieri*, 32 drivers and two *maniscalos* who wore the same uniform as the *artiglieri*, with the addition of the appropriate rank badges.

Artiglieri wore the infantry shako with brass lozenge plate embossed with the crossed cannon motif and crown. The cords and the carrot-shaped pompom were of red and chin scales were brass. Coats were of the usual infantry pattern of dark green with metal buttons, and all facings were red piped dark green. The horizontal pockets were piped red and had a single button at each point and the turnbacks were decorated with dark green grenade badges. Waistcoat and breeches were dark green and the gaiters black with white metal buttons. Equipment was as for the regiment's elite companies with a brass grenade badge on the pouch lid and red sabre-straps on the sabre-briquet. The musket was of the short dragoon pattern.

Drivers wore a shako as above with green pompom and cords but their coats were the single-breasted 'habit a la Kinski' style; a short-tailed tunic with double turnbacks of dark green with red facings on the collar, plain round cuffs and shoulder straps all piped dark green. The front of the coat was piped red, extending around the base of the coat and the dark green turnbacks. Breeches were buff leather and worn with high-cuffed riding boots with steel spurs. Drivers and *maniscalos* were armed only with the sabre-briquet, carried on a single shoulder belt. The sabre strap was white with green knot.

The *sergente-maggiore* of the company wore the usual rank distinctions plus black riding boots and was armed with the heavy cavalry pattern sword with a black leather scabbard with brass heel and fittings.

All officers were mounted and officers' distinctions were as used in the line infantry.

Shabraques were as for the infantry officers although that of the *sergente-maggiore* had white lace and grenade badges in place of silver.

---

25 A Joineau, 'L'Infanterie de la Ligne Italienne 1804–1808', *Figurines No. 20, Mars 1988* (Paris: Tradition, 1988), p. 26.

Reggimento Coloniale (Colonial Regiment)

History and Organisation
The Reggimento Coloniale was originally raised in 1803 as the Legione Italiana from vagrants, suspect foreigners and beggars fit for work; in 1805 it was renamed as the Battaglione Coloniale. The battalion was essentially a penal unit, even if not titled as such, and was recruited from prisons and the 'draft dodgers' brought in by the Gendarmeria. In 1808 the single battalion was expanded to a regiment of two battalions, each with an establishment of six centre companies, not surprisingly there were no elite companies as was usual with similar units. The battalion and, after 1808, the regiment was stationed on the Isle of Elba in order to deter desertion (although Elba was actually part of France, not Italy). In 1811 the unit was absorbed into the 6º Fanteria di Linea. Rawkins, who is usually very reliable, states that in 1813 a new Reggimento Coloniale of two battalions was raised but the author has been unable to confirm this from any other source,[26] and Carigniani and Boué[27] have no entry from the regiment after 1808.

Service
Although some elements of the regiment certainly served in Spain, the author has found nothing to confirm a formed battalion and it seems likely that they served only as separate and independent companies. The evidence is that they actually proved quite reliable despite their origins.

Uniform

Headwear
Light infantry pattern shako with a brass lozenge-shaped plate, embossed with a crown above the 'RC' cipher, and brass chin scales. The carrot-shaped pompom was light green. No source mentions the wearing of shako cords, again perhaps not surprising for what was essentially a 'penal regiment'. Fatigue caps were steel-grey with light green tassel and piping.

Coat
The coat was the short-tailed habit-veste as worn by the light infantry regiments and was steel-grey with light green collar and cuffs. The lapels, turnbacks, cuff flaps, shoulder straps and pockets were all steel-grey piped in light green. All buttons were white metal.

Breeches etc.
Breeches and waistcoats were steel-grey and the short gaiters were black with white metal buttons. The dark grey greatcoats were standard infantry pattern.

---

26 W. J. Rawkins, *The Italian Army, 1805–1814* (Aylsham: Anschluss Publishing, nd), no pagination.
27 Juan Carlos Carmigniani and Gilles Boué, trans. Marie-France Renwick, *Napoleon and Italy: A Military History of Napoleonic Italy, 1805–1815* (Paris: Histoire & Collections 2016), p. 242.

Equipment
All equipment was as for the *fuciliere* companies of line infantry.

Officers and NCOs
All rank distinctions were as for the line infantry. NCOs wore the twin shoulder belts of the infantry elite companies.

Officers wore surtouts of steel-grey with all belts of black leather. They were armed with the straight epée, carried in a black leather scabbard fitted in steel or brass. The shabraques of the field officers were steel-grey with silver lace.

Tamburi
As for the rank and file of the regiment, with usual distinctions.

Zappatori
The regiment did not have *zappatori*.

Reggimento Guardia Alla Città di Venezia (City of Venice Guard Regiment)

History and Organisation
The regiment was originally raised on 17 January 1808 as a single battalion with the title 'Guardia Sedentaria di Venezia', for local defence duties in the City of Venice and surrounding districts. In November 1810 the battalion was expanded to a two battalion regiment and took the title Reggimento Guardia Alla Città di Venezia. Each battalion had the usual infantry establishment of four centre and two elite companies and was presumably of the regulation establishment. In 1811 a regimental artillery company was added.

Service
The regiment did not see active service until the 1813–14 campaigns in the Po Valley against the British and Austrian forces, when it is recorded as being amongst the army's most reliable units.

Uniform

Headwear
All companies wore the infantry pattern shako with the national cockade at the front and a white metal lozenge plate embossed with the cipher 'GV'. Company distinctions were the same as those used in the Fanteria di Linea: white cords with green and white pompoms for Fucileri, red cords and plumes for the Granatieri, and yellow cords and plumes for the Volteggiatori. Chin scales were white metal. The fatigue caps were dark green with red piping and tassels.

Coat
The Guard wore dark green coats of the same cut as those worn by the line infantry, but with a red collar, red cuffs and red turnbacks, and all buttons were of white metal. The lapels, three-pointed cuff flaps and shoulder straps

THE FANTERIA DI LINEA (INFANTRY OF THE LINE)

of the Fuciliere companies were dark green piped red, the horizontal pockets were also piped in red. The elite companies wore full-fringed epaulettes of red for the Granatieri and yellow and green for the Volteggiatori. It should be noted that the facing colour of this regiment was a dull red rather than the bright red of the line infantry.

Breeches etc.
Breeches and waistcoats were white and the gaiters were black over-the-knee gaiters with white metal buttons. In 1811 the regiment adopted the shorter, below the knee, pattern of gaiters, again black but with black cloth covered buttons. Greatcoats were dark grey and of the regulation line infantry pattern.

Equipment
All equipment was the same as that used by the line infantry.

Officers and NCOs
Officers and NCOs used the same badges of rank and distinctions as in the line infantry regiments. Officers' greatcoats were dark green with white metal buttons.

Musicanti
Tamburi' distinctions were the same as those used in the regiments of line infantry.

A Boisselier study of two musicians of the Guard *c.* 1812[28] show them in a black bicorne with silver lace, tassels and cockade strap (securing the national cockade), and a white over green over red plume. The coat is red with sky blue 'plastron style' lapels, collar, Polish cuffs, lining and turnbacks; all edged with wide silver lace – the collar is laced along both the upper and lower edges and there is a diamond of silver lace at the junction of the turnbacks at the back. The buttonholes of the coat have fringed silver batons and the shoulder ornaments are silver full-fringed epaulettes, the turnbacks are plain and there are no pockets visible, or at least none that are laced or piped. All buttons are silver. The breeches are white and the hussar-pattern boots have silver lace and tassels.

Zappatori
Zappatori do not appear in the regiment until 1810; thereafter they were uniformed the same as the Granatieri but with the addition of the usual *zappatore* uniform distinctions and equipment as used by the *zappatori* of the line infantry regiments.

Regimental Artillery Company
The regimental artillery company had the same establishment as that of the line infantry and was uniformed as the rest of the regiment but with all facings dark green piped red and the addition of artillery distinctions as used by the line infantry's artillery companies.

---

28 Unpublished watercolour in the author's collection.

Battaglione Guardia Alla Città di Milano (The City of Milan Guard Battalion)

History and Organisation
The original battalion was formed from the Milan National Guard of the old Cisalpine Republic and although certainly in existence at the beginning of 1807 when it is recorded as being in Germany, at this point its history becomes rather vague and the unit would seem to have been disbanded, or at least put into abeyance, shortly afterwards. The battalion was, however, reformed as the garrison and police force of the Kingdom's capital by an order of 10 December 1811.

The battalion was organised as a standard infantry battalion of six companies, four centre and two elite, with presumably the standard battalion strength and organisation – although the author has found no contemporary confirmation of this. Only one officer and 72 other ranks from the battalion returned from the 1813 campaign in Germany[29] but the battalion was reformed during the winter of 1813/14 incorporating reinforcements drafted from the Pompieri Della Città di Milano, although given the low establishment of that unit (see below) it may have been that the whole unit had been absorbed.

Service
Although the battalion is recorded as being in Germany in 1807, it saw no recorded action until 1813 when, as Napoleon scoured the Empire and its satellites to reform the Grande Armée after the disaster of the Russian campaign, the battalion was called up as part of the Italian contingent. It left Milan under the command of *Capo di Battaglione* Varesi (or Varesio) with a strength 787 men and served in the 15th Division of Bertrand's IV Corps.

1813, Germany	2 May	Battle of Lützen
	19 May	Ambush at Königswartha
	20 May	Battle of Bautzen
	23 Aug	Gross-Beeren
	6 Sep	Battle of Dennewitz
	3 Oct	Battle of Wartenburg
	16–18 Oct	Battle of Leipzig
	30 Oct	Battle of Hanau.
	Nov?	Returned to Italy
1814, Italy	10 Mar	Battle of Pescheira (as part of Palombini's Division in the Po Valley)

---

29 This seems to be an incredibly low strength but is that given in Italian sources and it may be that some officers and men had been drafted into other Italian units in Germany.

THE FANTERIA DI LINEA (INFANTRY OF THE LINE)

Uniform

Headwear
The black felt infantry pattern shako had a brass lozenge plate embossed with either 'GM' or, possibly the Imperial eagle,[30] surmounted by the national cockade and a carrot-shaped pompom of red over white over green. The chin scales were brass and the black leather peak was trimmed with brass. The fatigue caps were sky blue piped red.

Coat
The coat was a sky blue habit of the pattern worn by the line infantry with squared lapels, three-pointed horizontal pockets, and Brandenburg cuffs with plain cuff flaps. The collar and cuffs were red; the lapels, cuff flaps and shoulder straps were sky blue piped red (based on an illustration in the collection of HM The Queen at Windsor Castle dated to *c.* 1807). Another source, however, records the cuffs as sky blue piped red and a yet a third shows both the collar *and* cuffs as sky blue piped red. It seems likely that all sources may be correct and the variations are simply differences in issues. The turnbacks were white, piped red, with red grenade badges. All buttons were white metal.

Breeches etc.
Breeches and waistcoats were white and the gaiters were black with white metal buttons.

Equipment
All equipment was the same as that for the fusiliers of the line infantry regiments, although the abovementioned illustration at Windsor shows the bayonet being worn at the left of the pouch rather than with the sabre-briquet. This arrangement is unknown apart from this watercolour but is also recorded as being used by the Milan Company of Firemen (Pompieri Della Città di Milano, see below) and thus may well simply be a variation manufactured in the city.

Officers and NCOs
All details of uniform variation, rank insignia, etc. are as for the line infantry. An illustration, copied from a contemporary source, in the New York Public Library's (hereafter NYPL) Vinkhuizen Collection shows an officer in sky blue breeches and English pattern 'jockey boots'.

Musicanti
Tamburi had red epaulettes but all other details and variations are as given above for *tamburi* of the line infantry.

---

30 Since both are cited by different sources, the author's suggestion would be that the GM plate was the earlier, and later changed to the Imperial eagle.

Battaglione Guardia Alla Città di Milano c. 1812. A copy of the contemporary illustration in the Anne S. K. Brown Collection. (General Research Division, The New York Public Library. 'Italy, 1812', *The New York Public Library Digital Collections*. 1910)

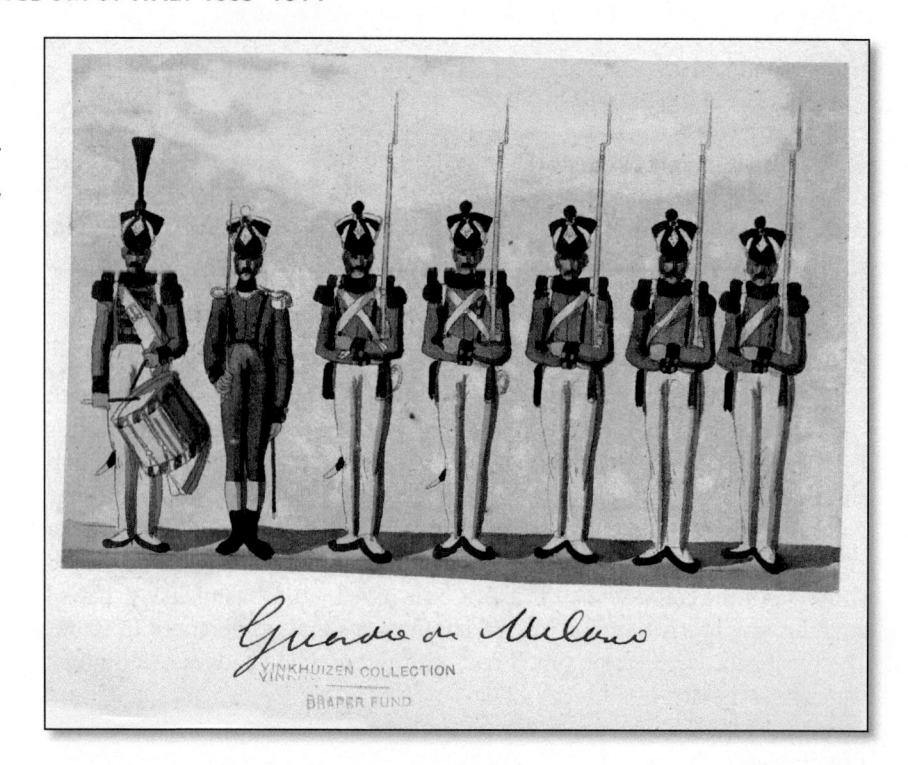

The NYPL illustration referred to above shows a *tamburo* with four double-width, red batons across the chest of his coat

Fanteria Leggera (Light Infantry)

History and Organisation

In 1805 when the organisation of the Army of the new Kingdom was formally established there were to be two regiments of Fanteria Leggera; a third regiment, with the honorary title of 'Real Bresciano', was raised in 1806 and a fourth regiment in 1811.

The battalion and company establishments of the Fanteria Leggera were identical to those of the Fanteria di Linea except that the title *Fucilieri* was replaced by Cacciatori and that of Granatieri by Carabinieri.[31] However, these were simply a change in titles reflecting those in the French Infanterie Légère on which the Italian Fanteria Leggera was modelled; it had no influence on the tactical usage of the companies. The post 1805 changes in the internal organisation of the Fanteria di Linea were reflected change for change in the Fanteria Leggerra. Likewise the 1808 changes that changed the status of the *aquile-alfiori* and added the two '*sergente-aquile*' were repeated in the Fanteria Leggera.

Regulations formally setting out the uniform of the Fanteria Leggera were not issued until 25 January 1811 when the 4° Regimentto was raised. Prior

---

31 Again, as with so many things concerning the Army of the Kingdom, this is a reflection of the titles used in the French Régiments Légère where the centre companies were 'chasseurs' and the elite companies 'carabiniers' and 'voltigeurs'.

THE FANTERIA DI LINEA (INFANTRY OF THE LINE)

to this date although the basic colouring was fairly standard across all three regiments the details of the uniforms were subject to a number of regimental variations. The uniform regulations laid down in 1811 were based on dress of the 1º Regimentto at that time.

Service

1º Regimentto
1806, Germany (end of year)
1807 (1st Bn) Germany
1807 (2nd Bn) Spain
1808 (1st and 2nd Bns, perhaps also the 3rd Bn) Spain
1809 (1st and 2nd Bns) Spain
1809 (3rd and 4th Bns) Germany
1810 (1st and 2nd Bns) Spain
1811 (1st and 2nd Bns) Spain
1812 (1st Bn) Spain
1812 (2nd and 3rd Bns) Germany
1813 (1st Bn) Spain. Probably returned to Italy by the summer of 1813
2º Regimentto
1806, Germany (end of year)
1807 (1st Bn) Germany
1807 (2nd Bn) Spain
1808 (1st and 2nd Bns) Spain
1809 (1st and 2nd Bns, and possibly the 3rd) Spain
1809 (4th Bn) Germany?
1810 (1st and 2nd Bns) Spain
1811 (1st and 2nd Bns) Spain
1812 (1st Bn) Spain
1812 (2nd Bn) Germany
1813 (1 Bn) Spain. Probably returned to Italy in the summer of 1813
3º Regimentto
1812 (1st, 2nd and probably 3rd Bns) Russia
4ᵉ Regimentto
No recorded deployments outside of the Kingdom

THE ARMY OF THE KINGDOM OF ITALY 1805–1814

5° Infanteria di Linea, 1809–1812, A 'sketch' watercolour by Henry Boisselier. (Author's collection)

THE FANTERIA DI LINEA (INFANTRY OF THE LINE)

Uniform

Pre-January 1811

These details are taken almost entirely from contemporary illustrations since, as stated above, there were no official regulations and it is almost certain that many of the recorded variations would have continued throughout 1811 and 1812. It should be noted that any dated statement is really only 'good' for the year of the illustration – we have no way of knowing whether it holds true for any prior or later period.

Headwear

In 1809 the Cacciatori and Volteggiatori companies were wearing the low early pattern of shako that did not have the reinforcing 'V' of leather at the sides and had less of a bell shape than later patterns. The shako had a white metal lozenge plate at the front embossed with the regimental number, and a national cockade surmounted by green ball pompom (Cacciatori) or plume (Volteggiatori) at the side. Both had white cords but the 'CM paintings' in the Anne S. K. Brown Collection show these cords as only at the back of the shako although still with the flounders at the right side.

The Carabinieri wore the light infantry pattern bearskin without front plate and with red cords and a red plume above the national cockade at the left side, but again the CM paintings of *c.* 1809 show the cords only at the back of the bearskin although with the usual flounders at the right side.

There is no evidence for the fatigue caps of the light infantry although, since they were almost certainly issued, the author's speculation is that these would have been dark green, piped with the regimental colour and decorated with the company insignia as in the line infantry.

In 1807/08 the Carabinieri of the 1st Regiment are shown wearing a black busby with a red bag, piped yellow at the right side, a red falling plume (falling towards the front) and red cords. The same source shows Volteggiatori of the regiment with a yellow over green falling plume and mixed green and yellow cords, their shako had a brass lozenge plate with a hunting horn badge and the regimental number in the loop of the horn.[32] Weiland shows a similar busby for the Carabinieri in 1806 but it lacks the bag and the tassels and racquets hang on the right-hand side.[33]

Coat

The coat was similar to that of the line infantry but with pointed lapels and pointed 'Polish' cuffs. Coats were dark green with green lapels and turnbacks and regimental facing colour collar and cuffs. The 'CM paintings' show these without piping but other sources indicate that the lapels and turnbacks were piped in the regimental facing colour as were the vertical pockets. All buttons were white metal. There are no turnback decorations shown for any

---

[32] Guy C. Dempsey Jr, *Napoleon's Soldiers: The Grande Armée of 1807 as Depicted in the Paintings of the Otto Manuscript* (London: Arms & Armour, 1994).
[33] Alain Pigeard (ed.), *Le Manuscrit de Weiland: Uniformes de l'Armée Français et de ses Alliés de 1806 à 1815* (Paris: Tradition, 1998), p. 28.

companies on the 'CM paintings'

Regimental facing colours:
1º Regimentto: Yellow
2º Regimentto: Red then Sky Blue[34]
3º Regimentto: White[35]

In 1809 all companies of the three regiments are shown wearing fringed epaulettes – green for the Cacciatori and Volteggiatori and red for the Carabinieri. The wearing of fringed epaulettes by 'centre' companies is another conceit apparently taken from the French Army where the chasseur companies of the Infanterie Légère habitually did so.

In 1807 the 1º Regimentto is shown with red square 'Brandenburg' cuffs with red cuff flaps, both piped yellow.

Weiland portrays a Carabinier *c.* 1806 wearing the above uniform, with a sky blue waistcoat, but with sky blue 'Brandenburg' cuffs and cuff flaps, both piped red and red piping on the sky blue coat collar. The gaiters also have a red lace and tassel in place of facing colour. The bearskin has the traditional form of cords but in white. It seems likely that these variations were those of the Carabinier company alone, although perhaps the gaiters were also worn by other companies. The painting is titled '… troisieme regiment des chasseurs Italienne' but the sky blue points to this being a Carabinier of the 2nd Regiment, not the 3rd.

Waistcoats were in the regimental facing colour with white metal buttons.

Breeches etc.
Breeches were dark green and worn with black under knee gaiters. These were of the light infantry pattern, which imitated the hussar-pattern boots having piping around the top edge and a tassel at a 'V' cut at the front. In 1809 the 1º Regimentto is shown without the lace and tassel whereas the 2º and 3º Regimentti had these in their facing colour. Carabinieri appear to have had red lace and tassel in all regiments. The buttons were of white metal or covered in black cloth on campaign. Greatcoats were almost certainly of the same pattern as worn by the line infantry.

Equipment
Equipment was of the same pattern as that carried by the Infanteria di Linea except that all companies carried the sabre-briquet, with a green knot and tassel for the Cacciatori and Volteggiatori and in red for the Carabinieri. There is no evidence of any decoration on the cartridge box lid for any companies.

---

34 In 1805 the regiment had red facings and this is usually cited in most modern works, but by 1806/7 it was already using sky blue and when the uniforms were regulated by an order of 1 July 1807 the sky blue was confirmed; however there is some evidence that red may have been restored in 1811.

35 In the 1811 regulations the 3rd were given orange as their facing colour but in 1809 they are shown still using white.

THE FANTERIA DI LINEA (INFANTRY OF THE LINE)

1 Fanteria Leggera c. 1808. Contemporary illustration by 'CM'. (Reproduced courtesy of the Anne S K Brown Collection)

Officers and NCOs

All rank distinctions were as for the Infantria di Linea with rank lace silver or white. Officers of all companies carried the curved sabre with silver sabre strap either on a white leather shoulder strap or from a white waist belt.[36] Officers habitually wore hussar-pattern boots with silver lace and tassel. 'CM' shows an officer of the 1° Regimentto in 1809 wearing laced and tasselled hussar boots even though the rank and file did not use laced gaiters.

The Weiland Manuscript[37] shows a *capitano* of the 1° Regimentto, c. 1806/07 in a regulation pattern uniform (with hussar boots, laced and tasselled silver) but with a triple inverted chevron of wide silver lace at the sides of the shako, the point of the outermost chevron resting against the black leather upper band.

1811 Regulations

Headwear

The Cacciatori and Volteggiatori companies wore the shako of the same pattern as the line regiments (by 1811, this would have been of the later pattern – slightly taller with slightly more of a bell shape) with a white metal

---

[36] Suhr shows a *capitano* of the 1° Regimentto in the regulation uniform, but with his sword supported from a white waist belt with silver buckle

[37] Alain Pigeard (ed.), *Le Manuscrit de Weiland: Uniformes de l'Armée Français et de ses Alliés de 1806 à 1815* (Paris: Tradition, 1998).

lozenge plate at the front embossed with the regimental number, sometimes within a bugle horn. Cockade and strap were as for the line infantry and shako cords were white for the Cacciatori and green for the Volteggiatori with pompoms as for the line infantry. The Carabinieri wore the light infantry pattern bearskin without front plate and with decorations as for the grenadiers, or shakos with red cords and pompom were worn for campaign. Fatigue caps were dark green, piped with the regimental colour and were decorated with the company insignia as for the line infantry. A contemporary illustration of a Carabinieri in Germany in 1807 shows a red 'falling' plume on his shako.[38]

Coat
The habit coat was similar to that of the line infantry but with pointed lapels and Brandenburg cuffs prior to 1812, after that date it was of the short-tailed habit-veste pattern. Coats were dark green with collar and cuffs of the regimental facing colour and with the lapels, turnbacks and pockets in dark green piped with the distinctive colour. Cuff flaps were dark green and all buttons were white metal. The turnbacks of the elite companies were decorated with insignia as for the line regiments of facing colour.

Regimental facing colours:
1° Regimentto:	Yellow
2° Regimentto:	Sky Blue
3° Regimentto:	Orange
4° Regimentto:	Crimson

The epaulettes of the elite companies were the same as used by the Fanteria di Linea and the shoulder straps of the Cacciatori were dark green piped in the facing colour.

Waistcoats were dark green, often with non-regulation regimental colour piping at the edge and around the pockets.

Breeches etc.
Breeches were dark green and worn with black knee-length gaiters with white metal buttons, usually with the top shaped in imitation of hussar boots and trimmed with company colour lace with a similar colour tassel at the front. A contemporary illustration of a Carabinieri in full dress c. 1807 uniquely shows white gaiters with a yellow trim at the top and a red tassel.[39] Overall trousers were issued for campaign and were white or dark green, the latter often with a facing colour stripe on the outer seam. Greatcoats were as for the Fanteria di Linea.

---

38 The illustration is annotated as the 2nd Regiment but the yellow facings confirm that it is of a soldier of the 1st.
39 This is almost certainly no more than a regimental or even just a company variation. The author has seen no confirmation from any other source, but the distinction is unique and unusual enough to be what the artist actually saw.

THE FANTERIA DI LINEA (INFANTRY OF THE LINE)

3 Fanteria Leggera c. 1809. Contemporary illustration by 'CM' (reproduced courtesy of the Anne S. K. Brown Collection). Though almost identical to the previous Illustration, there are enough small differences to indicate that the artist was drawing from life.

Equipment
Equipment was identical to that of the Fanteria di Linea, although the regulations laid down that only the elite companies were to carry the sabre-briquet there is evidence that many of the centre companies did so as well.[40]

Officers and NCOs
All rank distinctions were the same pattern as those of the line infantry with rank lace silver or white. Officers of all companies carried the curved sabre with silver sabre strap, usually worn from a white waist belt with a silver buckle. Officers' greatcoats were dark green and double breasted with two rows of white metal buttons. Although not strictly regulation, many officers wore hussar pattern boots with silver lace and tassels in imitation, as with so much of the Kingdom of Italy's Army, of their allies in the French Army.

Musicanti
The uniforms of *tamburi* and *cornetti* were essentially the same as those of the regiment's rank and file but with the addition of red and white lace trim to the collar and cuffs and the other uniform variation worn by the *musicanti* of the line infantry. Volteggiatore *cornetti* are sometimes shown wearing the colpack with facing colour bag and company colour cords, and tassel.

---

40   Yet again an emulation of the practice in the French Régiments Légère.

Prior to 1811 some *tamburi* and *cornetti* may have worn coats of reversed colours, although this was never a widespread practice.

1° Regimentto:
Tamburo-maggiore c. 1807:[41] black bearskin without plate with double gold cords and racquets falling at the right side. A tall red plume with, either side, three dark green falling feathers. Dark green coat of the same cut as the rest of the regiment with a dark green collar and cuffs piped with a wide gold lace. Yellow lapels edged with a wide white lace and laced in white across the front. The rank stripes on the cuff are gold, piped in red and the coat has gold, fringed epaulettes. Yellow waistcoat with pockets and edge laced white. Yellow breeches with white spearheads on the thighs. The boots are English pattern with buff turned-over tops. The black waist belt has a brass buckle embossed with a grenade badge in silver and supports an infantry officer style sabre fitted silver with a gold sword knot and strap and a black scabbard, also fitted silver. The *tamburo-maggiore*'s baton was brown wood with a silver top and ferrule and silver cords plaited along its length and ending in silver tassels (the illustration does not allow for any bearskin patch or cuff flaps to be seen and, remarkably, the figure is not wearing a sash).

2° Regimentto:
Tamburo-maggiori c. 1810:[42] black colpack with red bag piped silver and silver cords and racquets falling on the right-hand side. A tall white plume with a group of white ostrich feathers at the base and a single red and a single green ostrich feather at the front. Dark green coat of the same cut as the regiment with a red collar edged with a wide silver lace. Dark green lapels edged with a wide silver lace and with a similar lace on the buttonholes. The turnbacks appear to be dark green edged silver. The rank stripes on the cuff are silver and the seams of the coat's sleeves have wide silver lace. Silver fringed epaulettes. Red waistcoat with pockets and edge laced silver. All buttons on both coat and waistcoat are silver. Red breeches with silver Hungarian knots on the thighs and silver lace on both inside and outside seams. Yellow Hungarian boots with silver lace and tassel. The black waist belt has a brass buckle embossed with a grenade badge in silver and supports an infantry officer's style sabre fitted brass with a silver sword knot and strap and a black scabbard. His baton is brown wood with a silver top and bottom and silver cords plaited along its length ending in silver tassels. The *tamburo-maggiore* sash is red with silver lace edge and silver fringe along the edges, silver drumstick badge (the illustration does not allow for the cuffs or cuff flaps to be seen).

Zappatori
The *zappatori* of the light infantry wore the uniform of the Carabinieri company with the usual badges and equipment of the position added.

---

41 Guy C. Dempsey Jr, *Napoleon's Soldiers: The Grande Armée of 1807 as Depicted in the Paintings of the Otto Manuscript* (London: Arms & Armour 1994), pp. 246–247.
42 Unpublished watercolour by Henri Boisselier.

THE FANTERIA DI LINEA (INFANTRY OF THE LINE)

1° Regimentto: a *zappatore* of the 1° Leggera, *c.* 1807,[43] is with a lower than standard, flat-topped bearskin (looking like a cross between a bearskin and the colpack), without plate but with a red falling plume at the front, red double cords with racquets at the left. No national cockade is in evidence but it may have been at the front and thus covered by the falling plume. The coat is dark green with dark green lapels and collar, piped in a buff colour (from other evidence in the manuscript this may once have been a fairly bright yellow), and with a red crossed axe badge on each upper arm, and red, fringed epaulettes. The waistcoat is the same buff as the piping and the apron, of a buff colour close to that of the waistcoat, reaches almost to the ankles. The gauntlets are the same colour as the apron. The cartridge box is worn on the stomach on a black waist belt. All belts have brass fittings.

4° Regimentto sergente zappatore, *c.* 1811.[44] Boisselier illustrates the *sergente zappatore* in a uniform that reflects the custom in the French Army, and although the illustration is credited as the 4° Regimentto, the colouring would seem to be more suitable for the 2°. The *sergente* has a black colpack with no apparent bag but with a scarlet falling plume at the front and no other visible decoration. The coat is sky blue with dark green collar and lapels but neither the cuffs (covered by the gauntlets) nor the turnbacks are visible – although it may be assumed that both are dark green. Buttons are white metal. The rank stripes are silver edged with red as is the sappers' badge on the upper arm. The epaulettes have brass straps and crescent and a red fringe. The gauntlets are white with black cuffs. The *zappatore* carries two pistols in his waistbelt. Breeches are green and the short light infantry pattern gaiters are white with a red braid and tassel. The usual sapper's apron is white. The cartouche box belt has a large brass grenade badge on the breast where the two belts cross. The sword cannot be seen but is probably the heavy sapper's sword illustrated above.

Regimental Artillery Companies
All details are as for the *artigleria* companies of the Fanteria di Linia, but the coat was of Infanteria Leggera pattern with pointed 'Polish' cuffs.

Legione Reale Dalmata/Reggimento Reale Dalmata (Royal Dalmatian Legion/Regiment)

In 1806 the Kingdom of Italy annexed parts of Dalmatia and subsequently raised the Legione Reale Dalmata (Royal Dalmatian Legion), although there is no record that it ever comprised anything except infantry so was technically not a 'legion'.[45] In 1808 the legion was redesignated as the

---

43 Guy C. Dempsey Jr, *Napoleon's Soldiers: The Grande Armée of 1807 as Depicted in the Paintings of the Otto Manuscript* (London: Arms & Armour 1994), pp. 244–245.
44 Unpublished watercolour by Henri Boisselier in the author's collection.
45 'Legions' were a mid-eighteenth century eccentricity that continued into the nineteenth. They supposedly contained both horse and foot units and often artillery as well. Almost all European

Reggimento Reale Dalmata (Royal Dalmatian Regiment). Following the tradition of the Venetian Republic, from whom the area had been annexed, the unit was recruited from the native Slavs. In 1808 the unit was reformed, or more accurately redesignated again, as a light infantry regiment with the same establishment as that of the other *reggimenti leggera* of the Kingdom of Italy. The uniform changed at the time to bring it in line with the rest of the Kingdom's army, although no doubt the somewhat dramatic changes took some time to fully carry through the whole regiment.

Service

1809, Tyrol
1812 (1st, 2nd, 3rd Bns) Russia

Headwear

In 1806 the regiment was equipped with the 'Corsican hat': a wide-brimmed, black felt hat with a stovepipe crown and the left side of the brim turned up.[46] The turned-up side was decorated with the national cockade and cockade strap surmounted by a carrot-shaped pompom in red for the Carabinieri, green for the Volteggiatore and yellow for the Cacciatori.

In 1808, when the Legione was reformed and renamed, the Corsican hat was replaced by a regulation pattern shako, which had a white metal lozenge-shaped plate embossed with the Iron Crown above the letters 'RD'.[47] Shako cords and pompom were of the same colouring as previously worn on the Corsican hat. The Volteggiatore companies continued to wear the Corsican hat until around 1811, as is so often the case, probably wearing out old depot stocks.

Coat

The coat was the light infantry pattern as worn previously by the regiments of the Cisalpine Republic. This was a hip-length single-breasted coat cut square along the bottom and with the turnbacks at the front in the manner of the 1790s Austrian Army coat. The upright collar was closed at the throat and cuffs were of the pointed 'Polish' pattern. The coat was dark green with red collar, cuffs and turnbacks. The front was closed with eight white metal buttons. Shoulder straps were dark green piped red for the centre companies and the elite companies wore red, for the Carabinieri, or yellow, for the Volteggiatore, fringed epaulettes. It appears that in 1808 the coat changed to the usual light infantry cut in the same colours.[48]

Nations adopted the concept for many their 'non-mainstream' units.
46 This style of headwear echoed that of the post 1806 Austrian Jaeger Regiment.
47 A modern reproduction of the uniform on display in the Museo di Risorgimento in Milan has a brass plate but the contemporary sources all show white metal.
48 The author has never found formal confirmation of this although Cristini also follows this line (Volume 1, plates L and M). Perhaps it was simply that depot stocks of the old pattern of coat had been exhausted?

THE FANTERIA DI LINEA (INFANTRY OF THE LINE)

Breeches etc.
In 1806 the regiment wore breeches of the tight fitting 'Hungarian' pattern, similar to those worn by the Hungarian and Grenzer regiments of the Austrian Army. The breeches were dark green with a tight cuff that fitted over the top of the boot and laced beneath the instep. These breeches were worn with the Dalmatians' national-style 'Opanker' shoes; essentially these were leather open sandals, cross-gartered to mid-calf. In 1808 the regiment adopted the more usual pattern of infantry breeches in dark green, with black knee-length gaiters and the normal pattern of boots.

Equipment
All equipment was as for the Infanteria Leggera, however prior to *c*. 1808, the sabre/bayonet shoulder belt of the elite companies was often replaced with a waist belt. The sword strap of the elite companies was either red or yellow as appropriate.

Officers and NCOs
The NCOs of the Reggimento Reale Dalmata wore the same uniform as the rank and file with the addition of the silver rank badges, in the form of inverted chevrons, above each cuff.

Officers, except for full dress, usually wore the surtout with regimental lace and the rank badges of the light infantry. For full dress officers wore the habit with pointed lapels and Polish cuffs, with red facings as for the rank and file.

Musicanti
The regiment's *musicanti* were uniformed the same as the rank and file but with the addition of red and white lace trim to the collar and cuffs. Whether this continued after 1808 the author has been unable to confirm.

Battalione Cacciatori d'Istria (Istrian Light Infantry Battalion)

History and Organisation
The fairly short-lived Battalione Cacciatori d'Istria was raised in 1808[49] and then absorbed into 3° Infanteria Leggera at the end of 1810. It was recruited in the Trieste region ostensibly only from men of Slavic origin, although it seems likely that others were accepted.

Service
The battalion does not feature in any of the Orders of Battle of the Army of the Kingdom during the period of its existence and Martinien[50] records no casualties amongst its officers.

---

49 Cristini, however (Volume 1), records its raising as 1806.
50 Aristide Martinien, *Tableaux Par Corps et par Batailles des Officiers Tués et Blessées Pendant les Guerres de l'Empire (1805–1815)* (Paris: Henri-Charles Lavauzelle, 1899).

Uniform

The Battalione Cacciatori d'Istria was uniformed along the same lines as the Reggimento Leggero Dalmata (see above) except with the regimental pattern of shako in place of the latter's hat. The dark green coats had mid-blue facings replacing the red of the Leggero Dalmata. The d'Istria are also recorded wearing dark grey breeches in place of the green of the Leggero Dalmata, and one illustration shows silver-white Hungarian knots on the thighs.[51]

Musicanti

The uniform was essentially that of the rank and file although only a single shoulder belt was worn to support the sabre-briquet of regulation pattern with initially a white sword knot and tassel but by 1809 a green one. The drums had a brass barrel with the hoops painted in white–red–white–mid-blue–white diagonals.

Compagnie Dipartmentali di Riserva (Departmental Reserve Companies)

History and Organisation

A decree was issued on 11 October 1811 ordering the raising of 'reserve companies' in each of the Kingdom's 22 departments, along the lines of those that existed in France.[52] Milan and Venice were excluded from this decree since both already had their own guard battalions (as described above) and which served a similar function to that for which the new companies were intended. The companies were organised along the same lines as the fusilier companies of the line infantry, however the strength of the company varied according to the population of the department and thus the rank and file numbered anywhere from 120 to close to 250. Each company also had a small administrative staff and was customarily commanded by a *maggiore*.

Service

The companies saw no active service but were drafted wholesale into the Army in 1814, either as complete companies or broken up and their manpower used to bring the regular regiments up to strength.

Uniform

Headwear

The shako was of the usual regulation infantry pattern with a white metal lozenge plate bearing either the company number (the companies were numbered consecutively 1 to 22) or the letter 'R' for 'Riserva'. Two patterns of pompom appear to have been used by the companies, the first, of green

---

51 Cristini, Volume 1, plate N.
52 There is some evidence that similar companies had existed earlier and until at least 1805/06 but their uniform was not regulated, except by department, and they seem to have been less than effectively organised.

and white, identical to that in use by the *Fucilieri* of the Infanteria di Linea, and the second a carrot-shaped pompom of red over white over green. Shako cords were white and the chin scales white metal. Fatigue caps were dark green with white piping.

Coat
The habit was dark green with white piped red lapels and turnbacks, the latter decorated with red grenade badges. The collar and cuffs were red piped dark green, the cuff flaps were white and unpiped. Shoulder straps were dark green piped red.[53] The horizontal pockets were piped in red. All buttons were white metal.

Breeches etc.
Breeches and waistcoats were white. Gaiters were black over-the-knee pattern with white metal or cloth covered buttons. The grey greatcoats were of regulation infantry pattern.

Equipment
All equipment was the same as that used by the elite companies of the Infaneria di Linea, and the sword knot on the sabre-briquet was white.

Officers and NCOs
Rank badges and distinctions were as used by the line infantry.

Musicanti
Essentially the uniform was that of the *musicanti* of the line infantry with the addition of white swallow's nest epaulettes edged with red and white lace.

Reggimento Veterani e Invalidi (Veterans and Invalids Regiment)

History and Organisation
The regiment was formed in November 1811 by the amalgamation of the pre-existing Army and the Navy veteran battalions.[54] The regiment initially had an establishment of two battalions; 1° Invalidi Battalion of 480 men and a 2° Veterani Battalion of 1,440 men. By 1813 the establishment had increased to one *invalidi* battalion of four companies, and two *veterani* battalions, each of six companies.

---

53 Although a sketch illustration in Pier Giorgio Franzoni's *Napoleone in Italia: Soldati e Uniformi* shows red full-fringed epaulettes (Rome: Rivista Militare, 1987, p. 17).
54 Prior to this date the two 'units' existed separately with a strength of one battalion each. Their uniform had been the same except that both battalions wore the bicorne and the naval veterans wore a green waistcoat and green breeches. Similarly there is no evidence that the units ever participated in the field.

Service
There is no record of any field service by the regiment or its constituent battalions and it does not feature in any of the Italian Army's orders of battle.

Uniform
Headwear
The shako was the same model as that worn by the *Fucilieri* of the Infanteria di Linea with a white metal lozenge plate embossed 'VR', and with white shako cords. There is no evidence of a pompom being worn by the regiment, although with white cords being recorded a plain white pompom would seem probable.

Coat
The dark green habit had a white collar and cuffs, both piped red, red lapels and dark green cuff flaps without piping. The turnbacks and shoulder straps were dark green with red piping, the horizontal pockets were piped red, all buttons were white metal.

Breeches etc.
Waistcoats and breeches were white and the over-the-knee gaiters were white for full dress parades in summer, and black for campaign dress and winter, with cloth covered buttons. Greatcoats were of the same pattern as those of the line infantry, probably steel-grey.

Equipment
Equipment was the same pattern as that used by the *Fucilieri* of the Infanteria di Linea with a single cross-belt supporting both the black leather cartridge box, with a plain lid, and the bayonet in a brown scabbard. There were no elite companies in the regiment and sabre-briquets were not worn.

Officers and NCOs
All rank badges, uniform variations, etc. were the same as those of the officers and NCOs of the *Fucilieri* of the Infanteria di Linea. Officers' plumes were white.

Tamburi
Again, all uniform variations, equipment, etc. were as for the *tamburi* of the *Fucilieri* of the Infanteria di Linea.

THE FANTERIA DI LINEA (INFANTRY OF THE LINE)

Battaglione Franca di Bersaglieri

also termed

Bersaglieri di Brescia (Volunteer Rifle Battalion or Brescia Rifle Battalion)

History and Organisation
The Battaglione Franca di Bersaglieri was raised by an order of 30 August 1813, and was to be recruited from the men of the Forestry Department skilled in the use of rifles (there were attempts, with various levels of success, to raise similar units in other Napoleonic armies). The battalion's establishment was set as four companies, each with a strength of 140 all ranks, but by 13 December the Battalion numbered only 142 men, 60 of whom deserted a month later at the first hint of the unit being deployed (suggestive that the men were conscripted, or at least recruited under some sort of 'pressure', and not actually volunteers). With ongoing recruitment difficulties the unit never went beyond organising a single company, and it seems to have 'faded away' rather than being formally disbanded although it was listed amongst the units of the Army that were formally disbanded at the fall of the Kingdom in 1814.

Service
There is no record of the unit taking part in any actions, or even actually joining the army in the field.

Uniform
Headwear
The battalion wore a black felt Corsican hat, perhaps in imitation of the Austrian Jaegers who may have been the inspiration for the battalion.[55] The hat was turned up at the left side, which was decorated with a wide 'v' of green lace. The national cockade, at the upper edge of the turned up left side, was secured by a green cockade strap and surmounted by a green carrot-shaped pompom. The hat had a black leather chinstrap.

Bersaglieri di Brescia, c. 1813. Illustration by Henri Boisselier. (Author's collection)

---

55 Although it should also be noted that the French Imperial Guard raised two similar battalions around the same time – the Flanquers Grenadiers and the Flanquers Chasseurs, both of which were originally intended, it appears, to be rifle armed.

Coat
The dark green coat was of a similar cut to the 1812 pattern 'Spencer' habit-veste, with short tails and lapels closed to the waist. The lapels, collar, pointed cuffs and short turnbacks were mid-green, the lapels and cuffs piped dark green. The shoulder straps were dark green piped mid-green, the pockets were also piped mid-green. All buttons were of white metal.

Breeches etc.
Breeches were dark green with a facing colour stripe on the outer seam; the short gaiters were black with cloth covered buttons. On campaign the battalion wore grey overall trousers with a mid-green stripe on the outer seam. The pepper-grey greatcoats, of the regulation infantry pattern, had a mid-green collar.

Equipment
According to the regulations the rank and file were to have a black leather waist belt supporting the cartridge pouch at the centre front and the sabre-briquet and bayonet on the left hip. However there are references to the use of a white shoulder belt to support a sabre-briquet with green sword knot and bayonet, as for the infantry. It is improbable that both variations existed given the small size of the unit and it may be that the latter variation reflects what was available and issued as opposed to what was intended.

It had initially been planned to arm the battalion with rifles, but these were never issued and instead the unit was armed with the short dragoon pattern musket, although many of the men are known to have carried their own hunting rifles.

Officers and NCOs
NCOs wore the uniform of the rank and file with the usual distinctions and stripes, in the form of inverted silver chevrons above the cuff. Senior NCOs had a silver trim to the upper edge of the hat. The sword knot was mixed green and silver.

Officers wore a bicorne hat with silver trim and green plume or pompom. The coat was of a similar pattern to that of the rank and file but with long tails. Epaulettes were as worn in the line infantry but all officers carried the curved sabre with silver sword knot and tassel.

Musicanti
The regiment had no *tamburi*, only *cornetti*. These wore the uniform of the other ranks with the addition of white lace trim to the hat, collar and cuffs. The horns were brass with green cords.

Corpo Delle Guardia di Finanza (Customs Guards Corps)

History and Organisation
The Customs Department was not formally a part of the army, however, the unit was in constant action while performing its primary duty of patrolling

THE FANTERIA DI LINEA (INFANTRY OF THE LINE)

the borders of the Kingdom and maintaining the blockade against imported British goods under the 'Continental System' aimed at ruining Britain economically. In 1814 the unit was drafted wholesale into the Army during the campaign in the Po Valley.

Uniform

Headwear
The corps wore a plain black bicorne hat with national cockade and white cockade strap.

Coat
Coats were light blue-grey single-breasted 'surtout' style, fastened with nine brass buttons. The collar, round cuffs (without cuff flaps), turnbacks and shoulder straps were light blue-grey piped white.

Breeches etc.
Breeches and waistcoats were light blue-grey. The plain-topped black leather boots reached between ankle and calf, and were apparently worn without gaiters. Greatcoats were of the same pattern as those of the Infanteria di Linea.

Equipment
All equipment was the same as that used by the centre companies of the Fanteria di Linea. The cartridge box lid carried a brass plate with the inscription 'Regno d'Italia Guardia di Finanza'.

NCOs
NCOs of the Corpo Delle Guardia di Finanza used the same rank badges as the Fanteria de Linea but the actual titles of the ranks were unique to the corps:

Capo di I classe (*sergente-maggiore* – sergeant-major)
Capo di II classe (*sergente* – sergeant)
Sotto capo (*brigadiere/caporale* – corporal)

Their uniform was the same as that of the rank and file although all NCOs additionally wore the sabre-briquet with a white sword knot and tassel from a second cross-belt.

Officers
There were two grades of officer in the corps: *ispettori* (inspectors) and *subispettori* (sub-inspectors) but as they were technically not a part of the military, they did not wear military epaulettes of rank. Their rank was instead indicated by, respectively, a double and single edging of silver lace on the collar and turnbacks. Coats and waistcoats had all buttons silvered. Officers wore Hungarian pattern boots with silver lace and tassel. Armament was the straight, infantry pattern epée, worn in a black leather scabbard, fitted silver, and suspended from a yellow-leather waistbelt fastened with a silver buckle covered by a square silvered plate.

5

The Artigleria di Linea, etc. (Line Artillery and Support Units)

History and Organisation

The Artillery of the Kingdom of Italy was created from that of the Cisalpine Republic in November 1805 and organised into two regiments. The Reggimento di Artiglieria a Cavallo (Horse Artillery), which comprised both the Horse Artillery companies and the artillery train, and the Reggimento di Artiglieria a Piedi (Foot Artillery), which supplied the great majority of the Kingdom's artillery needs. The organisation was basically along the lines of the artillery regiments of the French Army and the guns and equipment were, mainly, the older French 'Gribeauval' pieces although there is some evidence that, at least in the earlier period, some captured Austrian pieces were used.

Reggimento di Artiglieria a Piedi (Regiment of Foot Artillery)

The Reggimento di Artiglieria a Piedi was created in November 1805 with two field battalions, each of 10 companies and numbered 1 to 20 straight through both battalions. Initially there were 10 artillery companies in each battalion but the following year companies 17 to 20 were disbanded and the artillery support companies integrated into the battalions. Thereafter the first battalion comprised eight companies of *artiglieri* (company Nos 1 to 8) plus a company each of *braccianti* (company No. 9) and artificer armourers (No. 10). The second battalion again had eight companies of *artiglieri* (companies 11 to 18) but with a company each of bridge engineers (No. 19) and *bombardieri* (No. 20).

On 20 August 1807, a small depot battalion was authorised with a permanent establishment of one *maggiore*, five other officers, 21 NCOs and two *tamburi*. The depot was responsible for processing recruits and passing them through to the field battalions.

LINE ARTILLERY AND SUPPORT UNITS

Artiglieria a piedi. A 'sketch' watercolour by Henri Boisselier showing various ranks of the regiment. (Author's collection)

163

By an order of 16 January 1808 Eugène reorganised the regiment into two battalions of artillery (the 1st and 2nd battalions) and a third battalion, which contained the support companies and had an establishment of:

2 *bracciante* companies
2 bridge engineer companies
1 artificer armourer company
1 *bombardiere* company
1 depot 'company'[1]

On 7 March 1808 the regiment absorbed the Compagnia di Artiglieria a Piedi of the Tuscan Army and on 7 May the two companies of the Roman Army.

The last reorganisation of the regiment was ordered on 4 February 1811, which increased the 1st and 2nd battalions' establishments to 10 companies of artillery and the 3rd battalion to:

3 *bracciante* companies
3 bridge engineer companies
1 artificer armourers company
1 depot 'company'

The companies of the field battalions each had eight guns: either six 12-pdr artillery pieces and two eight inch howitzers or six 8-pdr[2] artillery pieces and two short-barrelled six-inch howitzers, the latter establishment being the most common.

The number of men required to serve a gun varied according to the type of piece; a 12-pdr field gun or eight inch howitzer had a crew of 15 men of whom eight were specialist gunners; an 8-pdr field gun or six-inch howitzer required a crew of 13 men, again eight were specialists, and the 4-pdr field guns of the horse batteries had an eight man crew of whom five were specialists. The non-specialists were usually temporarily detached from infantry regiments for the duration of a battle, occasionally it appears that such draftees could serve with a gun for longer periods.

Regimental Staff

1 *colonnello*
1 *maggiore*
2 *aiutante*
1 *quartiermastro*
2 *sergente-aquile*
1 *tamburo-maggiore*

1 *colonnello sotto*
3 *capo di battaglione* (foot artillery)
6 *aiutante-sottufficiale*
1 *aquile-alfiori*

---

[1] Although titled as a 'company', the depot had an inflated officer and NCO establishment (see above) and a fluctuating rank and file strength as recruits came in or were passed out to the field battalions.

[2] This was the French 'pound', not the British. A French 8-pdr gun actually used a shot slightly heavier than the British 9-pdr.

LINE ARTILLERY AND SUPPORT UNITS

Company Establishment

1 *capitano*	1 *tenente*
1 *sottotenente*	1 *sergente-maggiore*
4 *sergenti*	8 *caporali*
1 *caporale-furiere*	1 *tambure*
64 *primo artiglieri*	46 *artiglieri*

Over the first couple of years of the regiment's existence there were a number of minor alterations to the initial establishment, mainly in the number of gunners.

At the general disbandment of the Army of Italy in 1814, the Reggimento di Artiglieria a Piedi (and parts of the artillery of the Royal Guard) was incorporated into the Austrian Infantry Regiment IR 2 Erzherzog Ferdinand, despite it being theoretically a 'Hungarian Regiment'![3]

Service

The Army's artillery, medical and support units fought alongside the rest of the Army at almost every engagement and skirmish and to list them all here would seem a particularly pointless exercise. Except in Russia none of these units suffered particularly heavy casualties.

An indication of the service of the regiment can perhaps be seen in a snapshot of the locations of the Reggimento di Artiglieria a Piedi in the summer of 1807:[4]

1st Battalion

1st Company	Mantua
2nd Company	Grande Armée
3rd Company	Verona
4th Company	Army of Naples
5th Company	Istria
6th Company	Ancona
7th Company	Dalmatia
8th Company	Dalmatia

2nd Battalion

9th Company	Ragusa
10th Company	Civitavecchia
11th Company	Pavia
12th Company	Pavia
13th Company	Dalmatia
14th Company	Dalmatia

---

[3] The infantry regiments of the Austrian Army of the period were designated either 'Hungarian', recruited (theoretically) only from Hungary, or 'German', recruited from all other provinces of the Empire.

[4] Jean-Pierre Perconte, 'Organisation et Uniformes de l'Artillerie à Pied du Royaume d'Italie, 2e Partie', *Soldats Napoleoniens: Les Troupes Françaises, Alliés et Coalisées, No. 4, Décembre 2004* (Paris: Éditions de la Revue Napoléon, 2004), pp. 37–44.

15th Company   Grande Armée
16th Company   Venice

Bracciante coy   Pavia
Blacksmith coy   Brescia, Milan, Verona
Bridging coy   Grande Armée
Maintenance coy   Venice

A comparison of the company locations on 1 February 1813[5] demonstrates that the companies of the battalion rarely served together:

1st Battalion
Company No. 1   Mantua
Company No. 2   Grande Armée
Company No. 3   Illyria
Company No. 4   Corfu
Company No. 5   Palmanova
Company No. 6   Trieste
Company No. 7   Grande Armée
Company No. 8   Spain
Company No. 9   Spain
Company No. 10   Spain

2nd Battalion
Company No. 11   Venice
Company No. 12   Corfu
Company No. 13   Mantua
Company No. 14   Grande Armée
Company No. 15   Venice
Company No. 16   Chioggia
Company No. 17   Ancona
Company No. 18   Ancona
Company No. 19   Peschiera
Company No. 20   Osopo

3rd Battalion
Bracciante Coy No. 1   Venice
Bracciante Coy No. 2   Pavia
Bracciante Coy No. 3   Mantua
Armourers Coy   Brescia
Bridging Coy No. 1   Grande Armée
Bridging Coy No. 2   Grande Armée
Bridging Coy No. 3   Grande Armée
Depot Company   Pavia

---

5 Jean-Pierre Perconte, 'Organisation et Uniformes de l'Artillerie à Pied du Royaume d'Italie, 2e Partie', pp.37–44.

LINE ARTILLERY AND SUPPORT UNITS

Uniform

Headwear

In 1805 the regiment wore a black bicorne with national cockade, white cockade strap and carrot-shaped red pompom, but by an order of 17 February 1808 this was replaced by a black shako, without peak and possibly even without the leather reinforcing top and bottom although one source shows the shako as having a red band around the upper edge. The front of the shako was decorated with a large brass crossed cannon badge, the shako cords and the carrot-shaped pompom were both red. The shako seems to have had variations with both brass chin scales and a black leather chinstrap being recorded.

By 1812 this unusual pattern of shako[6] had been replaced by the more conventional infantry pattern, with a brass lozenge plate embossed with crossed cannon below the Iron Crown or the Imperial eagle. The shako had the national cockade at the front above the plate and for full dress a red plume and cords, replaced when on campaign with a carrot-shaped red pompom.

The fatigue caps were dark green, piped red with a red tassel.

Coat

The coat for all of the Regiment of Foot Artillery was a dark green habit, with dark green shoulder straps piped red, red piped horizontal pockets, red turnbacks with dark green grenade badges. Details of other facings, etc. varied for each arm, viz.:

> *Artiglieri*: black lapels and collar piped red. Red cuffs and cuff flaps piped dark green.
> *Braccianti*: black collar piped red, red lapels with no piping. Red cuffs and cuff flaps piped dark green.
> Bridge workers: black collar piped red, sky blue lapels with no piping. Black cuffs and cuff flaps piped red.
> Blacksmiths: 'Aurore'[7] collar piped black, black lapels piped red.[8] 'Aurore' cuffs, cuff flaps and turnbacks, all piped black. Shoulder straps and pockets were dark green piped red.

Boisselier's drawings show a gunner for the period 1812–14 in a dark green 'Spencer' coat with the same colours as the habit coat except that the turnbacks are green piped red and without badges, and the shoulder straps have been replaced with red, fringed epaulettes. This would appear to follow the styles adopted in the French Foot Artillery regiments although it may not have ever been a widely issued uniform.

---

6   The present author makes a guess that this shako was 'old stock' from a warehouse somewhere and used, until stocks ran out, to save costs.
7   'Aurore', literally 'dawn', is a bright orange-red colour.
8   A project of April 1806 projected steel-grey lapels but there is no evidence that this was ever put into effect.

Breeches etc.
Breeches and waistcoat were dark green with white metal buttons. Black over-the-knee gaiters with white metal buttons for parade and cloth covered buttons on campaign. If the 'Spencer' coat mentioned above came into use it would be expected that the gaiters were replaced by the shorter, below-knee, pattern. The greatcoats were the same pattern as used by the infantry and are shown as dark blue in 1807 in an illustration by Massimo Fiorentino,[9] although other sources show grey, including by Fiorentino for 1812 – it may be that, as in the French Army, they were often intended to be blue but the exigencies of war caused them to be made in whatever suitable cloth was available (which would include all shades of grey and even brown).

Equipment
Equipment was of the same pattern as that used by the elite companies of the line infantry, with a brass grenade badge on the cartridge box lid. The sword strap was white with red knot and tassels.

Officers and NCOs
All rank distinctions and badges were the same as those used by the line infantry. *Primo artiglieri* wore the stripe of a *caporale* in white on the left cuff only.

Officers' distinctions and badges were the same as those used by the line infantry. Officers' greatcoats were dark green with a black collar and silver buttons. All belts were black leather with brass fittings. Field officers' shabraques were of infantry officers' pattern, of dark green with silver trim and a grenade badge in the rear corners.

Musicanti
Tamburi had the same lace and uniform differencing as the *tamburi* of the line infantry. Drums, equipment, etc. were also the same as those used by the line infantry.

Reggimento di Artiglieria a Cavallo (Regiment of Horse Artillery)

The regiment was created by a decree of 1 November 1805 and comprised a regimental staff, two companies of horse artillery and four companies of train, which had the been the strength of the similar regiment in the Army of the Cisalpine Republic.

The 1805 decree laid down the establishments as:

Regimental Staff

1 *colonnello*	2 *capo-squadrone*
2 *aiutante-maggiore*	1 *quartiermastro*

---

9   Jean-Pierre Perconte, 'Organisation et Uniformes de l'Artillerie à Pied du Royaume d'Italie, 2e Partie', pp. 37–44.

LINE ARTILLERY AND SUPPORT UNITS

1 *chirurge-maggiore*
8 *aiutante-sottouffìciale*   1 *tromba-maggiori*
1 *veterinario*
3 *maestro-artigiani* (master craftsmen: bootmaker, tailor, saddler)

Horse Artillery Company

1 *capitano comandante*	1 *sottocapitano*
1 *tenente*	2 *sottotenente*
1 *capo maresciallo*	6 *maresciallo delle case*
1 *furiere caporale*	6 *caporali*
2 *trombettieri*	
1 *sellaio* (not mounted)	1 *marshal-ferratura* (not mounted)
30 *primo cannoni*	60 *cannoni di 2° classe* (40 not mounted)

Train Company

1 *tenente*	2 *sottotenente*
1 *capo maresciallo*	4 *maresciallo delle case*
1 *furiere caporale*	4 *caporali*
2 *trombettieri*	2 *sellai* (not mounted)
28 *primo soldati*	54 *soldati di 2° classe*

There were some minor adjustments to this organisation over time, including the addition of a *maggiore* to the Staff on 2 February 1807, and an *aiutante chirurgo* and a *chirurgo secondario-principale* to the staff on 23 February of the same year. However aside from the increase to six train companies on 31 December 1807 none were significant until the train was moved off into a seperate regiment in February 1811.

Service

Perconte[10] gives a table for the period 1807–1810, which is reproduced here and is indicative of the service of the regiment during this period. The later service of the regiment would have been similar.

Date	Men	Horses	
Establishment of 2 companies of horse artillery and 4 of train: 624 men and 656 horses*			
1807, 15 October	789	1,012	444 men with 709 horses were outside Italy
1808, 16 January	716	847	
Establishment of 2 companies of horse artillery and 6 of train: 824 men and 1,320 horses			
1808, 31 May	803	872	
1808, 1 July	780	1,109	47 men were outside of Italy

---

10 Jean-Pierre Perconte, 'Artillerie à Cheval et Train d'Artillerie du Royaume d'Italie 1805–1814, 2e Partie,' *Soldats Napoleoniens: Les Troupes Françaises, Alliés et Coalisées*, No. 15, Décembre 2007. (Paris: Éditions de la Revue Napoléon, 2007), pp. 61–69.

1808, 16 September	796	1,008	244 men at Perpignan
1808, 1 October	784	996	250 men with 351 horse at Perpignan
1808, 16 December	789	995	250 men with 342 horses in Spain
1809, 1 February	936	1,291	252 men with 345 horses in Spain
1809, 1 March	934	1,328	253 men in Spain (horses not recorded)
1809, 1 November	913	1,270	246 men with 327 horses in Spain 515 men with 793 horses in Germany
1810, 16 February	848	1,140	245 men with 327 horses in Spain
1810, 16 March	905	1,102	241 men with 327 horses in Spain
1810, 1 April	901	1,120	241 men with 327 horses in Spain
1810, 1 June	869	766	220 men with 144 horses in Spain
1810, 16 August	806	746	152 men with 139 horses in Spain
1810, 1 September	805	741	149 men with 139 horses in Spain
1810, 16 October	813	712	160 men with 157 horses in Spain and Dalmatia

*No explanation is given in the document as to why the regiment was actually, and highly unusually, *over* establishment!

The regimental depot was at Pavia.

Uniform
Headwear
The first headdress issued to the Reggimento di Artiglieria a Cavallo was a lancer-style czapska with the lower part a black fur turban and the upper part black, trimmed with dark green along the edge and across the top. The trim was changed to red by a regulation of 1807 but this change would have taken some time to appear in the regiment. The chin scales were brass and the peak was black leather edged in brass. At the left front upper edge of the czapska was the national cockade, secured by a white cockade strap and surmounted by a red plume, in later issues the plume had a white over red ball pompom at its base. Below the cockade was a brass badge of crossed cannon with a crown above and a small pyramid of six cannonballs below. On campaign the plume was replaced with a red carrot-shaped pompom.

In 1811 the czapska was officially replaced with the infantry pattern of shako, identical to that in use by the foot artillery, although the czapska may have remained in use by some companies until at least the end of 1812.

The the fatigue caps of the Reggimento di Artiglieria a Cavallo fatigue caps were dark green with red piping, often shown with a red crossed cannon badge.

LINE ARTILLERY AND SUPPORT UNITS

Artiglieria a Cavallo, officer and gunner, c. 1812. Watercolour by Henri Boisselier. (Author's collection)

Royaume d'Italie
Regiment d'artillerie à cheval
1811–1812

Coat

In 1805 the regiment was uniformed in a dark green hussar-style dolman with red collar (Weiland[11] shows a dark green collar, piped red) and 'Polish' cuffs and red frogging with five rows of brass buttons. By the end of 1806 this uniform had been replaced by a dark green coat of the same cut as that worn by the regiments of light horse. The new coat had a black collar and 'Polish' cuffs both piped red, red turnbacks with dark green grenade badges, and red lace batons on the front. The dark green shoulder straps and the pockets were both piped in red. Some illustrations show red epaulettes in place of the shoulder straps and it may be that, like the French horse artillery regiments, these were taken into use quite unofficially. From 1812 the regiment seems to have adopted the short-tailed habit-veste with pointed lapels and Brandenburg cuffs with all facings identical to those of the 1st Regiment (Reggimento di Artiglieria a Piedi).

Breeches etc.

Waistcoats were dark green with white metal buttons. The breeches were also dark green, with red Hungarian knots on the thighs and a red stripe on the outer seam. The Hungarian boots had red lace and tassel and steel spurs. From at least 1811 dark green overalls with black leather inserts and cuffs were issued for campaign wear. The overalls had a wide red stripe and white metal buttons on the outer seam. Greatcoats were dark green with black collar and red lining, and were of the same pattern as used by the light cavalry. White gloves were worn for parades and white gauntlets on campaign.

A watercolour by Henri Boisselier in his series of studies of the Army of the Kingdom of Italy shows gunners, dated to 1807 in both sky blue and dark blue breeches with red side stripes and Hungarian knots on the thigh. A subsequent plate dated 1811 shows the more commonly illustrated green breeches.[12]

Equipment

All equipment was the same as that used by the light horse regiments and the cartridge box lid carried either a brass crossed cannon badge or a lozenge-shaped plate embossed with a crowned crossed cannon device. All belting was white and the sword strap was white with a red knot and tassel.

Artiglieri were not routinely issued with the carbine although dragoon pattern muskets and cartridge boxes of infantry pattern were available for picket duties. *Artiglieri* were armed with a brace of pistols, carried in the usual design of holster on the saddle.

Officers and NCOs

All rank distinctions and badges were the same as those used by the light cavalry. Additionally the *primo artiglieri* wore the white stripe of a *caporale* on the left cuff only.

---

11 C. F. Weiland published his work in Weimar in 1807. The best modern reprint is Alain Pigeard (ed.), *Le Manuscrit de Weiland: Uniformes de l'Armée Français et de ses Alliés de 1806 à 1815* (Paris: Tradition, 1998).

12 Unpublished watercolours by Henri Boisselier in the author's collection.

LINE ARTILLERY AND SUPPORT UNITS

Officers' distinctions and badges were also the same as those used by the light cavalry. The lace batons on the 1806 coat were often piped silver, apparently an individual conceit and preference and not a regulation. Fiorentino[13] shows a *capitano* with the batons and breeches decoration in silver, which again may be a personal conceit albeit that it looks impressive. Officers' greatcoats were dark green with black collar and silver buttons. All belts were white (black on campaign) leather with brass fittings.

Trombettieri

Even after the adoption of the shako *trombettieri* continued to wear the czapska. The upper part was dark green with black piping and the lower turban was of white fur. *Trombettieri* plumes are shown as both black and dark green,[14] both with a red tip. *Trombettieri* are later sometimes shown wearing the colpack with a red bag piped dark green and with the crossed cannon badge at the front. Coats were trimmed with mixed red and white lace at the collar and cuffs with a similar lace being used on the front of the 1806 coat. The fringed epaulettes were white with mixed red and white fringes and crescents. Trumpets were brass with red cords.

Fiorentino[15] shows a variation reconstructed from a description c. 1807–11. The czapska is trimmed red and has a red plume from the white over red pompom described for the troop. The coat is red with black collar and cuffs, both trimmed with wide silver lace, silver batons at the front, a single baton on the collar and two on each cuff. Silver, full-fringed epaulettes.

Horse Furniture

The dark green 1805 pattern shabraque was of the same pattern as used by the light horse regiments with a wide red stripe piped dark green. The rear corners were decorated with red grenade badges. The dark green valise was round with red lace on the ends. When not worn the greatcoat was strapped on top of the valise with the lining uppermost.

In 1811 the shabraque was replaced, for campaign dress, with a white sheepskin with a red dogtooth cloth edging. The battery number in white was added to the ends of the valise at around the same time.

Trombettieri' shabraques were red with white lace and grenades and when the sheepskin shabraque was introduced in 1811, it was black with red edging.

Officers' shabraques were of the same pattern as the men with the addition of a wide silver trim, piped red and silver grenades in the rear corners. Officers did not adopt the sheepskin shabraque but retained the cloth for all orders of dress.

---

13 Jean-Pierre Perconte, 'Artillerie à Cheval et Train d'Artillerie du Royaume d'Italie 1805–1814, 2e Partie', pp. 61–69. An unpublished watercolour by Henri Boisselier in the author's collection also shows an officer with silver batons.

14 It is possible, perhaps even probable, that the black plume is simply a misinterpretation of the dark green.

15 Jean-Pierre Perconte, 'Artillerie à Cheval et Train d'Artillerie du Royaume d'Italie 1805–1814, 2e Partie', pp. 61–69.

Treno di Artiglieria (Train of Artillery)

Headwear

The Treno d'Artiglieria wore the czapska, similar to that originally issued to the Reggimento di Artiglieria a Cavallo. This had a black upper part, piped black at the top and red down the vertical edges. The lower part was a black fur turban with a brass lozenge plate at the front bearing a device of crowned crossed cannon barrels over a pyramid of cannonballs. The national cockade had a white cockade strap and was surmounted by a light green carrot-shaped pompom.

In 1811 the artillery pattern peakless shako was introduced to replace the czapska. It had the same plate, cockade and pompom as the czapska but had light green cords and plume for parade dress.

Fatigue caps were mid-grey with light green piping and tassels.

Coat

The mid-grey coat was of the surtout style with short tails. The collar, Polish cuffs and turnbacks were mid-green and the vertical pockets and front of the coat leading down into the turnbacks were piped in the same colour. The front of the coat had green lace batons of the same design as the coats of the Reggimento di Artiglieria a Cavallo, and there were two similar batons on the cuffs (one above and one below the actual cuff). The full-fringed epaulettes were mid-green, and all buttons were white metal. In 1811 the companies serving the Reggimento di Artiglieria a Piedi made some changes to their coats (how far, if at all, these changes were reflected by the other companies is unknown): the epaulettes were replaced by mid-grey shoulder straps piped in mid-green and the cuffs were changed to the Brandenburg pattern with cuff flaps, all still in mid-green, with two mid-green batons, worn one above the other but both on the cuff, although a painting in the collection of HM The Queen shows the cuffs without these lace batons.

Breeches etc.

Waistcoats were mid-grey with white metal buttons and breeches were soft buff leather with white metal buttons on the outer seams and were worn with high, cuffed riding boots with steel spurs. Members of the regiment who were not mounted wore white or mid-grey breeches and black gaiters as for the infantry. Whitened leather gauntlets were worn for parade and buff gauntlets on campaign. The light grey greatcoats were of light cavalry pattern, with a light green collar and lining.

Equipment

The drivers wore the light cavalry pattern pouch belt and cartridge box with the crossed cannon badge, and the twin shoulder belts supported an infantry pattern sabre-briquet in a black leather scabbard with light green sword strap and a white knot with light green tassel. Short dragoon pattern muskets were carried on the saddle.

LINE ARTILLERY AND SUPPORT UNITS

Treno di Artiglieria *c.* 1812. *Tenente* (left) and driver (right). Watercolour by Henri Boisselier. (Author's collection)

Officers and NCOs

Insignia was as the same as that used by the light cavalry and *brigadieri* were equipped as for the drivers. Senior NCOs and all officers carried the light cavalry sabre and waist belt, and on campaign both favoured the bicorne hat with silver lace and tassels. Officers' uniforms followed the style of the officers of the Reggimento di Artiglieria a Cavallo. Greatcoats were dark grey with a light green collar.

Musicanti

The regiment's *trombettieri* were uniformed as for the rank and file but with the addition of white lace to the edges of the collar and cuffs and red cords and plume to both the czapska and shako. *Trombettieri* carried the light cavalry sabre with a red sword strap and tassel. Trumpets were brass with green or red cords.

Tamburi had the same distinctions as the *trombettieri* but wore mid-grey breeches and black gaiters. All equipment, drums, etc. were the same as that of the *tamburi* of the line infantry regiments.

Horse Furniture

All draft horse harness was plain brown leather with brass buckles and fittings. The outriders' saddles were brown leather with a plain grey saddle blanket and a mid-grey round valise piped in light green at the ends.

Sergenti and other senior NCOs were mounted and used a mid-grey version of the 1805 pattern dragoon shabraque, with wide light green edging piped mid-grey. The pistol holsters were also light green edged white, in turn piped light green.

In 1811 the half-shabraque was taken into use; the cloth was the same colouring as the 1805 issue and the white sheepskin had a light green dogtooth edge.

The square valise was mid-grey with a light green lace on the ends.

Trombettieri' shabraques were mid-grey with red trim and the sheepskin was black with a red dogtooth edging.

Officers' shabraques were of the 1805 dragoon officers' pattern in mid-grey with silver lace decorations and grenades, the silver lace was piped with light green.

All wooden items – ordnance, caissons, limbers, halter collars, etc. – were painted dark green (not the olive green used by the French artillery).

Guardiacosta Artiglieri Compagnia (Coast Guard Artillery Companies)

History and Organisation

The Guardiacosta Artiglieri Compagnia were commissioned on 7 July 1810, initially with an establishment of seven batteries, but an eighth battery was raised in 1811. Ostensibly recruited locally to their location, the Guardiacosta Artiglieri were intended to offer some defence against raids by the Royal Navy. The batteries were equipped with heavy 'fixed position' guns, often of naval

LINE ARTILLERY AND SUPPORT UNITS

pattern and battery establishments varied according to the crew requirement of the particular gun or guns.

Service
The Guardiacosta Artiglieri was, of course, sedentary and saw little action although *Capitano* Riron of the battery of Goro was killed by unspecified enemy action on 2 October 1813.

Uniform
Headwear
The headwear was a black felt bicorne hat with national cockade and white cockade strap, the plume and pompom were of the national colours of red over white over green, although the reverse is also shown. Fatigue caps were dark green with white piping and tassels.

Coat
The dark green habit was the same as that worn by the Foot Artillery Regiment, with dark green collar, cuff flaps and shoulder straps and black lapels and cuffs. The turnbacks, pocket piping and shoulder strap piping were mid-grey and the turnback badges were dark green grenades. All buttons were white metal.

Breeches etc.
Breeches and waistcoats were mid-grey and worn with black over-the-knee gaiters with white metal or cloth covered buttons. Greatcoats were of the regulation infantry pattern and usually grey.

Equipment
The sabre-briquet, with a white sword strap and tassel, was the gunners' only personal weapon and was worn on a single shoulder belt. As always the sabre-briquet hilt was in brass and the scabbard was of black leather, fitted with brass. Highly unusually there is no record of the Guardiacosta Artiglieri being issued with muskets.

Officers and NCOs
The uniform was of the same colouring as that of the rank and file with all rank badges and distinctions of the same pattern as those used by the foot artillery.

The coastal artillery does not appear to have had either *tamburi* or musicians and arguably there would have been no purpose for them.

Battaglioni dei Transporti (Transport Battalions)

Uniform
Headwear
The 1st Battalion was initially issued with the Corsican hat of black felt with national cockade, white cockade strap and red over white over green carrot-

shaped pompom. In 1809 this was replaced with the infantry pattern shako with brass lozenge plate embossed with the letters 'TM' surmounted by the Iron Crown. Cockade and cockade strap were as on the Corsican hat and the pompom was tricoloured, and both carrot-shaped and round examples are recorded. Fatigue caps were red-brown with crimson piping and tassel for the 1st Battalion and yellow for the 2nd.

Coat
The coat was the short-tailed habit-veste in red-brown, it had square lapels and Brandenburg cuffs with three-pointed cuff flaps. The collar and turnbacks were crimson and the lapels, cuffs, cuff flaps and shoulder straps were all red-brown piped in crimson.

The coat of the 2nd battalion, raised in 1811, was identical to that of the 1st but substituted yellow for crimson as the facing colour.

Breeches etc.
Waistcoats and breeches were buff leather for the 1st battalion and red-brown for the 2nd battalion. Outriders wore high-cuffed riding boots and the drivers who sat upon the wagons wore black gaiters and infantry boots. The 2nd battalion's cloth breeches had black leather inserts. The men assigned to duties with the oxen teams walked beside their charges and had black gaiters but also often white or red-brown overall trousers. The red-brown greatcoats were of the cavalry pattern for the mounted troops with facing colour lining and collar. The dismounted men wore the infantry pattern in grey with facing colour lining and collar. Buff leather gauntlets were worn by the drivers and mounted troops.

Equipment
All rank and file wore pouch-belts and cartridge boxes of the light cavalry pattern. The belt was of whitened leather with brass fittings and the pouch is often shown decorated with a brass plate of the same design as that of the shako. Mounted men carried the light cavalry belt and sabre and the wagon drivers and foot conductors carried the infantry pattern shoulder belt with sabre-briquet and bayonet; both sabres and sabre-briquets had white sword straps and knots. Mounted men were armed with the light cavalry carbine carried on a light cavalry pattern white leather carbine belt, and dismounted men carried infantry pattern muskets.

Officers and NCOs
NCO rank stripes were as used by the infantry but all equipment was that of the light cavalry.

Officers almost invariably wore the bicorne with silver lace and cockade strap and white plumes. The officers' coat was the long-tailed habit of the same colouring as the men's coats. Waistcoats and breeches were either red-brown or white and worn with cuffed riding boots with silvered spurs. All rank distinctions were as used by infantry officers and all equipment was as used by light cavalry officers, with all leatherwork in black. Officers'

LINE ARTILLERY AND SUPPORT UNITS

greatcoats were of cavalry pattern and were dark brown with a facing colour collar.

Musicanti
The *trombettieri* of the transport battalions wore the same uniform as the other ranks with the addition of mixed facing colour and white lace to the collar and cuffs and white epaulettes with mixed facing colour and white crescents and fringes. Shako plumes were white tipped with the facing colour or red. The *trombettieri* of the 1st battalion had brass trumpets with green cords and tassels, those of the 2nd battalion used brass infantry-style bugle horns with green cords.

2nd Battalion *trombettista c.* 1812/1813: headwear was a czapska but the illustration shows it covered with its oilskin protection so any colours are unknown. The coat was yellow with a red-brown collar and cuffs, edged with red and white lace, and plain red-brown turnbacks. The overalls were red-brown with white metal buttons and all belting was black. Horse furniture was the black sheepskin without any apparent edging.

Horse Furniture
Outriders' saddlery was of the same pattern as used by the artillery train. Those mounted conductors acting as attendants to heavy draft animals that could not be ridden had red-brown shabraques and sheepskins of the pattern used by the artillery train. The edgings were of facing colour. Sheepskins were white with facing colour dogtooth edging. The square valise was red-brown with facing colour lace on the ends.

Trombettieri had black sheepskins with facing colour edge and the shabraques were facing colour with white lace.

Officers' shabraques were of the 1805 officers' pattern in red-brown with silver trim, piped with the regimental colour.

Harness for the heavy draft animals was plain brown leather and the wooden halter collars were painted the same dark green as the ordnance.

Battaglione d'Zappatore e Minatore del Genio (Sappers and Miners Battalion)

History and Organisation
The Battaglione d'Zappatore e Minatore was raised in 1807 with an establishment of seven companies of sappers and two companies of miners. Despite its relatively small size the battalion was responsible for all engineering work for the Army but, as required, would draw additional labour from any nearby infantry unit.

Uniform
Headwear
All companies wore the black bicorne with national cockade, white cockade strap and carrot-shaped pompom, in yellow for the *zappatore* companies

THE ARMY OF THE KINGDOM OF ITALY 1805–1814

Treno di Genie, officers c. 1812. Watercolour by Henri Boisselier. (Author's collection)

LINE ARTILLERY AND SUPPORT UNITS

and red for the *minatore*. In 1812 the battalion adopted the infantry pattern shako. This lacked the usual front plate, but had white metal chin scales, national cockade and carrot-shaped pompom as had been worn on the bicorne; the full dress cords were of the pompom colour. Fatigue caps were dark green with yellow piping for the *zappatori* and red for *minatori*.

Coat
The dark green habit had black lapels, collar, cuffs and three-pointed cuff flaps, all piped red, the red turnbacks had dark green grenade badges. The horizontal pockets were piped red. All companies wore full-fringed epaulettes, the *zappatori* in yellow and the *minatori* in red.

Breeches etc.
Breeches and waistcoats were dark green. Gaiters were of the over-knee pattern in black with cloth covered buttons. Greatcoats were standard infantry pattern in grey.

Equipment
All equipment was of the same pattern as that used by the foot artillery. Sword knots were yellow for the *zappatore* companies and red for the *minatori* companies, following the company distinctive colour.

Officers and NCOs
All rank, badges, distinctions, etc. were as used by the foot artillery. The *capo di battaglione* and the company *capitani* were mounted with shabraques of infantry pattern in dark green, edged with a single wide silver lacing edged with red.

Musicanti
The company *tamburi* were uniformed the same as the rank and file but with red and white lace on the collar and cuffs. All other details and equipment was the same as for the *tamburi* of the infantry.

Treno di Genie (Engineers' Train)

History and Organisation
Raised in 1807, at the same time as the Battaglione d'Zappatore e Minatore, the Treno di Genie had an establishment of a single company and the sole (and obvious) function of moving the engineering equipment. The initial strength was two NCOs and 15 drivers but by 1812 this had expanded to an establishment of three officers, including the *capitano* commander, 17 NCOs, two *trombettieri* and 56 conductors with 35 specialist wagons. Of the 56 other ranks, 32 were mounted and 24 dismounted, although they actually marched and moved on the wagons. In 1813 when the Army was reformed after the Russian campaign the company was absorbed into the artillery train and the uniform changed to conform to that regiment.

Uniform

Headwear
The company wore the bicorne with national cockade and white strap, white tassels and a yellow carrot-shaped pompom. The fatigue cap was dark green with yellow piping and tassel.

Coat
The coat was a dark green, long-tailed surtout, with black collar and Polish cuffs and dark green turnbacks; the turnbacks and vertical pockets were piped black. The front of the coat was decorated with eight yellow lace batons and the collar and cuffs had narrow yellow batons as for the artillery train. The coat had yellow full-fringed epaulettes.

Breeches etc.
Waistcoats were dark green with white metal buttons and the breeches were buff leather. Mounted troops wore high-cuffed riding boots with steel spurs, dismounted men had black over-the-knee gaiters with cloth covered buttons. Gauntlets were buff leather and the grey greatcoats were of cavalry pattern.

Equipment
Mounted rank and file carried the light cavalry pattern sabre with a yellow sword strap with white knot and yellow tassel, and the light cavalry pattern cartridge box. Dismounted rank and file were armed with the infantry pattern sabre-briquet and bayonet with the dragoon pattern musket and the infantry pattern cartridge box. The dismounted troops' sabre-briquet sword knot was the same as that of their mounted comrades,

Officers and NCOs
All badges and rank distinction were the same as those used by the Treno di Artiglieria.

Musicanti
The two *trombettieri* were uniformed the same as the rank and file but with white lace edging to the collar and cuffs and they did not wear the pouch belt. The plume on the bicorne was red with a yellow tip. Trumpets were brass with green cords.

Horse Furniture
Outriders' saddles were the same as those of the Treno di Artiglieria and the mounted conductors' shabraques were of the later dragoon pattern half-shabraque of a white sheepskin with yellow dogtooth edging over a dark green cloth with white edging. The dark green valise was square, trimmed white and with the letters 'TG' on the ends.

Officers' shabraques were of the 1805 pattern with a silver lace edge piped dark green.

LINE ARTILLERY AND SUPPORT UNITS

Pompieri Della Città di Milano (City of Milan Company of Firemen)

History and Organisation
In 1811 a single company of pompieri was raised in Milan to assist with engineering and to combat fires in the event of the city coming under siege. Although privately financed, as so often with such units the company was organised and uniformed as a military unit of 85 officers and men. In 1813 the company provided drafts to the Milan city guard.

As a small side note, today titled as the Corpo dei Vigili del Fuoco di Milano, this is the only unit of the Army of the Kingdom of Italy still in existence (insofar as it actually was a part of the Army of Italy).

Company Establishment
1 *capitano*	1 *tenente*
4 *sergente*	2 *caporale*
2 *tamburi*	75 *pompieri*

Service
The company saw no formal field service although in 1814 it was attached to the Battaglione Guardia Alla Città di Milano and may therefore have been present with that unit at the Battle of Pescheira.

Uniform
Headwear
The company wore a brass dragoon-style helmet without the black fur turban or horsehair crest and with a red houpette and plume. The front of the helmet was embossed with the unit's title. The chin scales were brass and fitted with sun-burst bosses. Fatigue caps were light blue with red trim.

Coat
The coat was a light blue, short-tailed habit-veste, as worn by the light infantry, with light blue lapels and turnbacks, both piped red, turnback ornaments were red grenades. The collar and 'Polish' cuffs were red and the pockets were piped red. All buttons were brass. The company wore red full-fringed epaulettes.

Breeches etc.
Breeches and waistcoats were light blue. Gaiters were black and knee length, with white metal buttons.

Equipment
All rank and file wore twin white leather shoulder belts. The first supported the cartridge pouch, with a brass badge of a grenade superimposed upon crossed axes on the lid, against the right hip, with the bayonet frog attached to the left side of the pouch; the only other unit recorded using this unusual placement of the bayonet is the Battaglione Guardia Alla Città di Milano (The City of Milan Guard Battalion, see above). The second belt supported

the sabre-briquet, which had a red sword strap and tassel. The company carried short, dragoon pattern, muskets.

Officers and NCOs
All rank badges and distinctions were the same as those of the line infantry but the NCO rank stripes were, as was usual with the Polish cuff, in the form of inverted chevrons.

Officers carried the light infantry-style curved sabre and customarily had all belts of black leather.

Tamburi
Tamburi coats were of the same pattern as the rank and file but in red with sky blue facings, and with white lace trim to the collar and cuffs. All other details as for the infantry.

Corpo di Medicina & Ambulanza Compagnia (Medical Corps and Ambulance Companies)

The Italian Army had an organised medical corps as early as 1802 and with the formation of the Kingdom's army in 1805 the corps was reorganised as part of the new army.

The corps was commanded by a director general and consisted of three departments: *medici* (physicians/doctors), *chirurgi* (surgeons), and *farmacisti* (apothecaries), with 1st, 2nd and 3rd class grades and cadet officers.

Following the French example, four ambulance companies were raised on 27 August 1811, each with an establishment of two administrative officers, one *trombettista* and 79 'attendants'. The companies were equipped with the French pattern two-wheeled ambulances, each drawn by two horses, harnessed in-line. The author speculates that these were painted the same dark green as the artillery, though having seen no confirmation.

Medico Ufficiali (Medical Officers)

Uniform
Headwear
All medical officers wore the black bicorne with national cockade and silver cockade strap.

The hat of the *ispettore generale* (inspector general) was faced with black velvet and had silver lace edging and tassels.

Coat
The dark green full dress surtout closed with nine silver-plated buttons, embossed with the words 'SANITA MILITARE' around the edge. The collar and cuffs were of departmental colour, red for the *chirurgi*, black for the medici and dark green velvet for the farmacisti. The *ispettore generale* had the collar and cuffs of his coat in black velvet. Turnbacks were dark green

and the coat had horizontal pockets with three buttons. The cuffs were plain but had three buttons horizontally at the front and outside. The full dress waistcoats were red for *chirurgi* and dark green for the other officers and all had silvered buttons.

On campaign all officers wore the dark green surtout with turned-over 'Swedish' collar of departmental colour and pockets 'a la Soubise' piped in the same. All buttons were silver. Waistcoats were white or dark green.

Rank Insignia
The coats of the *ispettori generali* were heavily embroidered with nine 32 mm-wide silver laurel leaf lace batons, with pointed ends, across the front. The collar and cuffs were trimmed with the same lace, 20 mm wide, and a further 5 mm strip outside that – the two separated by a narrow piping of the cuff colour. The pockets and the edges of the waistcoat were trimmed with 5 mm of the lace. The undress surtout was trimmed only on the collar and cuffs.

Senior departmental officers wore the same uniform as the *ispettore generale* but with lace batons only 20 mm wide.

The coats of 1st class officers of all three departments again had the same lace batons but 10 mm wide and extending approximately 150 mm each side of the front. The collar was decorated with four 15 mm-wide horizontal batons and the cuffs and pockets each had three vertical batons of the same width. The undress coat was decorated with only the cuff and collar batons.

The full dress coats of 2nd class officers had only three batons on the collar and cuffs. The undress surtout was laced only on the collar.

The full dress coat of 3rd class officers had two batons of the lace on the collar and cuffs, and the undress tunic was decorated with two batons of lace on the collar only.

Medical officer cadets wore the undress surtout without lace but with departmental colour collar, dark green cuffs and turnbacks and white metal buttons.

Breeches etc.
Dark green breeches were worn in full dress and white or dark green for undress uniform and on campaign, although white or dark green trousers were more common for campaign wear. All officers wore English pattern boots, which had turned-over tops showing the buff leather lining. The dark green greatcoats were of the cavalry pattern and were lined in the facing colour, the collar was in the dark green of the coat. White gloves were worn for full dress.

Equipment
The waist belts were in black leather and supported the straight bladed epée with embossed silvered hilt, carried in a black leather scabbard with brass fittings. The sword strap was gold with a heavy bullion fringe for the *ispettore generale* and the same but in silver for the senior officers. 1st class officers had silver sword straps with finer fringe on the tassel, as worn by infantry officers. The 2nd class officers had the same but with a narrow red stripe in the knot and the 3rd class officers had the same but with two stripes. Officer

cadets had sword straps of mixed white silk and wool with silver fringing.

Horse Furniture
The dark green shabraques were of the Dragoni della Guardia pattern with brown leather saddles and a wide silver edging piped dark green. The edging was 55 mm wide for the *ispettore generale,* 45 mm for the senior officers, 40 mm for 1st class officers, 35 mm for 2nd class, and 30 mm for 3rd class. Cadets had the same shabraque with a 20 mm-wide lace. Pistol holsters were dark green and trimmed in the same way as the shabraque. Girth straps were grey and all harness was black leather with brass fittings.

Ambulanza Compagnia (Ambulance Companies)

Headwear
The companies wore the regulation infantry pattern shako, with a white ball pompom, black leather chinstrap and the national cockade with a white cockade strap. The shako plate was a white metal lozenge shape, embossed with the latter 'A'. Fatigue caps were red-brown, piped grey with a grey tassel and a white, or just possibly grey, 'A' at the front.

Coat
The coat was a red-brown habit-veste with squared lapels and Brandenburg cuffs. The collar, cuffs, turnbacks and shoulder straps were red-brown with grey piping and the lapels and cuff flaps dark grey piped red-brown. All buttons were white metal.

Breeches etc.
Breeches and waistcoats were dark grey and the high gaiters black with white metal buttons. The infantry pattern greatcoats were dark grey.

Equipment
The single white shoulder belt supported the infantry sabre-briquet with a white sword strap.

Officers and NCOs
The two *sergenti* and four *corporali* of each company wore rank insignia as used by the line infantry.

The company was commanded by an officer known as the '*centurione*', assisted by a '*sottocenturione*'; for unknown reasons these did not rank as commissioned officers and were not allowed the privilege of wearing epaulettes of rank or sword straps. The *centurione* was distinguished by a wide silver lace band around the top of the cuff and on the collar and the *sottocenturione* had the same lace but only on his cuffs. Coats were red-brown surtout style with red-brown collar, cuffs of plain round pattern, and turnbacks all piped dark grey. All buttons were white metal. The bicorne was decorated with the cockade and silver cockade strap only. Breeches and waistcoats were white and the boots were of the English pattern. A straight epée was carried on a black leather waist belt in a scabbard of black leather fitted in white metal. Officers' shabraques were of the infantry pattern and red-brown with a wide silver edging.

Musicanti
The shakos of the *trombettieri* had a white plume tipped red and the coat was as for the rank and file with white and red lace on the collar and cuffs. *Trombettieri* were mounted and wore the light cavalry sabre and their shabraque was as for the officers but with white lace. The infantry pattern bugle horn was brass with green cords.

6

Naval Units

The small navy of the Kingdom of Italy saw almost constant, albeit small-scale, service in the Mediterranean from its creation with the Kingdom in 1805 until it, and the Kingdom, were dissolved in 1814 when the remaining personnel passed into the service of the Austrian Empire. Whilst it is not the purpose of this study to cover the ships and personnel of the navy a number of naval units served with the Army.[1] These units were:

> Navale Artiglieri Battaglione (Battalion of Naval Gunners)
> Navale Bracciante Compagnia (Naval Workers Companies)
> Compagnia Due Militari Guardaciurme (Military Company of Ships Guards)
> Navale Verterani Battaglione (Naval Veterans Battalion)

These units were often commanded by, or in part at least officered by, naval officers so it is worthwhile to cover the uniform of the *capitaine* and other ranks of the Navy. Even when serving on land or with the Army, naval officers appear to have retained their full naval uniform, probably as much out of pride as for any other reason (British Royal Navy officers did the same).

Naval Officers

Officers wore the bicorne, usually 'fore and aft', with the national cockade held by a silver cockade strap on the left side, and silver tassels.

Two patterns of coat were in use by naval officers: The first was of a surtout style in dark green with red collar, turnbacks and cuffs and seven batons of white lace with pointed ends, across the breast. All buttons were silvered and silver epaulettes following the system set out below.

The second pattern of coat, which seems to have been service dress, was again a dark green surtout but with all facings dark green piped silver. Rank was again indicated by silver epaulettes.

---

1 Similarly the French Navy supplied a number of units, particularly artillery, for service with the French army.

The system of naval officers' rank epaulettes was:

Capitano (3 years' service): two full heavy-fringed epaulettes[2]
Capitano (under 3 years' service): as above, but on the right shoulder only
Comandante: as above, but on the left shoulder only
Tenente: as for *comandante* but with a thinner fringing

Officers' breeches were dark green for parade and white for wear onboard ship and for service dress on land (this appears the reverse of what would be intuitive but it is what the sources indicate …) The green breeches had silver Hungarian knots on the thigh and the full dress boots were of Hungarian pattern with silver trimmed lace along the top and silver tassels. On board ship officers wore either sea boots or shoes and white stockings, for service on land they may have worn either the Hungarian boots or perhaps English-style 'jockey boots'.

Navale Artiglieri Battaglione (Battalion of Naval Gunners)

History, Organisation and Service

The battalion was raised to defend the coast between Rimini and the marshes of the delta of the River Po.[3] Its organisation was as four companies of gunners, one ordnance company, one apprentice company and one bombardier company. Each company comprised one *sergente-maggiore*, four *sergenti*, four *corporali*, a *caporale-furiere*, two *tamburi* and 95 other ranks. The absence of any officers on the company establishment as it is recorded is almost certainly an error and it should perhaps be expected that there were three officers in addition to the above.

By definition the battalion was sedentary but Martinien records *Tenente* Santolini as wounded in the Battle of Lissa on 13 March 1811, although this was a naval action so he may have been serving on board, perhaps 'on attachment'?

Uniform
Headwear
The hat was a narrow-crowned leather 'top hat' with a curled and polished brim and with black fur roll forming an inverted V trim to the front and rear of the crown. The front of the hat was decorated with a large triangular brass plate embossed with crossed cannon superimposed over an anchor between two grenades. A red carrot-shaped pompom with tufted tip was worn at the left side, above the national cockade secured by a white strap with a white metal button. The dark green fatigue cap was the same pattern as that of infantry, with red piping and tassel, and a red grenade badge.

---

2   Higher ranks in the navy had their rank indicated by varying numbers of stars on a similar pattern of epaulettes. *Capitano* and below had plain straps.
3   Why this battalion should have been a part of the navy, and not a coastguard artillery unit of the army, is unknown.

Coat
The coat was a dark green Spencer tunic, with dark green collar, lapels and cuffs piped red and red turnbacks and cuff flaps, both piped dark green. Turnbacks could be either plain or decorated with a dark green grenade badge. Pockets were piped red. The Bombardiere Compagnia and *primo artiglieri* wore red, fringed epaulettes, all other personnel had red contre-epaulettes. All buttons were white metal.

Breeches etc.
The Hungarian-style breeches were dark green, full length and tight fitting with a cuff that fitted over the top of the shoes and strapped beneath the instep. The buttons at the sides of the calf were white metal. The infantry pattern greatcoat was dark grey.

Equipment
All equipment was of the same pattern as that used by the foot artillery of the line. The cartridge box lid was decorated with a brass crossed cannon and anchor badge.

Officers and NCOs
NCOs wore rank badges the same as those of the foot artillery. *Corporali* had red, fringed epaulettes; other NCOs had epaulette fringes of mixed red and silver with a plain red strap.

Officers' distinctions would probably have been the same as those used by the Army.

Tamburi
All *tamburi* distinctions were the same as those in the Army, as was their equipment, drums, etc.

Navale Bracciante Compagnia (Naval Workers Companies)

History, Organisation and Service
The original purpose of these companies was for shipbuilding but in 1813 two companies were sent to Germany as bridge-builders for the Italian Army. Each company had, besides officers, four *sergenti*, four *corporali*, one *tamburo* and 96 *braccianti* (literally 'labourers', which says much for their original function).

Headwear
The Bracciante Compagnia wore the infantry pattern shako with a brass lozenge plate embossed with crossed axes and the anchor. Chin scales were brass and the national cockade, worn at the front above the plate, was surmounted by a red carrot-shaped pompom. *Braccianti 1° classe* may have had a red trim to the upper edge of the shako. Fatigue caps were dark green with red piping.

NAVAL UNITS

Coat
The dark green 'Spencer' habit-veste had a black collar, black lapels and cuffs piped red, red turnbacks and red cuff flaps. All buttons were white metal. One source shows dark green turnbacks piped red with white crossed axes and anchor badges.

1º classe bracciante wore red, fringed epaulettes, *2º classe* red contre-epaulettes and the *3º classe* had dark green shoulder straps piped red.

Breeches etc.
The dark green breeches were worn with black knee-length gaiters that had white metal buttons. The grey greatcoat was of the usual infantry pattern and worn with epaulettes the same as those worn on the coat.

Equipment
All as for the elite companies of the line infantry with white sword strap and red knot and tassel.

Officers and NCOs
The NCOs wore the uniform of the company with badges and distinctions as for the line infantry.

The companies were commanded by naval officers.

Musicanti
Tamburi wore the uniform of the company with equipment and distinctions as for the army.

Compagnia Di Militari Guardaciurme (Military Company of Ships Guards)

Compagnia Di Militari Guardaciurme was originally raised as a unit of the Venetian Navy to guard galley slaves but by the time that the Venetian Navy was absorbed into the Italian Navy in 1806 it had become simply a unit of marines supplying guards to the docks and the 'sharpshooters' for service on warships.[4]

The unit was commanded by naval officers and had an establishment of two *tamburi*, eight *sergente-maggiori*, 14 *sergenti*, and 14 *corporali*, commanding 200 marines organised into eight squads.

Uniform
Headwear
The Guardaciurme had a black shako with a white metal lozenge plate at the front embossed 'MG' (for Militari Guardaciurme). It had white metal chin scales and national cockade above the plate but, unusually, no pompom. The fatigue caps were dark green with light grey piping.

---

[4] The use of such 'sharpshooters' was usual in the navies of most nations. For example the French navy used selected infantry regiments onboard its ships – see Stephen Ede-Borrett, *Swiss Regiments in the Service of France 1798–1815* (Warwick: Helion & Co, 2019).

Coat
The infantry pattern dark green habit had collar, lapels, turnbacks and cuff flaps of light grey and cuffs and shoulder straps of dark green with light grey piping. All buttons were white metal and the pockets were piped light grey.

Breeches etc.
Breeches and waistcoats were light grey and the knee-length black gaiters had white metal buttons. Greatcoats were grey and of the same pattern as the infantry.

Equipment
As for the elite companies of infantry with brass anchor on the cartridge box lid, white sword knot.

Officers and NCOs
The NCOs had infantry rank badges on uniforms following the pattern of the rank and file. Officers were naval personnel.

Musicanti
Tamburi had distinctions as for the infantry.

Navale Veterani Battaglione (Naval Veterans Battalion)

The battalion was raised in 1807, and merged into the Reggimento Veterani e Invalidi (Veteran and Invalids Regiment) in 1811 but, in the interim, was responsible for the guarding of the Navy's bases.

Uniform
Headwear
Black felt bicorne with national cockade surmounted by a carrot-shaped pompom of red over white over green. Fatigue caps were dark green with white piping.

Coat
The coat was a dark green habit with white collar, plain round cuffs, red lapels, turnbacks and shoulder straps piped dark green. The pockets were piped red. All buttons were white.

Breeches etc.
White waistcoats and white breeches worn with black over-the-knee gaiters with white metal buttons. Greatcoats were the infantry pattern of grey.

Equipment
All as for the elite companies of the Fanteria di Linea. Sword knots were white with a red tassel.

NAVAL UNITS

Officers and NCOs
All distinctions and rank badges as for the Fanteria.

Tamburi
All distinctions as for the Fanteria di Linea.

Appendix I

The Order of the Iron Crown

The Order of the Iron Crown was instituted as Article VIII of the original Constitution of the Kingdom on 5 June 1805 and was conceived as an Italian equivalent of the French Légion d'Honneur. The Order was to be in three classes and by its initial rules it was to comprise a maximum of 20 Grand Cross Dignitaries, 100 Commanders and 500 Knights. The Order was also to be available to French Citizens who had fought in Italy as well as citizens of the Kingdom of Italy, indeed the nominees for the first 20 Grand Cross Dignitaries on 25 March 1806 were all French Generals (although the list included, unsurprisingly, Prince Eugène himself).

When the Kingdom was annexed by Austria in 1815 the Order was, very surprisingly, not abolished as all the other Napoleonic institutions were but became the Imperial Order of the Iron Crown, in which form it survived until 1918 and the fall of the Habsburg Monarchy.

Facing page: The Order of the Iron Crown 'medal' (top) and breast star (bottom). The medal ribbon was aurora bordered in dark green.

Overleaf: Covering letter and confirmation of the appointment of Giuseppe Ajassa of the Royal Guard Artillery as Chevalier of The Order of the Iron Crown. Dated 27 September 1813. Ajassa served until the fall of the Kingdom but (at present) his subsequent career is unknown.

Note that Napoleon, even on such documents, terms himself 'Imperatori de Francesi, Re d'Italia' (Emperor of the French, King of Italy)

Photograph courtesy of Patrick T. del C. Nisbett, a descendant of the family.

THE ORDER OF THE IRON CROWN

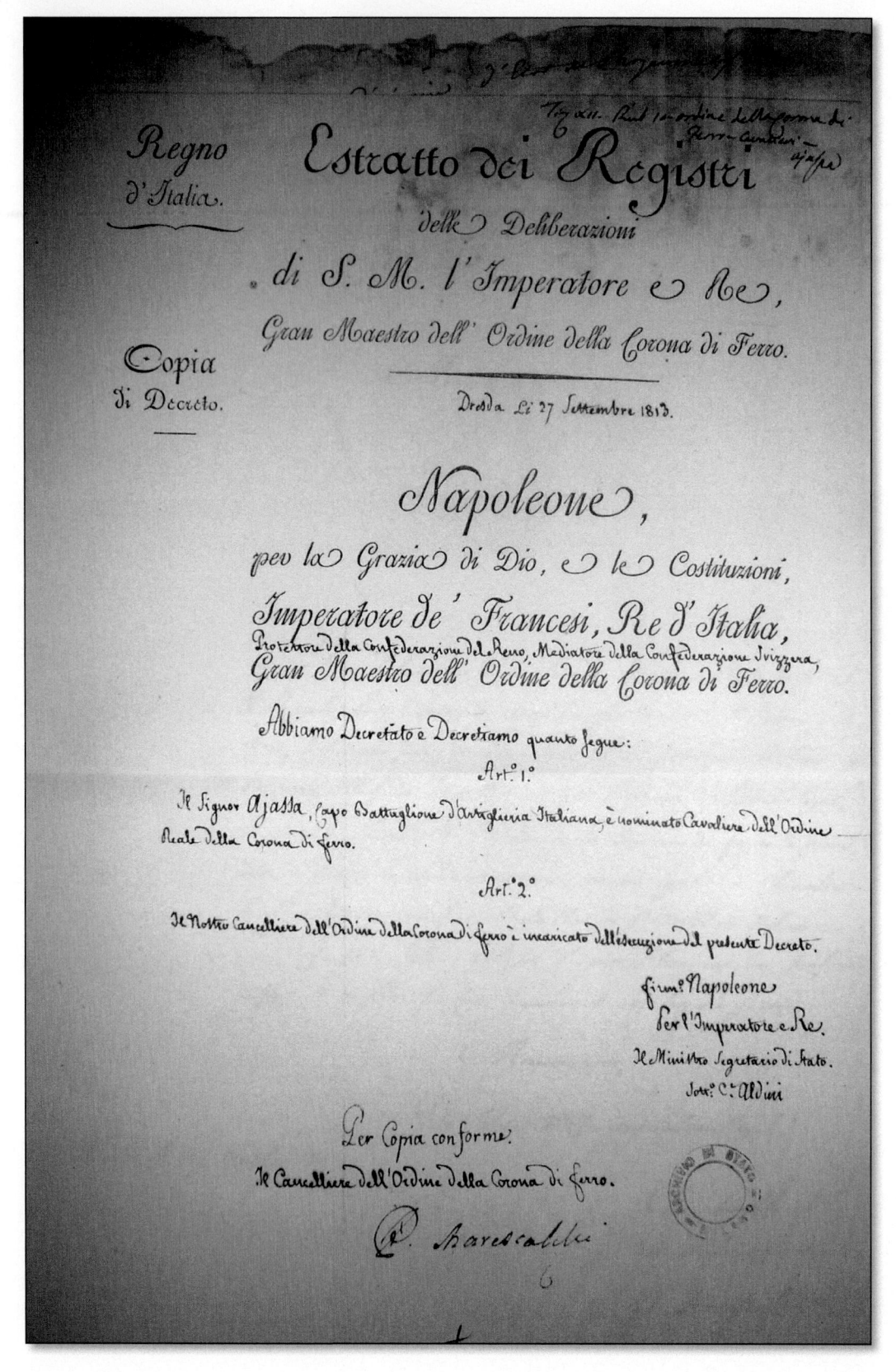

THE ARMY OF THE KINGDOM OF ITALY 1805–1814

THE ORDER OF THE IRON CROWN

Renvoyé aux [...]
Vienne le 5. 9bre 1813.

Monseigneur,

J'ai l'honneur d'adresser à Votre Altesse Impériale & Royale les Copies de deux Décrets de S. M. l'Empereur & Roi, le premier, daté de Pirna le 19 7bre der. par lequel le Sieur De Goux, Chef de Bataillon au 33.e Régiment d'infant. de ligne, est nommé Chevalier de l'Ordre de la Couronne de fer, et le second, daté de Drèsde le 27 du même mois, nomme également Chevalier le Sr. Ajasso, Chef de Bataillon de l'Artillerie Italienne.

Je prie Votre Altesse d'agréer l'hommage du profond respect, & du plus parfait dévouement avec lesquels je suis,

Monseigneur,

De Votre Altesse Impériale et Royale,

Paris, le 27 Octobre 1813.

le très humble &
très obéissant serviteur.

Marescalchi

Appendix II

Illustrative Strength Returns

The Strength of the Royal Guard, 1 July 1807

Guardie D'Onore

	1st Coy Milano	2nd Coy Bologna	3rd Coy Brescia	4th Coy Romagna	5th Coy Venezia
Capitano	1	1	1	1	1
Tenente	1				
Sottotenente	2	1	2	1	
Maresciallo d'alloggio capo		1	1	1	
Marescialli d'alloggio	2	2	3	2	3
Brigadiere furiere	1	1	1	1	1
Brigadieri	5	5	5	4	3
Guardie	49	25	60	33	44
Veterinario	1				
Maniscalchi	1	1	1	1	1
Trombe	2	2	2	1	2
Tamburi	1	1	1	1	1
Total	66	40	77	46	56

Dragoni

Colonnello	1
Capo-squadrone	1
Capitani	6
Tenente 1° classe	5
Tenente 2° classe	6
Sottotenente	6
Ufficiali di Sanita	3

Maresciallo d'alloggio capo	5
Veterinario	2
Maestro-artigiani	23
Brigadieri	37
Mariscalchi	4
Musicanti	12
Dragoni	300
Total	411

Granatieri & Cacciatori and Veliti

	Granatieri & Cacciatori	Veliti
Colonello		
Maggioro	1	1
Capo di battaglione	2	2
Capitano	12	14
Tenente 1° classe	10	15
Tenente 2° classe	9	16
Sottotenente	10	12
Ufficiali di Sanita	3	2
Aiutante-sottuficiale	8	10
Sergenti and *artigiani*	47	28
Caporali and *zappatori*	116	96
Tamburi	19	30
Musicanti	29	30
Soldati	770	1,029
Total	1,036	1,255

The Italian Division at Kolberg, 1 April 1807

1° Fanteria di Linea: 58 officers and 1,508 men. Plus 297 in hospital, 1 under arrest, 9 in prison, 19 missing

1° Fanteria Leggera: 52 officers and 1,428 men. Plus 365 in hospital, 23 under arrest, 15 in prison, 16 missing

2° Fanteria Leggera: 65 officers and 1,568 men. Plus 265 in hospital, 2 under arrest, 9 in prison, 19 missing

4° Compagnia d'Zappatore: 3 officers and 78 men. Plus 16 in hospital, 1 under arrest.

2 Compagnie di Artiglieria[1]: 5 officers and 54 men, plus 4 in hospital. These companies had 2 x 12-pdr guns, 8 x 6-pdr guns, 2 howitzers and a mortar.

Granatieri a Piedi & Carabinieri a Piedi Della Guardia in 1811 and 1812

1811, August: 50 officers, 1,086 NCOs and men, 32 NCOs and men in hospital, 26 in prison, 6 under arrest, 10 invalids.

1812, September, Moscow: 1,078 officers and men, plus 56 in the depot, 25 in hospital, 6 prisoners of war, 28 'lost en route'.

The Italian Contingent in IV Corps, 25 June 1812

	Officers	Men	Officers' Horses	Men's Horses	Train Horses
Royal Guard Division					
Gardes d'Honneur, 5 coys	17	274	40	269	16
Granatieri and Carabinieri, and artillery coy	45	1,137	3		54
Veliti, 1st and 2nd Battalions and artillery coy	43	1,105	3		52
Coscritti, 1st and 2nd Battalions and artillery coy	40	1,084	3		49
Dragoni, 1st and 2nd squadrons	19	392	49	371	8
1° Dragoni di Linea ('Regina'), 1st–4th squadrons	37	616	86	595	8
Artiglieria, 1st (foot) and 2nd (horse) battalions Treno d'Artiglieria	10	373	11	70	327
Zappatore battalion, 4th Company (line)	3	81			6
1° Transporti Militari, 1st and 3° coys	3	239	4		352

---

1   The author has been unable to identify which companies these were.

	Officers	Men	Officers' Horses	Men's Horses	Train Horses
Sailors	3	99			
Total	220	5,400	199	1,305	872

15th Infantry Division

	Officers	Men	Officers' Horses	Men's Horses	Train Horses
1º Leggera, 4th Battalion	22	742			8
3º Leggera, 1st, 2nd, 3rd, 4th Battalions and artillery company	87	3,039	3		61
2º di Linea, 1st, 2nd, 3rd, 4th Battalions and artillery company	86	2,690	4		61
3º di Linea, 1st, 2nd, 3rd, 4th Battalions and artillery company	89	2,892	3		62
Reale Dalmata, 1st, 2nd, 3rd Battalions and artillery company	65	1,681	3		53
Artiglieria a Piedi, 14th Company Artiglieria a Cavallo, 2nd Company Treno d'Artiglieria, 3rd and 4th Companies *Braccianti*, 2nd Company	13	406	20	87	290
Zappatori, 6th Company	3	101			6
Transporti Militari, 2nd Company	2	152	6		286
Total	367	11,703	39	87	827

15th Light Cavalry Brigade

	Officers	Men	Officers' Horses	Men's Horses	Train Horses
2º Cacciatori a Cavallo, 1st, 2nd, 3rd, 4th squadrons	39	608	89	587	8
3º Cacciatori a Cavallo, 1st, 2nd, 3rd, 4th squadrons	33	601	76	590	8
Total	72	1,209	165	1,177	16

The Strength of the Royal Guard, Late 1812 / February 1813 (Germany in late 1812, Italy in February 1813)

Guardie D'Onore

	Germany		Italy	
	Officers	Men	Officers	Men
Staff		4		1
1st Coy Milano	3	54	1	30
2nd Coy Bologna	1	49	2	20
3rd Coy Brescia	3	53		21
4th Coy Romagna	1	67	1	17
5th Coy Venezia	4	60		28
Total	16	283	5	116

Dragoni & Gendarmeria

	Germany		Italy	
	Officers	Men	Officers	Men
Staff	7	5	2	4
1st Squadron, 1 Company	4	104	1	15
1st Squadron, 3 Company	4	109		12
2nd Squadron, 2 Company	4	107		16
2nd Squadron, 4 Company	4	106		12
Total	23	431	3	59
Gendarmeria		9	1	30

Granatieri

	Germany		Italy	
	Officers	Men	Officers	Men
Staff	12	31	1	4
1st Battalion, 1 – 4 Coy	14	521		
1st Battalion, 5 Coy			3	54
2nd Battalion, 1 – 4 Coy	17	526		
2nd Battalion, 5 Coy			3	45
Detached	1	48		
Total	44	1,126	7	103

ILLUSTRATIVE STRENGTH RETURNS

Veleti

	Germany		Italy	
	Officers	Men	Officers	Men
Staff	11	32	1	6
1st Battalion, 1 – 4 Coy	15	482		
1st Battalion, 5 Coy			2	204
2nd Battalion, 1 – 4 Coy	16	506		
2nd Battalion, 5 Coy			2	186
Detached	2	47		
Total	44	1,067	5	396

Cacciatori

	Germany		Italy	
	Officers	Men	Officers	Men
Staff			2	2
1st Battalion, 1–4 Coy	15	545		
1st Battalion, 5 Coy			3	29
2nd Battalion, 1–4 Coy	15	524		
2nd Battalion, 5 Coy			2	299
Detached	2	101		
Total	32	1,170	7	330

Artiglieria

	Germany		Italy	
	Officers	Men	Officers	Men
Staff	6	3	1	2
1st Company (Horse)	5	75		
Depot (Horse)				4
1st Company (Foot)	4	102		4
2nd Company (Foot)	3	94		
1st Company (Train)	3	94		
2nd Company (Train)	2	93		
Depot (Train)				12
Total	23	461	1	22

Appendix III

The Armée d'Italie at the Battle of the Mincio, 8 February 1814[1]

This is an illustrative and typical order of battle of the Army of Italy and it can be seen that, even in 1814, the French still provided the majority of the combat troops of the field army. This order of battle also shows the relative weakness of the Italian units by this time.

Commander-in-Chief: Prince Eugène de Beauharnais, Viceroy of The Kingdom of Italy.

First Army Corps: Général de Division Paul Grenier

2ᵉ Division Rouyer

Brigade Schmitz
9ᵉ de Ligne	2,266
52ᵉ de Ligne	1,010
67ᵉ de Ligne	1,042

Brigade d'Arnaud
35ᵉ de Ligne	2,144
1ᵉʳ Régiment Étranger	2,144
1 horse battery	
1 foot battery	

---

1 Juan Carlos Carmigniani and Gilles Boué, trans. Marie-France Renwick, *Napoleon and Italy: A Military History of Napoleonic Italy, 1805–1815* (Paris: Histoire & Collections, 2016), p. 269. The unit titles show that even at this late stage the majority of the Amy of Italy in the field was actually French.

THE ARMÉE D'ITALIE AT THE BATTLE OF THE MINCIO, 8 FEBRUARY 1814

4ᵉ Division Marcognet

Brigade Jeanin
6ᵉ de Ligne	863
20ᵉ de Ligne	1,242
102ᵉ de Ligne	849

Brigade Deconchy
131ᵉ de Ligne	1,149
132ᵉ de Ligne	518
36ᵉ Légère	813
102ᵉ de Ligne	1,712
106ᵉ de Ligne	2,136
2 foot batteries	

6ᵉ Division Zucchi

Brigade Saint Paul
1° Fanteria Leggera	885
2° Fanteria Leggera	752
Volontari[2]	555

Brigade Paolucci
4° Fanteria di Linea	560
5° Fanteria di Linea	869
1 horse battery (Italian)	

Cavalry Divison: Général de Division Julien Mermet

Brigade Perrymond
1° Dragoni Regina	308
1ᵉʳ Hussards	795

Brigade Bonnemain
31ᵉʳ Chasseurs à Cheval	819
4° Cacciatori a Cavallo	261
1 horse battery	

---

[2] The author has no further information on whom exactly these 'voluntari' comprised. Their numbers preclude them being the Battaglione Franca di Bersaglieri.

Italian Royal Guard: Général de Division Giuseppe Lecci

Infantry Brigade
Granatieri a Piedi della Guardia   522
Carabinieri a Piedi della Guardia   1,324
Veliti della Guardia Reale   638

Cavalry Brigade
Dragoni della Guardia Reale   289
Guardia Reale d'Onore   119 (1 company)
2 horse batteries (Italian)
1 foot battery (Italian)

Second Army Corps: Major-Général Jean-Antoine Verdier

1er Division Quesnel

Brigade Campi
92e de Ligne   2,795
1er Légère   1,319
14e Légère   830
10e de Ligne   1,772

Brigade Soulier
35e de Ligne   765
84e de Ligne   2,319
1 horse battery
1 foot battery

3e Division Fressinet

Brigade Forestier
1er de Ligne   519
16e de Ligne   731
62e de Ligne   597
42e de Ligne   1,891

Brigade Pegot
7e de Ligne   1,037
53e de Ligne   1,912
1 foot battery

Appendix IV

Glossary of Uniform Patterns and Types

There are some uniform patterns and styles that were essentially identical throughout the Army so, rather than endlessly repeat the same description the illustrations and descriptions below will cover most of these.

It is always worth noting that the colour of many items such as greatcoats, shako/bearskin covers, etc. often depended on the availability of materials. Thus although greatcoats may be stated as being 'grey' or 'dark blue', these were often issued in other 'neutral colours' such as various shades of brown, darker shades of grey, etc. The same stricture applies to items like shako covers that are seen in many other colours than the prescribed black, even in Guard units. In Spain the problems of supply produced local solution whereby even coats were made in the local brown cloth.

The other consideration to bear in mind has already been mentioned, that of older patterns of uniform and equipment continuing to be issued from store well after they had officially been replaced. Equipment, of course, lasted much longer than cloth items such as coats. For example, although the helmets of the Guards of Honour may have been simplified it is unlikely that existing members ever needed to replace theirs, although, of course, new recruits would receive the new pattern and thus both patterns would have been seen alongside each other for a number of years, and this continuation and longevity of helmets probably accounts for the initial use of the czapska by the light horse regiments.

Incidentally, the national cockade, as used by the military, had a white outer ring, then red, and green at the centre, in other word it was the same as the French with the centre simply substituting green for blue.

THE ARMY OF THE KINGDOM OF ITALY 1805–1814

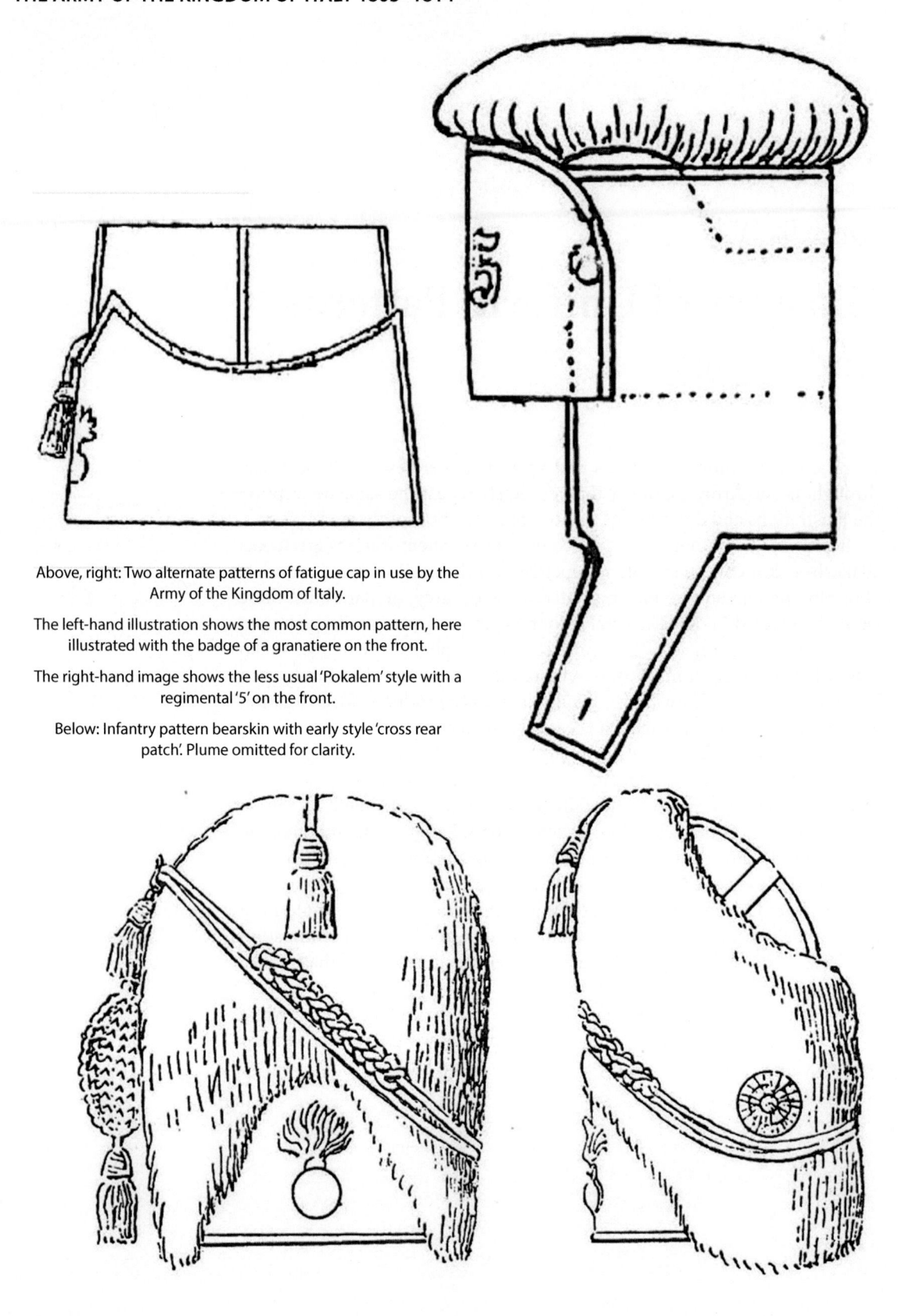

Above, right: Two alternate patterns of fatigue cap in use by the Army of the Kingdom of Italy.

The left-hand illustration shows the most common pattern, here illustrated with the badge of a granatiere on the front.

The right-hand image shows the less usual 'Pokalem' style with a regimental '5' on the front.

Below: Infantry pattern bearskin with early style 'cross rear patch'. Plume omitted for clarity.

GLOSSARY OF UNIFORM PATTERNS AND TYPES

Upper: full dress shako with plume and cords of a grenadier company of the 5° di Linea. The leather reinforcing 'V' can be clearly seen although it is actually less clear on surviving examples. The ball and tuft pompom is sometimes shown for campaign use.

Lower: shako of a fusilier of the 4° di Linea, devoid of all decoration as used on campaign. The 'disc' pompom is of the type shown in the illustration from the Anne S. K. Brown collection and in use from *c.* 1809, see colour plates.

THE ARMY OF THE KINGDOM OF ITALY 1805–1814

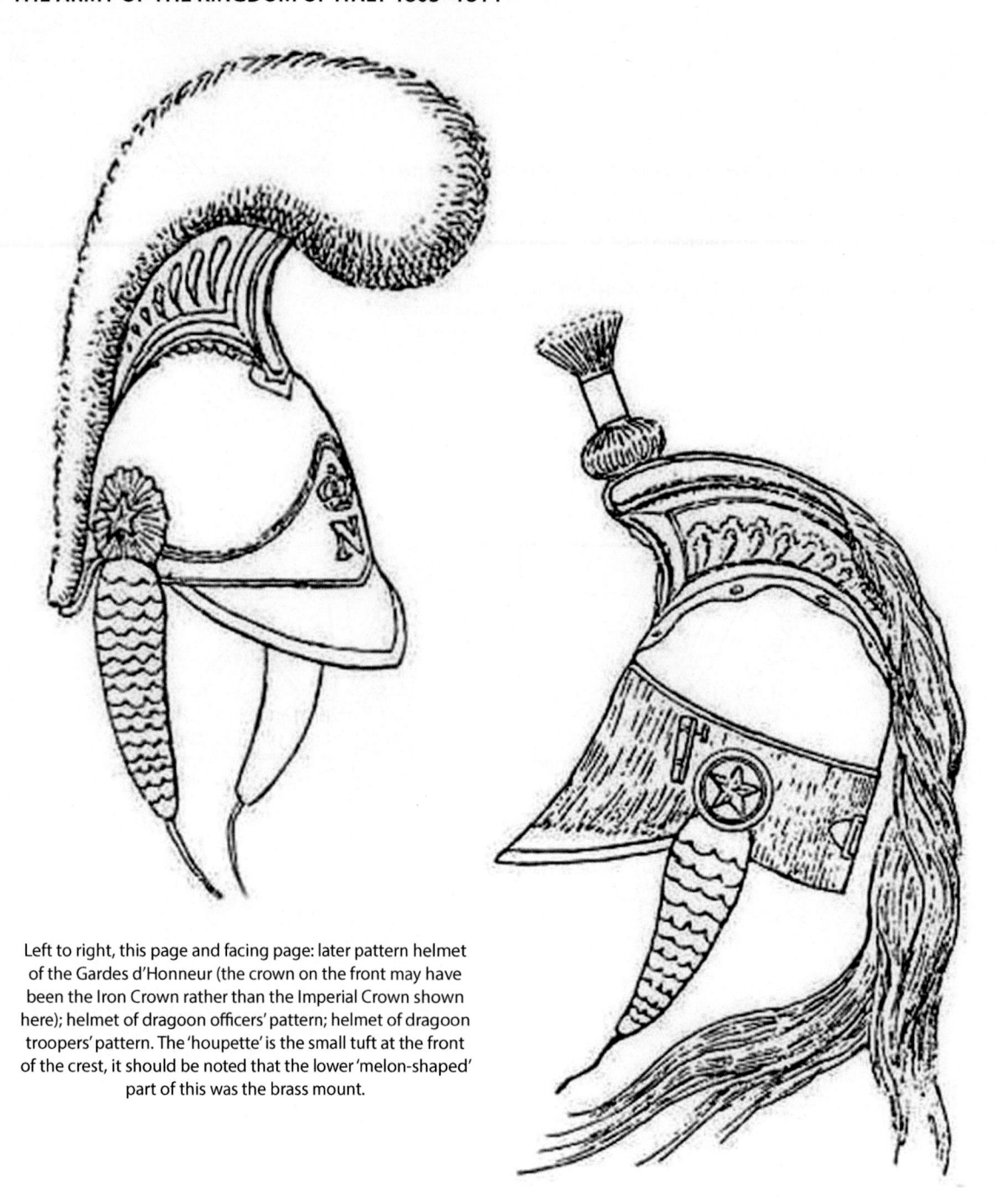

Left to right, this page and facing page: later pattern helmet of the Gardes d'Honneur (the crown on the front may have been the Iron Crown rather than the Imperial Crown shown here); helmet of dragoon officers' pattern; helmet of dragoon troopers' pattern. The 'houpette' is the small tuft at the front of the crest, it should be noted that the lower 'melon-shaped' part of this was the brass mount.

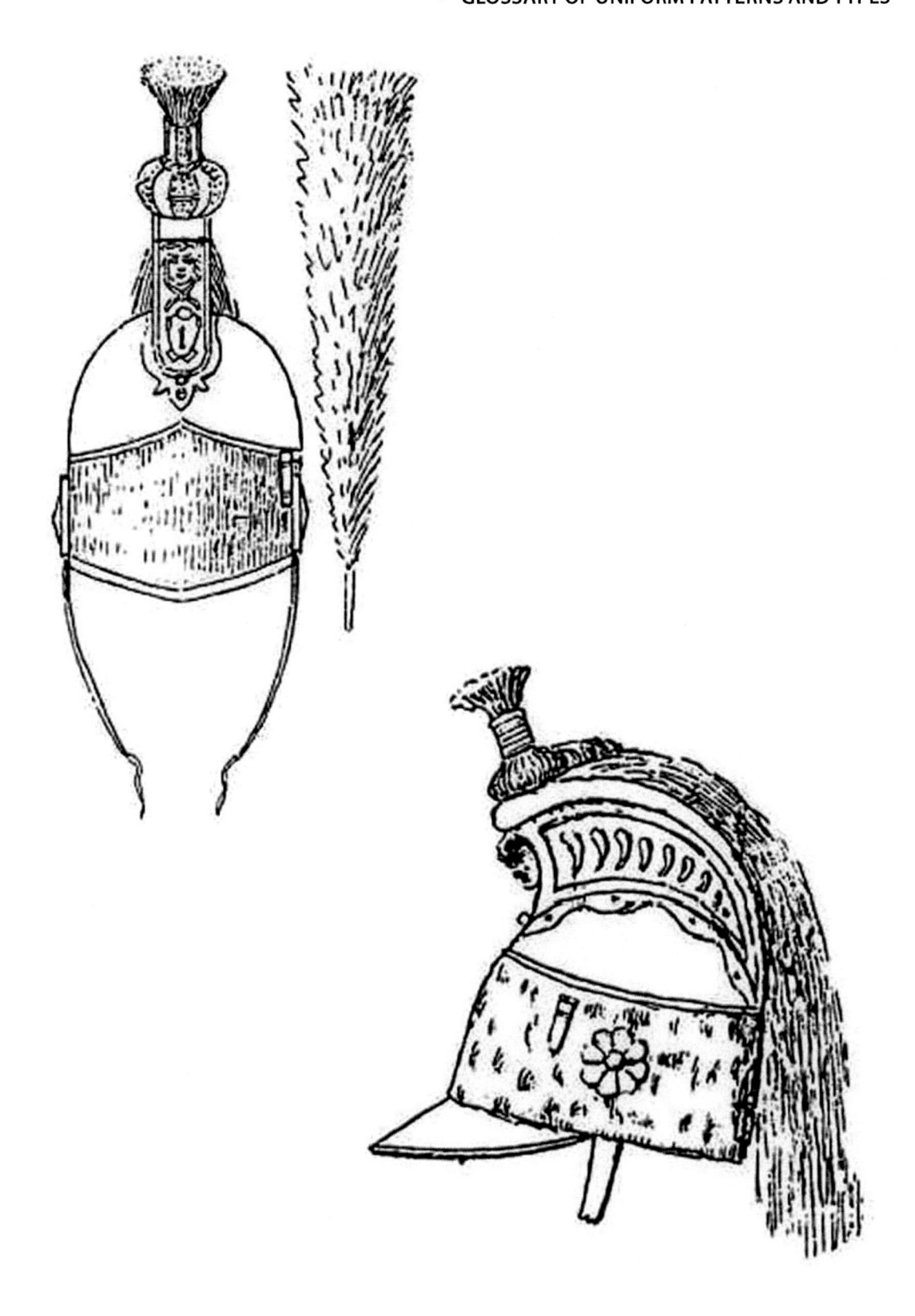

GLOSSARY OF UNIFORM PATTERNS AND TYPES

THE ARMY OF THE KINGDOM OF ITALY 1805–1814

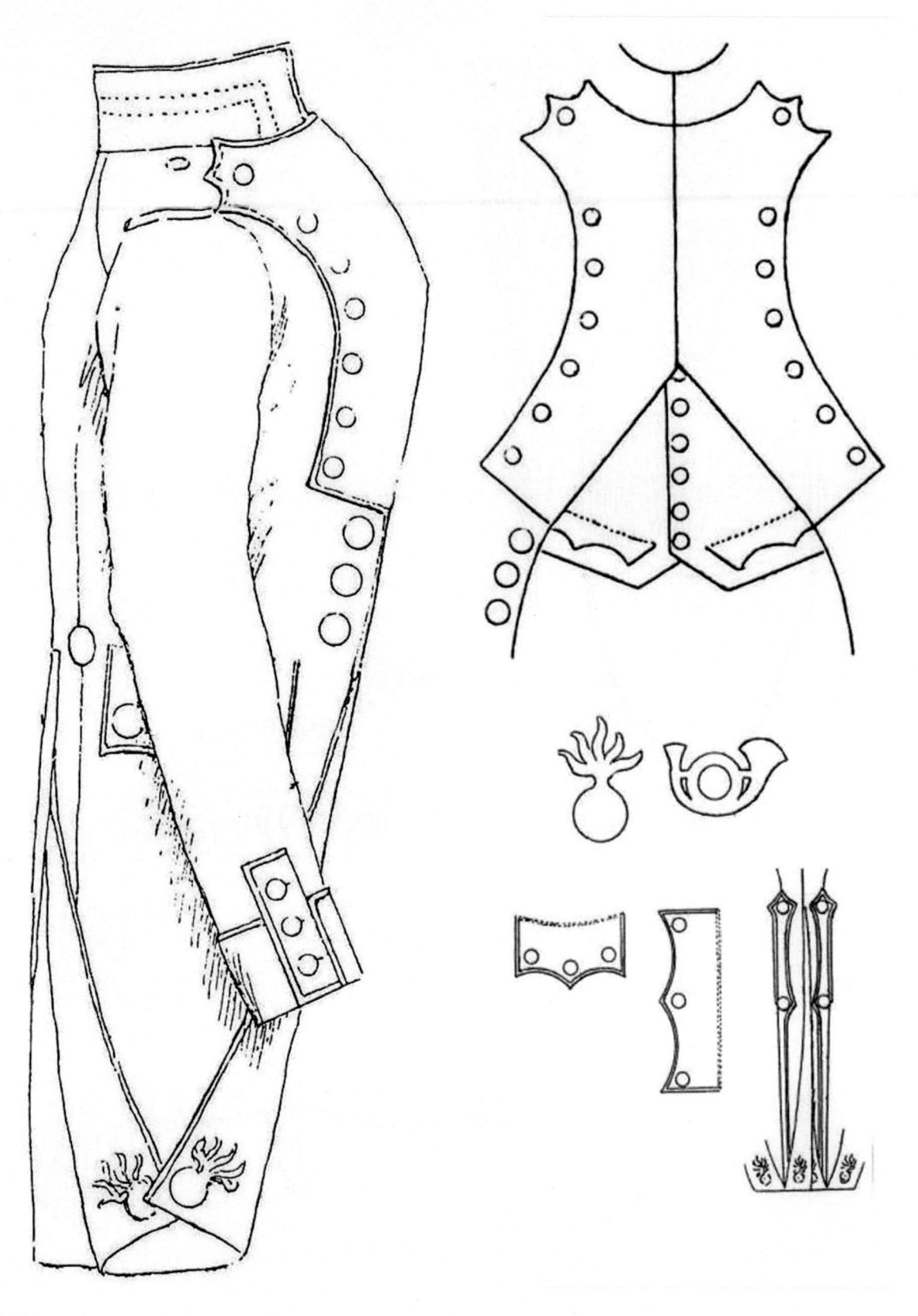

GLOSSARY OF UNIFORM PATTERNS AND TYPES

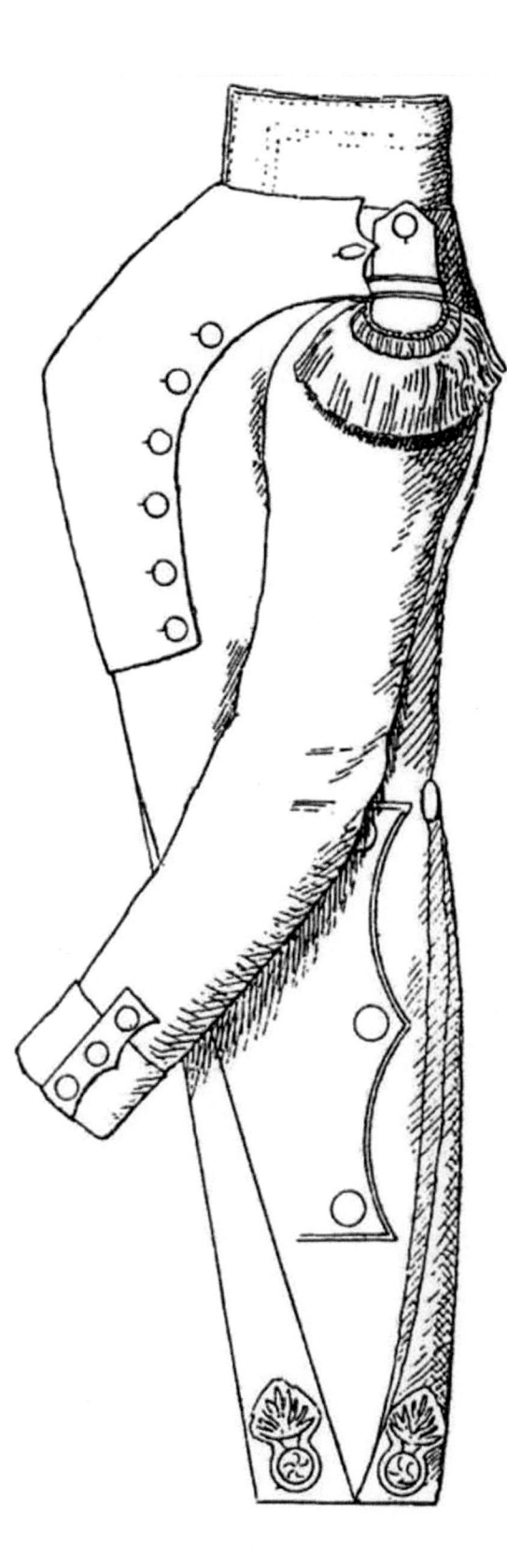

Left, and facing page: the habit coat as worn by most of the units of the Army, at left is that of a line grenadier *c.* 1805, note the square lapels and the epaulette retaining strap, the plain cuff flaps and the early-style turnbacks. At right is that of a grenadier of the Royal Guard *c.* 1812 with Guard pattern three-pointed cuff flaps and the later 'false' turnbacks.

The smaller inset illustrations show, upper, the turnbacks badges of a grenadier and of a voltigeur; lower, the three pocket styles, left to right, horizontal, vertical and 'soubise'.

THE ARMY OF THE KINGDOM OF ITALY 1805–1814

Habit coat with pointed lapels as used by the Fanteria Leggera. Note the late period false turnbacks on this coat and that on the facing page.

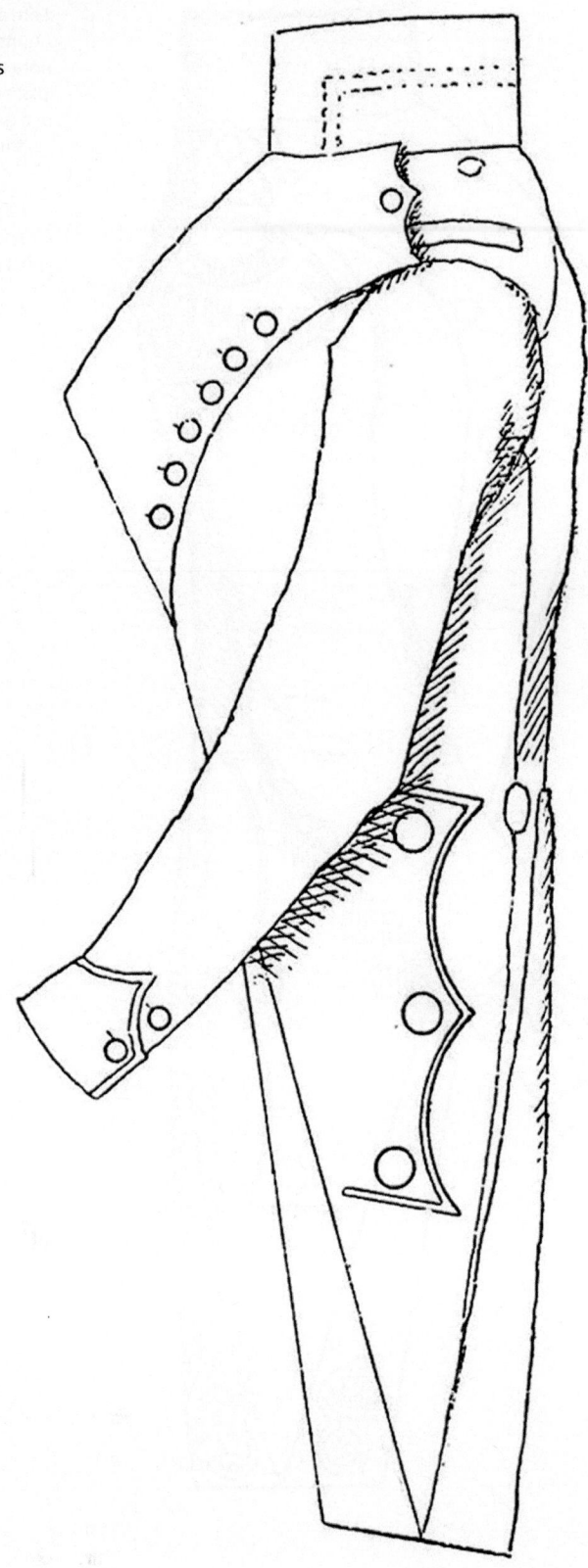

GLOSSARY OF UNIFORM PATTERNS AND TYPES

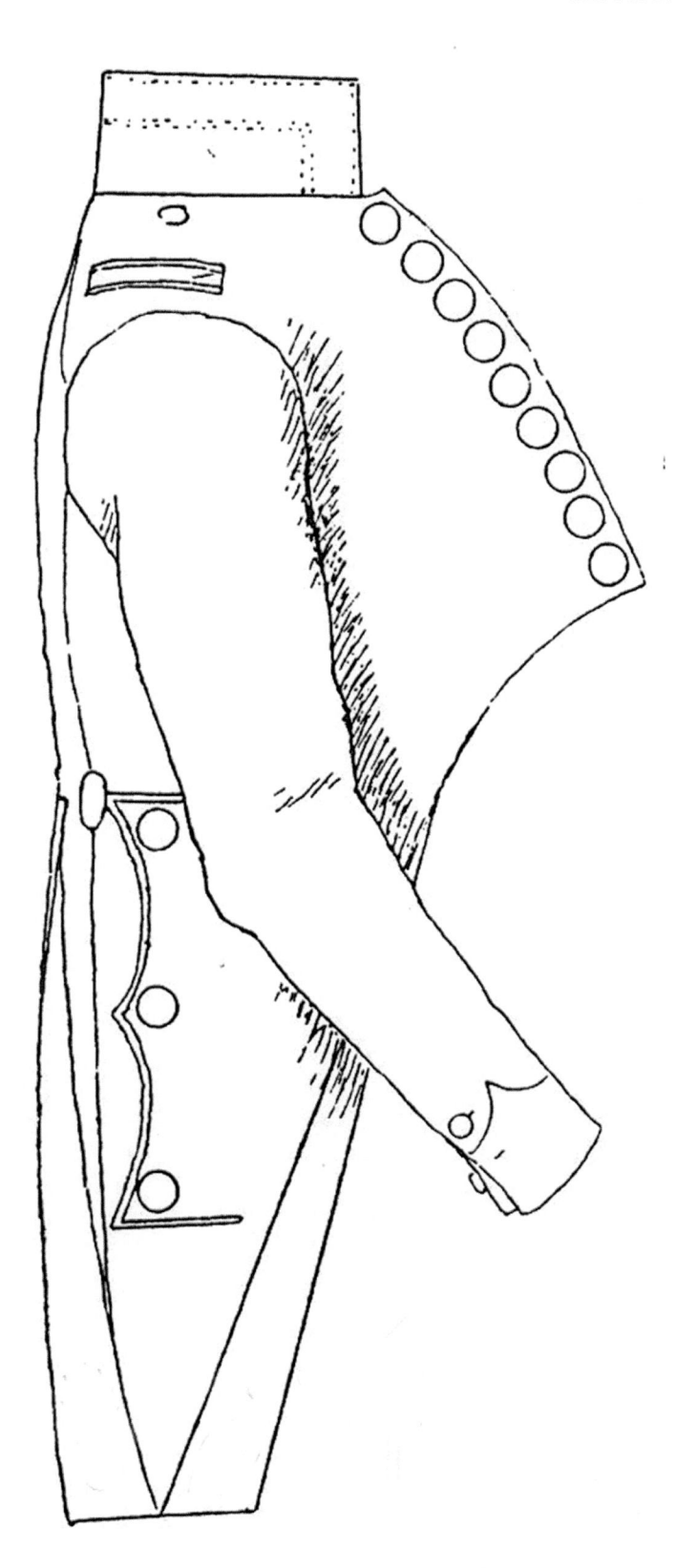

Surtout coat with Polish cuffs. These coats often had vertical pockets even when the unit's habit coats used horizontal.

THE ARMY OF THE KINGDOM OF ITALY 1805–1814

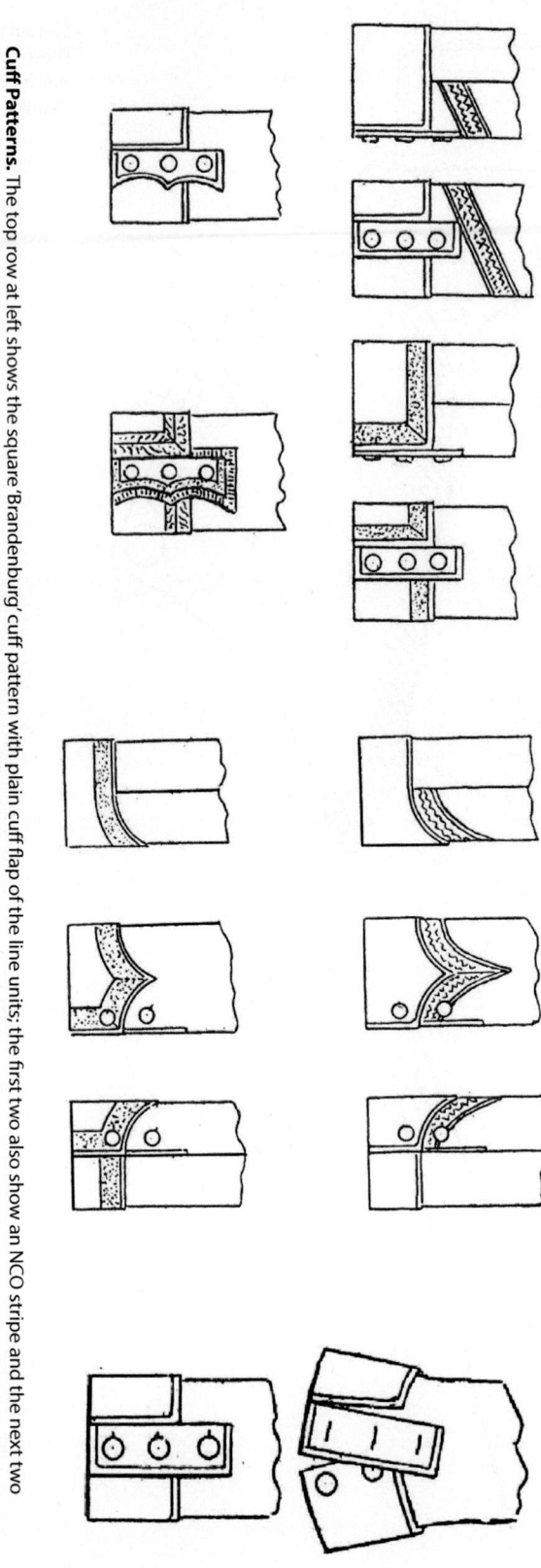

Cuff Patterns. The top row at left shows the square 'Brandenburg' cuff pattern with plain cuff flap of the line units; the first two also show an NCO stripe and the next two drummer's lace. The lower row at left shows the three-pointed flap of the Guard units, again the right-hand example shows a laced cuff, although this has the extra lace of, perhaps, the drum major.

The centre illustration shows the 'Polish' style of cuff with an NCO's stripe on the upper row and drummer's lace on the lower.

The right hand illustration shows how the cuff opened.

216

GLOSSARY OF UNIFORM PATTERNS AND TYPES

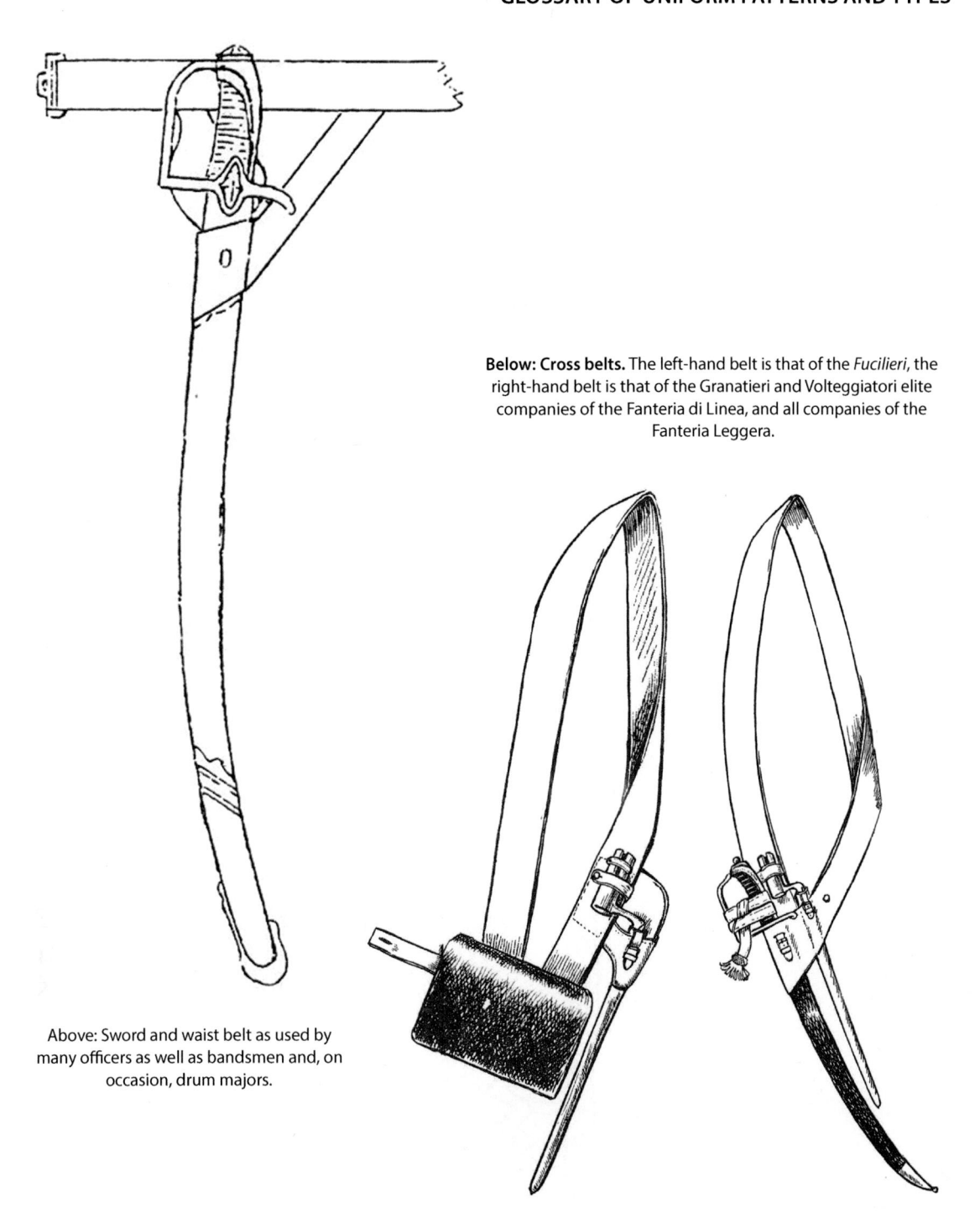

Below: Cross belts. The left-hand belt is that of the *Fucilieri*, the right-hand belt is that of the Granatieri and Volteggiatori elite companies of the Fanteria di Linea, and all companies of the Fanteria Leggera.

Above: Sword and waist belt as used by many officers as well as bandsmen and, on occasion, drum majors.

217

THE ARMY OF THE KINGDOM OF ITALY 1805–1814

Cavalry pattern overalls worn by most mounted units. The inner part of the legs and the cuffs are black leather. The outer cloth part was of regimental colour, although dark green was commonly used by all regiments, and the outer seam, pockets and zigzag divide between the cloth and leather were of the regimental facing or piping colour.

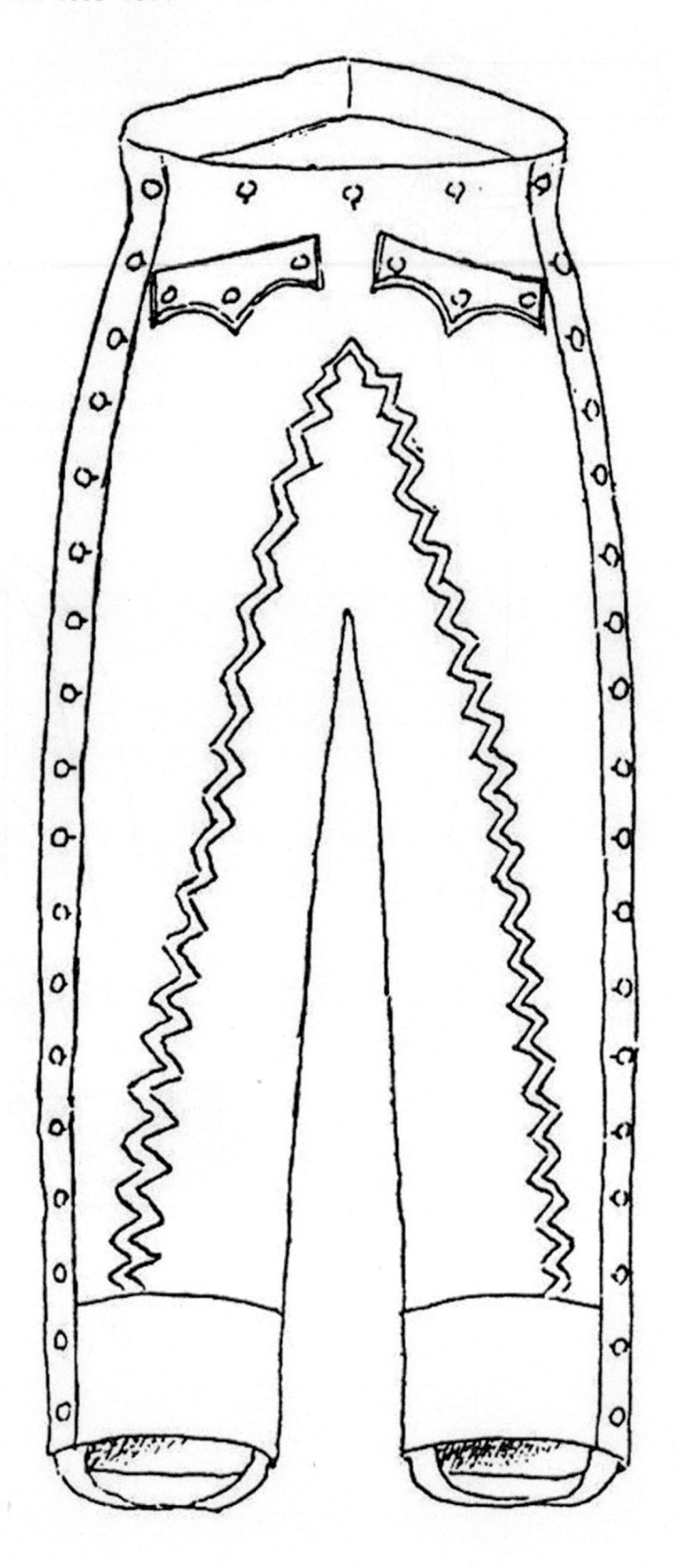

GLOSSARY OF UNIFORM PATTERNS AND TYPES

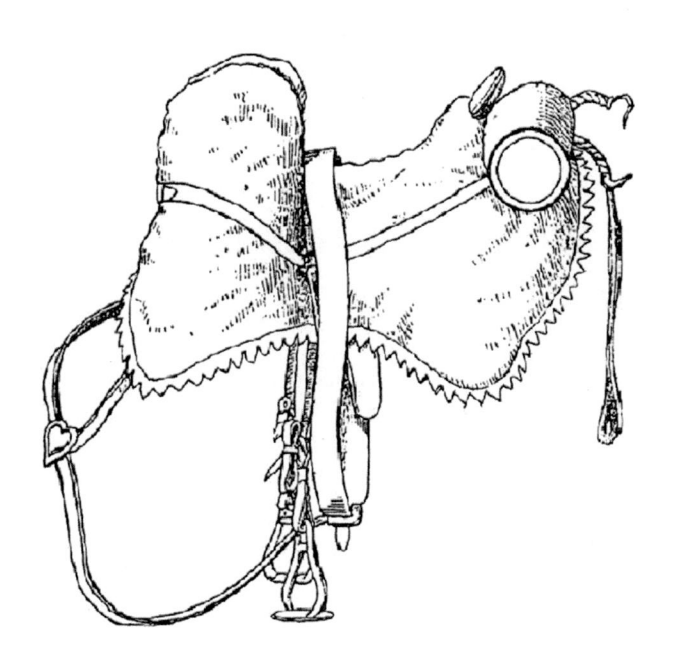

Sheepskin shabraque with the round portmanteau of the light cavalry regiments. The pistol holsters are hidden under the front of the saddlecloth in front of the saddle.

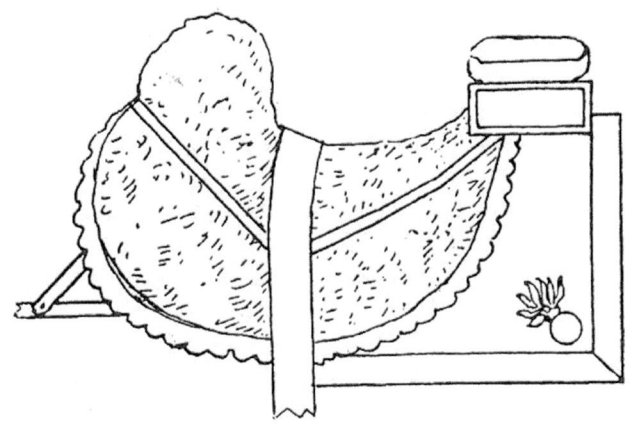

Half shabraque with square portmanteau, as used by the line dragoon regiments after about 1808.

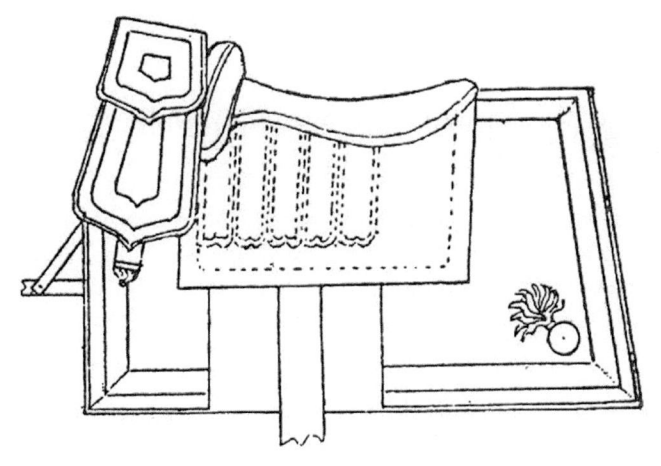

Cloth shabraque of the pattern used by the Guard dragoons, by the line dragoons 1805–c. 1808 and by mounted officers of infantry regiments. The cavalry regiments would have used the same portmanteau as shown above.

Colour Plate Commentaries

All plates except Plate P are from a previously unpublished series of watercolours of the Army of the Kingdom of Italy 1805–1814 by Henri Boisselier (1881–1959), © the author's collection. Boisselier painted a similar series devoted to the pre-Kingdom Italian Republics and a smaller third series on the post 1805 Italian principalities.

Born in Paris on 13 April 1881, Henri Boisselier was the son of a veteran of the Franco-Prussian War of 1870–1871. He studied art at the Boulle school and, a lover of militaria, he rubbed shoulders with the collector Léonce Bernardin and the uniformologists Eugène Louis Bucquoy and Louis Fallou; 'It was the chance of a meeting around 1908 in a small postcard store in the Rue de Richelieu that met and got to know Boisselier, and right from the first, we 'clicked …' All of the collections of the period contain some of Boisselier's innumerable unpretentious watercolors …' Bucquoy entrusted Boisselier with the illustration of a great many of the plates and cards of his famous series.

He was also in contact with Herbert Knötel, the son of the German standard setter Richard Knötel, and for whom he painted a number of the plates for the 'Neue Folge' ('new series', issued after the end of the First World War) of the *Grosse Uniformenkunde* that Herbert Knötel published to complete his father's work.[1] In the late 1940s and into the 1950s, Boisselier painted to order a great many plates for numerous collectors. After the Second World War, he collaborated with the Society of Historical Figurine Collectors (publishers of *Le Sabretache*). He was still active in the late 1950s, participating in a SCFH meeting on September 12, 1959, but three days later, while working on some plates for the Society, he died suddenly.[2]

Plate A. Eugène de Beauharnais, Viceroy of Italy, Duke of Leuchtenberg (1781–1824)

Son and heir of Alexandre de Beauharnais and Joséphine Tascher de la Pagerie, later the wife of Napoleon. Eugène became Napoleon's adopted son and heir to the Kingdom of Italy, although not to the Imperial title, although officially known as 'His Imperial Highness' from 1804. He was created 'Prince

---

[1] Richard Knotel died in 1913 having published eighteen series of *Grosse Uniformenkunde*. Sadly the 'New Series' ran to only two volumes.
[2] <https://fr.wikipedia.org/wiki/Henri_Boisselier>. Author's translation and editing.

de Venise' on 30 March 1806, and heir to the Grand Duchy of Frankfurt in 1810 thus nominally became the Grand Duke when Karl von Dalberg, Archbishop of Regensburg and Grand Duke abdicated on 26 October 1813. Although as the Grand Duchy was by then occupied by the Allies the title was no more than nominal.

In 1806 Eugène married Augusta, the daughter of Maximilia, King of Bavaria, and was created Duke of Leuchtenberg by his father-in-law. The title became extinct in 1974 with the death of Sergei, the 8th Duke, although it is claimed (disputed) by the de Leuchtenberg family through a morganatic marriage.

He is buried in St Michael's Church in Munich.

Top: Eugène from a contemporary illustration by Albrecht Adam in a simplied version of full dress. As always with the Prince he is shown with his distinctive affectation of buttoning his coat. The orange, edged green, sash visible below the coat is that of the Grand Cross of The Order of the Iron Crown, as is the star on the left breast. The medal on a red ribbon is the Légion d'Honneur. The coat tails are decorated with gold Imperial eagles. The baton in his right hand whilst resembling that of a Marshal is not formally so although it does appear near identical.

Bottom Left: Eugène in the full dress uniform as Viceroy of Italy. See above for comments on the sash, etc.

Bottom Right: Eugène, again from an illustration by Albrecht Adam, in a simplified campaign dress in Russia in 1812. Again note the distinctive coat fastening and the sash of the Order of the Iron Crown. His right hand holds a telescope, not a baton. Note also the simplification of the shabraque from the full dress version.

Plate B. Dragoni Della Guardia Reale, 1812

Left: Officer in full dress as described in the text.

Centre: Trumpeter in full dress. The appearance of this trumpeter is virtually identical to that of a trumpter of the French Imperial Guard, save only the red mane to the helmet – which *may* be (and this is pure speculation) the reason for its adoption. The absence of turnback badges is probably an error on the artist's part.

Right: Dragoon in stable dress wearing the greatcoat/cape. Note the absence of the coat, the pattern of fatigue cap and the fullness of the greatcoat which, when worn mounted, would also protect the flanks of the horse.

Plate C. 2º Dragoni, Napoleone, 1811–1812

Left: colonel. The absence of turnback badges is probably simply an error on Boisselier's part.

Centre: officer. Note, Boissselier has illustrated the epaulettes incorrectly, the epaulette on the right shoulder should be fringed.

Right: dragoon.

All details as in the main text.

Plate D. 2º Dragoni, Napoleone, c. 1810

Left: drummer. Right: trumpeter of the elite company, indicated by the white full-fringed epaulettes. Note the trumpeter's sword hooked directly to the belt for ease when dismounted – this practice was customary throughout the Army (and other armies of the period). Also notable is the otherwise unrecorded red mane on the drummer's helmet.

Plate E. 1º Cacciatoria a Cavallo 'Reale Italiano'. Senior officer, full dress, c. 1808.

The full dress leopardskin shabraque is also recorded as being used by all officers of the elite company of both the 1º and 4º Regimentti. The white plume indicates an officer on the regimental staff, elite company officers used either the same yellow plume with a dark green tip as for the rest of the regiment, or possibly a red plume.

Plate F. 1º Cacciatoria a Cavallo 'Reale Italiano'. Colonel (left) and troopers, c. 1810.

Uniformed according to the regulations, except for the oddity of no thigh decorations for the colonel and the left-hand trooper, and the Hungarian Knots in place of spearheads on the right-hand trooper. All are recorded variations, although the simplicity of the colonel's uniform suggests perhaps campaign wear. Note also the 'inverted V' leather reinforcements on the right-hand trooper's shako. This style seems to have been common throughout the Kingdom's Army and may have more to do with the manufacturer's methods than any deliberate variation from the usual French style of a simple 'V' shape.

COLOUR PLATE COMMENTARIES

Plate G. 2° Cacciatoria a Cavallo 'Reale Principale'. Trumpeter (centre) and troopers, *c*. 1812.

Noteble is the unusual shape of the thigh decoration lace, essentially a hybrid between true Hungarian Knots and the plain spearhead style. The lack of any shako plate on all three figures is also unusual, but the left-hand figure does give a good (and rarely shown) rear view of the carbine and cartridge box belts.

Plate H. 2° Cacciatoria a Cavallo 'Reale Principale'. Elite company trooper, campaign dress, Russia 1812.

Based on contemporary eyewitness description and illustrations, this shows how far, in many instances, what should have been worn was adapted in the field. Note the unadorned colpack, apparently without even its bag, but the use of the cloth shabraque in place of the regulated sheepskin. The trooper also appears to have dispensed with the carbine belt but may have kept the carbine itself, perhaps attached to the shabraque or saddle as many French units did.

Plate I. 3° Cacciatoria a Cavallo elite company trumpeters. Full dress *c*. 1806 (top left), campaign dresss *c*. 1810 (top right); campaign dress *c*. 1813 (bottom).

Trumpeters uniforms varied almost from year to year, as each issue may well have varied from the previous simply at the whim of the colonel or the availability and cost of particular items. The white breeches with white decorations on the 1806 trumpeter are particularly striking. As mentioned in the text, the trumpeter of 1813 is probably wearing a dolman below his pelisse, although this is by no means certain.

Plate J. 3° Cacciatoria a Cavallo. Sapper (top) and trooper, campaign dress, 1812.

Notable is the plain surtout-style coat of the trooper and the retention of the baton-laced coat of the sapper, although otherwise he is uniformed pretty much the same as the trooper. The lance was commonly carried by sappers in mounted regiments although the small national flag pennon is unusual and definitely non-regulation. Also notable is the lack of a bag on the sapper's colpack, which has a red patch with a green lace cross, suggesting that the bag has not just been removed for campaign wear but in fact does not form a part of the colpack even in full dress.

Plate K. 4° Cacciatoria a Cavallo. Trooper, campaign dress, Russia 1812 (left); colonel in full dress 1813–14 (centre); trooper in full dress 1813 (right).

The trooper at left wears overalls and has an oilskin cover to his shako (with a highly practical neck cover). He appearance is probably typical of that of most troopers on campaign.

The colonel might often have been expected to wear this sort of almost 'tenue de fantasie' even on campaign. He has adopted the cylindrical shako and whilst overall the unform reflects that of the regiment, it has too many unique aspects to list them all. However, notably he has taken to the hussar style of his elite company. All lace, braid etc. on the colonel's uniform would have been silver. Note the sabreatche design of the Imperial eagle under the Iron Crown of Lobardy.

The trooper at right wears essentially an earlier French Chasseur à Cheval uniform not otherwise recorded in any sources that the author has seen, but perhaps he has been equipped from obsolete French stocks in the absence of supply from the Kingdom's arsenals and depots. Cerainly the facings etc. are those of the Italian 3rd.

Plate L. 1° Fanteria di Linea. Mounted colonel and fusilier, full dress 1811–1812

Uniformed according to regulations, but note the lack of turnback badges (although on the back of the plate Boisselier notes that a green crowned 'N' badge is a possibility). Note also the colonel's heavy cavalry-pattern boots which would have made service on foot highly difficult, and may have been replaced on campaign with the more practical English 'jockey-boots' style (even a colonel can lose his horse in action).

Plate M. 2° Fanteria di Linea, grenadier (rear view), grenadier (front view), sapper, grenadier company drummer, full dress c. 1808–09

Uniformed entirely according to regulations, although note that the grenadier's sword knot is shown white on the rear view and red on the front view. The author has been unable to ascertain whether this is an actual variation or simply a colouring error.

Plate N. 4° Fanteria Leggera, drum major, drummer, cornet, c. 1810

As with the French Army, the fact that these uniforms are shown as 'c. 1810' does not mean that they matched how the individuals appeared in 1809 or 1811. Coats, as with the rank and file, were issued annually and each issue could vary with the whim of the colonel, or simply due to what cloth was available at whatever price he wanted to pay.

COLOUR PLATE COMMENTARIES

Plate O. 3 Fanteria Leggera, officer of chasseurs and chasseurs, c. 1806–07

The uniforms conform to that described in the text, although the officer's hussar-cut boots without tassels are unusual and the lack of lace or tassel on the light infantry pattern gaiters is also unusual. These may simply represent a variation, although of course an error in the original source is not impossible.

Plate P. Guardia d'onore Milano 1809 (top); Guardia Reale Dragon 1809 (bottom).

These two illustrations are typical of the series of plates by 'CM' in the Anne S. K. Brown Collection in Providence, Rhode Island, and are reproduced with their kind permission. The illustrations are all dated 'c. 1809' although many have attributes that suggest that the uniforms they show are actually 1807–08. However the Kingdom of Italy's Army almost certainly continued to issue coats etc. that were in the regimental depot long after patterns or designs had changed. This was customary practice in every army of the era (cf. the debates as to when the 1812 'Belgic' shako was actually issued to Wellington's Army, or when the 1812 pattern 'Spencer coat' arrived with much of the French Army).

Bibliography

Publications

Adam, Albrecht, et al.,*Voyage Pittoresque Et Militaire De Willenberg En Prusse Jusqu'à Moscou Fait En 1812: Pris Sur Le Terrain Même* (Munich: Hermann & Barth, 1828)

Ales, Stefano, *L'Esercito del Regno Italico: Uniformi, Equipaggiamento, Armamento* (Milan: Intergest 1974)

Brandani, Massimo, Pietro Crociani and Massimo Fiorentino, *Le Uniformi Militari Italiane Del 800 – Periodo Napoleonico* (Rome: Rivista Militaire, 1984)

Carmigniani, Juan Carlos and Gilles Boué, trans. Marie-France Renwick, *Napoleon and Italy: A Military History of Napoleonic Italy, 1805–1815* (Paris: Histoire & Collections, 2016)

Cristini, Luca Stefano and Guglielmo Aimaretti, *L'Esercito Del Regno Italico 1805–1814. Volume 1: La Fanteria* (Lodigliano: Soldiershop, 2010)

L'Esercito Del Regno Italico 1805–1814. Volume 2: La Cavalleria (Lodigliano: Soldiershop, 2011)

L'Esercito Del Regno Italico 1805–1814. Volume 3: Corpi Speciali (Lodigliano: Soldiershop, 2011.

Crociano, Piero, *L'Esercito Italico 1805-1814: Guardia Reale* (Parma: Albertelli, 2005)

Currie, James, *The Kingdom of Italy: Infantry, 1805-1814*, Napoleonic Association, no date or place of publication

Dempsey, Guy C. Jr, *Napoleon's Soldiers: The Grande Armée of 1807 as Depicted in the Paintings of the Otto Manuscript* (London: Arms & Armour, 1994)

Franzoni, Pier Giorgio, *Napoleone in Italia: Soldati e Uniformi* (Rome: Rivista Militaire, 1987)

Galliani, G., G. R. Parisini, G. M. Rocchiero, *La Cavalleria di Linea Italica, 1796–1814* (Genova: Interconair, 1970)

Gibellini, Valerio, *I Soldati Del Primo Tricolore: Le Uniformi* (Rome: Rivista Militare, 1993)

Hourtoulle, F. G., *Borodino, The Moskova: The Battle for the Redoubts* (Paris: Histoire & Collections, 2000)

Hourtoulle, F. G., *Wagram: The Apogee of the Empire* (Paris: Histoire & Collections, 2002)

Hourtoulle, F. G., *From Eylau to Friedland: 1807 The Polish Campaign* (Paris: Histoire & Collections, 2007)

Hourtoulle, F.G., *The Crossing of the Berezina : A Victory During the Retreat* (Paris: Histoire & Collections, 2012).

Knötel, Richard, *Mittheilungen zur Geschichte der Miltärischen Tracht, No.5 Mai 1892* (Rathenow: Max Babeuzien, 1892)

Knötel, Herbert, Richard Knötel, Herbert Sieg, *Handbuch der Uniformkunde* (Hamburg: Diepenbroick-Grüter & Schulz 1937)

Lienhart, Dr, and R. Humbert, *Les Uniformes de l'Armée Française. Recueil d'Ordonnances de 1690 à 1894, Volume 5* (Leipzig: Ruhl 1894)

Malibran, H., *Guide à l'Usage des Artistes et des Costumiers* (Paris: Combet et Cie, 1907)

Martinien, Aristide, *Tableaux Par Corps et par Batailles des Officiers Tués et Blessées Pendant les Guerres de l'Empire (1805-1815)* (Paris: Henri-Charles Lavauzelle, 1899)

Nafziger, George and Marco Gioannini, *The Defense of the Napoleonic Kingdom of Northern Italy, 1813-1814* (Westport, Connecticut, USA: Praeger, 2001)

Nafziger, George (trans.), *Historical Account of the Military Operations of the Army in Italy in 1813 and 1814* (Pisgah, Ohio, USA: Nafziger Collection, 2005)

North, Jonathan, *Napoleon's Army in Russia: The Illustrated Memoirs of Albrecht Adam, 1812* (London: Leo Cooper, 2005)

Oliver, Michael, and Richard Partridge, *Napoleonic Army Handbook, Volume 2: The French Army and her Allies* (London: Constable, 2002)

Oman, Carola, *Napoleon's Viceroy: Eugene de Beauharnais* (London: Hodder & Stoughton, 1966)

Pigeard, Alain (ed.), *Le Bourgeois de Hambourg : Représentation des Uniformes de Toutes les Troupes qui ont été Casernées à Hambourg, de l'Année 1806 à l'Année 1815* (Paris: Tradition, 1998)

Pigeard, Alain (ed.), *Le Manuscrit de Weiland: Uniformes de l'Armée Français et de ses Alliés de 1806 à 1815* (Paris: Tradition, 1998)

Pivka, Otto von (Digby Smith), *Napoleon's Italian and Neapolitan Troops* (London: Osprey, 1979)

Rawkins, W. J., *The Italian Army, 1805-1814* (Aylsham: Anschluss Publishing, ND)

Schneid, Frederick C., *Soldiers of Napoleon's Kingdom of Italy: Army, State, and Society, 1800-1815* (Boulder Co., USA: Westview Press, 1995)

Smith, Digby, *The Napoleonic Wars Data Book* (London: Greenhill 1998)

Smith, Digby, *Armies of 1812* (Staplehurst: Spellmount, 2002)

Zanoli, Alessandro, *Sulla Milizia Cisalpino-Italiana. Cenni StoricoSstatistici dal 1796 al 1814* (Milan: Borroni e Scotti, 1845

Journals

Bauer, Dr Gerhard, 'Comme Les Licteurs Romains', *Soldats Napoleoniens: Les Troupes Françaises, Alliés et Coalisées. Hors-série No.1, Avril 2003* (Paris: Éditions de la Revue Napoléon, 2003), pp. 60-62

Bauer, Dr Gerhard, 'Les "Dragoni Napoleone" en 1813: Beacoup de Pistes à Éclaircir…', *Soldats Napoleoniens: Les Troupes Françaises, Alliés et Coalisées. Hors-série No. 1, Avril 2003* (Paris: Éditions de la Revue Napoléon, 2003), pp. 62-63

Boissellier, Henri, 'L'Infanterie de la Garde Royal Italienne sous Napoléon'. *Bulletin de la Société des Collectionneurs de Figurines Historiques No.3, Mai 1955* (Paris: SCFH, 1955), pp. 45-47 and plates 157-164

Carles, Lt-Col P., 'Trompettes des Gardes d'Honneur du Royaume d'Italie, 1810-1814', *Carnet de la Sabretache No. 31* (Paris : SCFH, 1971) pp. 81-82 and plate 59

Carles, Lt-Col P., 'Trompettes des Dragons de la Garde Royale Italienne', *Carnet de la Sabretache No. 9* (Paris: SCFH, 1976), pp. 7-8 and plate 3

Crociano, Piero, 'Napoleon's Italian Army'. *Tradition Magazine No. 43, No. 44, No. 46, No. 47, No. 48* (London, Belmont-Maitland 197?)

Crociano, Piero and Massimo Fiorentino, 'La Garde Royale Italienne: Les Velites 1805-1814', *Tradition Magazine*:
 No. 153, Février 2000 (Paris: Tradition, 2000), pp. 17-22
 No. 162, Décembre 2000 (Paris: Tradition, 2000), pp. 16-22

Crociano, Piero and Massimo Fiorentino, 'Les Dragons de la Garde Royale Italienne, 1805-1814', *Tradition Magazine*:

       No. 177, Avril 2002 (Paris: Tradition, 2002), pp. 19–22 and 30–31

       No. 178, Mai 2002 (Paris: Tradition, 2002), pp. 11–18

Crociano, Piero and Massimo Fiorentino, '"Dragoni Napoleone", Un Nom Porté Avec Honneur', *Soldats Napoleoniens: Les Troupes Françaises, Alliés et Coalisées. Hors-série No. 1, Avril 2003* (Paris: Éditions de la Revue Napoléon, 2003), pp. 51–54

Crociano, Piero, Massimo Fiorentino and Alfred Umhey, 'À Propos de l'Esponton des "Dragoni Napoleone…"', *Soldats Napoleoniens: Les Troupes Françaises, Alliés et Coalisées. Hors-série No. 1, Avril 2003* (Paris: Éditions de la Revue Napoléon, 2003), pp. 78–84

Crociano, Piero and Massimo Fiorentino, 'Dragoni Napoleone, Un Nom Porté Avec Honneur', *Soldats Napoleoniens: Les Troupes Françaises, Alliés et Coalisées. Hors-Série No. 1, Avril 2003* (Paris: Éditions de la Revue Napoléon, 2003), pp. 55–65

Crociano, Piero, Fiorentino, Massimo and Umhey, Alfred, 'À Propos de "l'Esponton" des Dragoni Napoleone', *Soldats Napoleoniens: Les Troupes Françaises, Alliés et Coalisées. Hors-Série No. 2, Octobre 2003* (Paris: Éditions de la Revue Napoléon, 2003), pp. 78–84

Crociano, Piero and Massimo Fiorentino, 'Les Italiens en Allemagne, 1806–1808', *Soldats Napoleoniens: Les Troupes Françaises, Alliés et Coalisées. No. 10, Juin 2006* (Paris: Éditions de la Revue Napoléon, 2006), pp. 55–65

Darbou, Lt-Col René, 'La Cavalerie de la République Cisalpine et du Royaume: Italie, 1797–1814', *Bulletin de la Société des Collectionneurs de Figurines Historiques No. 5, Septembre 1957* (Paris: SCFH, 1957), pp. 61–69 and plates 2–11

Fiorentino, Massimo, 'Eugene de Beauharnais, Prince de Venise 1807', *Tradition No. 174, Janvier 2002* (Paris, Tradition 2002), pp. 11–14

Mangin, Jean-Marie (ed.), *Soldat No. 12: Les Italiens de Napoléon* (Paris: Editions Heimdal, 2019)

Papi, Ricardo, 'Les Chasseurs à Cheval du Royaume d'Italie, 1805–1814', *Carnet de la Sabretache* No. 107 (Paris: SCFH, 1991), pp. 44–52 and plates 4–7

Papi, Ricardo, 'Le 3e Régiment de Chasseurs à Cheval Italiens', *Soldats Napoleoniens: Les Troupes Françaises, Alliés et Coalisées. No. 26, Juin 2010* (Paris: Éditions de la Revue Napoléon, 2010), pp. 58–63

Perconte, Jean-Pierre, 'Les "Napoleone" en 1813', *Soldats Napoleoniens: Les Troupes Françaises, Alliés et Coalisées. Hors-série No. 1, Avril 2003* (Paris: Éditions de la Revue Napoléon, 2003), pp. 54–55

Perconte, Jean-Pierre, 'Les Uniformes des "Napoleone" en 1813', *Soldats Napoleoniens: Les Troupes Françaises, Alliés et Coalisées. Hors-série No. 1, Avril 2003* (Paris: Éditions de la Revue Napoléon, 2003), pp. 56–60

Perconte, Jean-Pierre, 'Organisation et Uniformes de l'Artillerie à Pied du Royaume d'Italie, *Soldats Napoleoniens: Les Troupes Françaises, Alliés et Coalisées*:

    1er Partie, No. 2, 2eme Trimestre 2004 (Paris: Éditions de la Revue Napoléon, 2004), pp. 37–45

    2e Partie, No. 4, Décembre 2004 (Paris: Éditions de la Revue Napoléon, 2004), pp. 37–44

Perconte, Jean-Pierre, 'Artillerie à Cheval et Train d'Artillerie du Royaume d'Italie 1805–1814', *Soldats Napoleoniens: Les Troupes Françaises, Alliés et Coalisées*:

    1er Partie No. 7, Septembre 2005 (Paris: Éditions de la Revue Napoléon, 2005), pp. 45–52

    2e Partie, No. 15, Décembre 2007 (Paris: Éditions de la Revue Napoléon, 2007), pp. 61–69

Pigeard, Alain, 'Les Gardes d'Honneur du Royaume d'Italie'. *Tradition No.117, Janvier 1997* (Paris: Tradition, 1996) pp. 12–16

Viotti, Andrea, 'The Veliti of the Italian Royal Guard, 1805–1815 [sic]', *Campaigns Magazine No. 29, July/August 1980* (Los Angeles: Campaigns, 1980), pp. 52–54

Uniform Plates

Anonymous series of watercolours of the Army of the Kingdom of Italy in the Collection of HM The Queen at Windsor Castle[1]

Boisselier, Henri, Unpublished series of watercolours and plates on the Army of the Kingdom of Italy, all in various private collections

Knötel, Richard, *Grosse Uniformenkude* (Rathenow: Max Babeuzien, 1890–1914). Plates: III/17, III/18, III/25, III/29, III/45, III/58, III/59, VI/42, XVI/45

Lelièpvre, Eugene, Notes and paintings to accompany the Historex model kits of Italian infantry

North, Rene, 'North's Paint Your Own Cards' (London: self-published, *c*. 1980). Set 106.

Rigondaud, Albert, 'Rigo, Le Plumet' (Paris: self-published, 1960–1980). *D Series* D.8, D.11, D.15, D.17, D.23, D.27, D.31, D.35; *Pl Series* 107.

Websites

Napitalia. The Eagle in Italy, <http://napitalia.org.uk/eng>

Le Règlement du 1er juillet 1807, <http://www.histunif.com/italie/italie2/RGT1807/ital002.htm>

---

[1] The author first became aware of these through Otto von Pivka's (Digby Smith's) book and extends his gratitude to him.